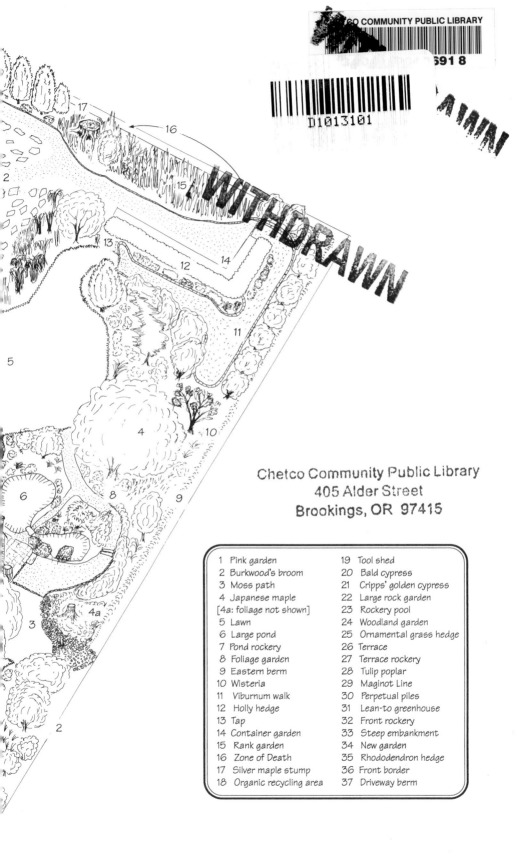

Chetco Community Public Library
405 Alder Street
Brookings, OR 97415

1	Pink garden	19	Tool shed
2	Burkwood's broom	20	Bald cypress
3	Moss path	21	Cripps' golden cypress
4	Japanese maple	22	Large rock garden
	[4a: foliage not shown]	23	Rockery pool
5	Lawn	24	Woodland garden
6	Large pond	25	Ornamental grass hedge
7	Pond rockery	26	Terrace
8	Foliage garden	27	Terrace rockery
9	Eastern berm	28	Tulip poplar
10	Wisteria	29	Maginot Line
11	Viburnum walk	30	Perpetual piles
12	Holly hedge	31	Lean-to greenhouse
13	Tap	32	Front rockery
14	Container garden	33	Steep embankment
15	Rank garden	34	New garden
16	Zone of Death	35	Rhododendron hedge
17	Silver maple stump	36	Front border
18	Organic recycling area	37	Driveway berm

635
GRISSEL Grissell, Eric
A journal in
thyme

DATE DUE

A Journal in Thyme

by Eric Grissell

With linocuts by Henry Evans

TIMBER PRESS
Portland, Oregon

The author gratefully acknowledges the editor of *GreenPrints* for permission to reprint the following essays, which have been excerpted or rewritten in slightly different form: "The Fall of Winter" (1990), "The New Year in Review" (1991), "Path Mistakes" (1991), and "Wasp Ways" (1991).

Printed in Singapore

ISBN 0-88192-276-5

TIMBER PRESS, INC.
The Haseltine Building
133 S.W. Second Ave., Suite 450
Portland, Oregon 97204-3527, U.S.A.

Library of Congress Cataloging-in-Publication Data

Grissell, Eric.
    A journal in thyme / by Eric Grissell ; with linocuts by Henry Evans.
        p.   cm.
    Includes index.
    ISBN 0-88192-276-5
    1. Gardening. I. Title.
SB455.G73   1994
635.9′092—dc20   93-29522
                                                                         CIP

Contents

Illustrations

For my mother,
a master gardener
of her kind

Preface

For nearly as long as gardens have existed there have also been gard[den] writers and gardening readers. The role of the garden writer has always been to nag, while that of the gardening reader has always been to work. From this simple interplay of give and take evolved a form of communication, or irritation, known as the "Garden Kalender" or "Gardener's Year"—essentially a garden writer's journal of sage wisdom and sound advice. This counsel consisted of weekly or monthly admonitions on when and how to do what needed to be done.

In the past we needed this help desperately because there were darn few gardening magazines and newspaper columns to tell us what to do. Neither were there garden centers nor endless numbers of seed, bulb, and plant catalogs to guide our education as gardeners. It was imperative that those who lived by the garden should know and deeply respect the seasonal cycles of the year, and we relied upon professional garden naggers such as Philip Miller to guide us. We acquired all manner of knowledge from these writers, knowledge that was of immensely practical value to our survival. For example, in Miller's 1725 edition of *The Gardeners*

Kalendar, we are told that in December we should "carry dung into the quarters of the kitchen-garden . . . that it may be mellowed by frost" and to "dung . . . the ground of orchards . . . which will be of great service to them, and cause the fruit to be fairer and better tasted." This was the advice of a true gardening friend, one who had personally worked out the relationship between manure and taste. It makes one realize that friends are no longer what they used to be.

In our century, when Czech writer Karel Čapek speaks out upon the subject of dung in *The Gardener's Year* (1929; reprint, Madison: University of Wisconsin Press, 1984), we hear a totally different pronouncement: "Only cowardly shame prevents the gardener from going into the street to collect what horses have left behind." Čapek's rebuke is less instructional than Miller's but decidedly more insightful. His thought evokes not so much the 200 years separating these garden writers as it does just how far we, as a society, have become separated from the horse's behind.

Today, when our lives do not depend upon our ability to grow our own food, it may be inconvenient to ignore the seasons and the garden naggers, but it is no longer a matter of life or death. For anyone desperate enough, brussels sprouts, okra, and peas are only as far away as the fresh produce counter or freezer section of the local market. Even flowers may be purchased at the grocery store. Centuries ago, ignoring the garden meant starvation and deprivation. Today it simply means more time to wash the car.

In the present everyone everywhere is only too happy to tell us what to do, when to do it, and exactly how to do it the correct way—that is, their way. In spite of all this so-called advice, we gardeners still must teach ourselves to follow the cycles of the calendar. But now we garden because we want to, not because we have to. We toil because we know that next season's garden is as near as today's thought. We grow flowers for the soul and let agribusiness, ably assisted by the friendly chemical conglomerates, grow our food.

What separates us from Miller's time is not tallied so much in years as in perspective. Whether the writer is Thomas Hyll, writing in 1563 of *A Most Briefe and Pleasaunt Treatyse, Teaching Howe to Dress, Sowe, and*

Set a Garden, or the 1990 edition of Thalassa Cruso's *The Gardening Year,* I am struck by how much these gardeners have in common. Their observations, though they span hundreds of years, are timeless. When they write of gardening through the year, it is as if nothing had changed but the language. And if anything might be found to differ, it is that, over the centuries, gardening journals have strayed from the strict path of garden instruction to follow an elusive and meandering course of instruction about the gardener. Oftentimes in present-day writing we learn as much about the gardener as about the garden. Occasionally more than we would care to.

For years I have kept what might charitably be called garden records—equipment and supply purchases, plant purchases, seed sowing dates, bloom times, garden diggings, propagations, and the like—nothing of interest to anyone but me, and then not really to me, either. (Who has the time to go back over all this data, anyway?) A journal it could never be called. So it came as a surprise even to me that in a recent and appropriately dismal November I began writing a gardening journal as if possessed by a sense of purpose. As if some constrained need to nag had erupted.

At first I was leery of this sudden urge: writing on a daily or weekly schedule is not the easiest commitment to live up to. I know because I've tried it dozens of times—since I was a wee lad, as a matter of fact. I've always found anything of a routine nature to be suspiciously like plain hard work. Like endless weeding. Who knows better than I that plans begun in the twilight of fall, when winter's dark and cold embrace seems but hours away, are often shattered by spring's surfeit of brutal work?

But having a suspiciously stubborn and, perhaps, latently masochistic personality, I soon found that I almost enjoyed writing about the day's or week's events. It even helped, on occasion, to put life in perspective. Writing, I found, opened vistas not suspected before pen had been set to paper. Little irritations (such as my life and job) suddenly became bearable. And a chance to complain on a routine basis was not without its charm.

These essays do not present a detailed account of everything I've done every minute of every day over the past year. Although this idea had occurred to me, I decided it was not the right approach to take. Not only would you abandon the garden in all due haste, but I'd be close behind. Besides, I can't remember half the things I did an hour after I did them. Hell, I can't even remember half the things I'm supposed to do that never get done. Details are, to put things entirely in perspective, not my forte.

The essays in this book are a distillation of the weekly pleasures and pain I've found in the garden this past year. As a gardener I much prefer to dream about the future than to itemize the past, but unlike the old writers, I promise not to nag incessantly—just as much as I have to. This book is, in a sense, a sequel to *Thyme on My Hands*. In that book I set the stage of the garden. It is now five years later and I am almost a year wiser. And just as the garden is always changing—adding new seedlings here, dying out there—a gardener is always pruning thoughts, adding ideas, rearranging the endless clutter.

The past year was more cluttered than most, and I was busier than is absolutely necessary. I didn't take the time to be as sociable as I could have been. So perhaps sometime when it is too wicked to work outside, you'll pull up a chair and let me describe what's been going on in the garden and with the gardener. There is no hurry in this. There will be many bad days ahead—too many, I predict. Days when garden work has lessened or been rained out. Days when either you or I don't feel much like gardening. Days when we want to garden but can't. Or simply days when a little garden chitchat is about all we can handle.

Please don't hesitate to drop by and visit for a while. If no one answers the front door, just walk on around back—chances are I'll be working somewhere out in the garden. There's always so much to do, and if you don't find me raking the pathways or trimming the lawn, I might just be sprawled out across the rock garden weeding the thyme. I can always use a break.

A Journal in Thyme

1

NOVEMBER

The way I garden there is no telling exactly what will be done by day's end—if anything. My garden plans often begin the day before, when I am not faced with any real work. Then during the night, when my subconscious takes over, plans somehow change drastically in form. The subconscious has a marvelous avoidance to work, and that is why I rely on its wisdom so much.

Take today, for example. My intent, upon retiring last night, was to begin the morning with another lawn-removal project. This is one of those never-ending jobs connected with creating a garden where before there was only sod. Last night I told myself this needed to be done, but fortunately I rarely listen to myself. When I awoke it was a glorious fall day, far too nice to be spent at hard physical labor. Something enjoyable had to be thought up, but something not as brutally worklike as sod busting. So with coffee in hand, I escaped for an impromptu inspection of the grounds.

Rarely am I allowed the privilege of a garden walk. There is always too much work to do, and the guards here at the asylum are fussy about letting me out without my straitjacket. This morning all was in nearly proper order—a rare occasion to be certain—but one area was looking a bit shabby: the large rock garden. No doubt some odd job could be found therein.

I have several rock gardens, or rockeries, scattered about the place, the largest of which is sited toward the northwest rear of the garden. It is an equilateral triangle about thirty feet on each side. There are also small rockeries off the terrace, the large pond, and the front of the house. As you might imagine, I greatly enjoy rock gardens, and it does not matter much whether they have plants or not. An assortment of shapely and well-placed rocks is, in fact, much more aesthetic to me than an ill-conceived pile of stones smothered under ill-chosen plants.

To assay the rock garden for potential chores in need of attention, I sat down at the rockery overlook that I'd built some years back. It is a simple garden bench with a straight-ahead, focused view of the large rock garden and a sideways, oblique view of the woodland garden. As my mind wandered through the many work-related options at my disposal, my eyes drifted over to the woodland view. A secondary focal point, it now unfortunately overlooked my neighbor's rear yard. An old, rotten apple tree had just been removed, leaving a huge, heart-rending gap in plain view. I suddenly realized what my garden project would be: to fill the void!

I'd been working halfheartedly on this area for several weeks without much conviction as to its design. The site demands an uplifting brightness as well as a certain amount of woodland disarray. I'd already begun a potential list of both native and woodsy-type trees and shrubs, most of which I'd been unable to find locally. I wanted at least two or three medium trees of multiple-season interest as well as an understory of smaller shrubs. I wanted texture, fragrance, fall color, fruits, and even flowers if possible. I'd already sent for and received plants of *Hovenia dulcis*, the Japanese raisin tree, and *Calycanthus floridanus*, Carolina allspice. Both have large shiny leaves and fragrant flowers. The raisin tree grows to thirty feet with insect-attractant white flowers that produce red edible fruits in late summer. Carolina allspice is a moderate-size native shrub with two-inch brown-red flowers and aromatic leaves and seed pods. Both plants also color up in the fall: allspice turning yellow and the raisin tree red.

This was a start, but much space still remained, especially up in the air. Leaving the bench, I went inside, grabbed my list of potential "investments" (as we gardeners refer, rather defensively at times, to our excessive plant expenditures), and headed off to the local planteria. It is a great place, this nursery, covering some ten acres with an inexhaustible variety of plants. But in spite of its vastness, I found only one plant on my list, the native sourwood tree, *Oxydendrum arboreum*. This tree is much like a thirty-foot-tall *Pieris* with drooping panicles of white, waxy, bell-like flowers. It blooms in midsummer—when some overhead excitement is needed—and has brilliant red to purple fall foliage. Its spring leaves are a crisp, glossy green. Altogether a multitude of priceless virtues that cost only twenty-five dollars. A bargain at twice the price.

This was not enough, however. It would not do to return home with but a single plant. So I shopped for another two hours, accumulating all the treasures I could possibly stuff into my tiny car and thinking how much better off I would be if only I had a bus—or maybe an eighteenwheeler.

Among the spoils was *Callicarpa japonica* 'Alba', the white-berried beauty bush, loaded now with staggering amounts of fruit. (I once cast a disparaging remark at the insipidly vile, purple-colored berries of beauty bush in *Thyme on My Hands*, but no more—I have learned my lesson. No sooner do I condemn a plant for ugliness than I find I like it in spite of myself. Or, perhaps, *to* spite myself.) There was *Itea virginica* 'Henry's Garnet', an improved eastern U.S. native shrub with fragrant white flowers in summer and velvety purple leaves in fall, a fine backdrop for the more open white beauty bush. Then came *Hamamelis* × *intermedia* 'Diane', a late-winter bloomer with bundles of small red straplike petals and leaves that turn brilliant orange and red in the fall. Next there was *Vaccinium* 'Blue Chip', a blueberry that produces late-spring white flowers, edible purple fruit, and absolutely fire-breathing red foliage in the fall. And finally, snowberry, *Symphoricarpos* × *chenaultii*

'Hancock', a subshrubby ground cover with purplish red to pink-white berries in the fall.

I still needed some additional ground-level plants, but I'd already done quite enough financial damage for one afternoon. The plan, now, was to go home and do some work. Although this autumnal day was glorious, winter's arrival was expected at any moment.

This was another bulb-planting week. I spent the day setting out tulips. Every year I remind myself not to plant the damn things and almost every year I plant them all the same. It is tiresome never to listen to myself, especially when I know I'm right. Tulips take a lot of time to plant—considering the reward—and they are more of a nuisance than a flower. Generally, the flowers last only a short while in our sudden spring heat waves, then the foliage hangs limp about the garden forever. It looks like nothing much and it is in the way when you want to plant something useful—annuals, for example. If you wait for the foliage to die back, it is almost too late to plant anything in their place. Since the bulbs seldom reflower, and then only with a lot of specialized care, the best thing is to dig them up and compost them right after they bloom. But this takes work, and in the spring I have enough to do without creating more. So, in spite of myself, I let the few tulips that winter over do the best they can and then plant more. It is not rational, but then I'm only a gardener after all.

My planting scheme for tulips this year is rather milk-toasty: 'Maureen' (white), 'Blue Amiable' (also called 'Bleu Aimable', purportedly blue but probably purple), and 'Pink Diamond' (a rather intense pink). I made two plantings staggered on opposite sides of the front pathway, each consisting of thirty bulbs—ten of each color. The blue separates the white from the pink. All are varieties chosen to bloom at the same time. I want to get them out of the way in one single outburst. There is almost nothing worse than a patch of tulips all blooming at different times and in different stages of collapse. Well, two patches might be even worse, and I'm certain I'll find out some time next spring.

I'm not overly keen on those fiery red and orange sorts of tulips that our friendly municipal planners here in the Washington, D.C., area think must be on display. Apparently, the philosophy is that spring should be announced by blaring trumpets and crashing timpani. Workers plant out thousands of square feet of flaming tulips that blast winter-weary eyes with radiant vibrations. I suppose this is one approach to celebrating the end of winter, but it would seem kinder to lead unaccustomed eyes gracefully into spring.

These great plantings, erupting in the nation's capital as they do (and in many other public areas I am certain), seem like an awful waste of money to me. Tulips are labor intensive both to plant and to rip out. Not only is the labor intensive, but I have no doubt that it is also expensive. The bulbs, too, are expensive, considering that they are removed right after flowering. And then there is the problem of the winter mud fields. Invariably, tulips are placed in big beds that remain bare all winter long. They come up and flower for a week or two, then are dug out. That leaves a large space mostly empty most of the time. It doesn't make sense to me. But then I learned a long time ago that very little makes sense to me; otherwise, I would have stopped planting tulips when I hit puberty. If you enjoy tulips, you can thank the gods of gardening that I am not on your city payroll because I'd probably use all that space to grow something useful in the winter—like rutabagas. Or turnips. In fact, maybe I'd compromise and grow tulips between the turnips.

I've either just hit upon a brilliant idea or winter's getting to me early. As some of my friends would likely tell you: "Given *that* choice, put your money on winter."

Week Two _____

So much for warm fall days. Winter is here, along with its complimentary frost. At an air temperature of 42 degrees there is little incentive to stick your bare arm through a thin sheet of ice into two feet of water and muck, but when it's been chilly for several days, the ice doesn't always melt as it's supposed to. Sometimes a fellow has to be braver than the gardening manuals call for. Today was such a day, and what required bravery was removing a tropical water lily from the large pond. I've built two ponds in the garden: a large, wasp-waisted one just off the terrace, surrounded by a small rockery, and a small pool in the midst of the large rock garden.

There is, at present, a grand national lust for ponds directed, in part, by the pond purveyors and their seductive catalogs. What they often neglect to mention is that occasionally you must do something other than dote on your aquatic accomplishments. In other words, there are assorted pond cleanup chores that must be performed, the details of which are conveniently overlooked in the excitement of commercial pond-pitching. Details, however, are what a gardener is made of, and we well know that nothing in gardening is without its modicum of cleanup.

In my ponds, fall cleanup amounts to removing excess organic matter from the water so that it won't form a mat of oxygen-depriving rot during the trying times to come. In this region the pond may be covered with four to six inches of solid ice, and it is important to keep as much oxygen as possible in the water for the fish's sake. They still have to breathe, after all, even when they can scarcely move about in the frigid water. I've rarely lost goldfish to winter's ravages except when there were too many fish for the amount of oxygen. Unfortunately, this is a self-righting system, and the only way I can tell that I didn't do a good job of fall cleanup is by the number of dead fish floating on the pond come spring. This is not a pleasant start to the gardening year, so it is best to keep things balanced in the fall.

Several weeks ago I cleaned the large pond of leaves. I just raked it along with all my other leaf-raking chores. One simply rakes the leaves from under the water. Instead of dragging the rake across the top of the pond, I slide it vertically into the water, making certain I don't drive its tines into the liner, turn it horizontally, and bring it upwards beneath the surface. This catches all the floating leaves. Then I use the rake as a scoop, gently dredging leaves up from the bottom, trying not to disturb the film of black ooze that resides permanently at the pond's base. The water always roils up a bit, but next day it is as good as new. Or at least as good as it is going to get.

Although I've had the large pond for six years, this year was my first adventure into tropical water lilies. In the past they'd always seemed so expensive and so transitory as to be easily ignored. This year, however,

I caught the urge—that well-known gardening phenomenon in which the will becomes subservient to the whim. My whim arrived after seeing a number of tropicals in bloom at Lilypons Water Gardens, the nearby (and national) mail-order aquatic nursery.

The tropicals are magnificent plants, full of pure saturated colors not usually seen in hardy water lilies. Not only that, some bloom in early evening through late morning so that I'd have a chance to see their flowers, unlike the hardy sorts that bloom only at midday (and which I can see only on weekends). It seemed almost thrifty, actually, to plunk down thirty-five dollars (plus tax) for a plant I might get to see blooming on a daily basis. I purchased 'Red Flare', a cultivar with red flowers and reddish leaves. It's a real beauty even when not in flower, and although the flower is described as "red," it might more accurately be called "day-glo hot vermilion."

From the day I placed the huge plant (two feet across) in my pond, it has been everything a plant ought to be: handsome, floriferous, fragrant, colorful, exciting, pest-free, and a conversation piece. There is only one slight problem: the plant is not hardy. That would be asking too much, I suppose. The term "tropical" says it all.

In northern climes, the recommendation of most books (and aquatic nurseries, I might add) is that plants be discarded at the end of the year. This practice may make sense (actually dollars) to the nursery but does not sit well with me. I do not believe in throwing money away or in taking a beautiful plant that has served with vigor and glamor and repaying its kindness by tossing it on the compost heap.

Although water-gardening books give advice on many things, their suggestion for tropical water lilies amounts to a cryptic "store them over winter." I can often get by without such helpful, informative advice. At such times that I *do* need advice, I usually turn to my friend and colleague Dug Miller in the U.S. Department of Agriculture. You may recall this Master of Manure from my previous book. The inspiration for my pond came from Dug, who built the first pond on the block and inspired three more of us to do the same. Naturally, he is the first person I turn to when faced with questions concerning the pond. Although a great proponent of tropical water lilies, he has personally killed more plants than anyone has a right to. He has had no success overwintering them in his heated greenhouse, and since I have a cold greenhouse (very cold at times), I haven't seen much point in listening to his advice on the issue of tropical water lilies. I needed a higher authority.

Henry Mitchell, the exceptionally knowledgeable and often irascible garden columnist for the *Washington Post*, has also done battle with tropical water lilies. He points out that small nodules form on the mother plant in the fall. He removes these and overwinters them in jars of moist sand. I may try this, but my first inclination is to let the plant go dormant (as it has), bring its plastic tub indoors (as I did today), let it gradually dry out (as it will), and then store it in a cool, dry place for the winter. This will have one of three effects on the plant: kill it outright, kill it slowly, or allow it to live through the winter so that I can kill it in the spring.

For weeks the refrigerator has been full of bulbs, over 500 at last count. Slowly they've all been planted out—except for the paper-white narcissi. Today was *their* day. These narcissi are forcing bulbs, and although it doesn't seem right somehow to force bulbs into unnatural acts, they apparently don't mind at all. At least they pretend as if this were their usual mode of existence. To give them as Christmas gifts might seem perverted, but I do it anyway, and most people don't seem to mind. I also keep a few pots for myself as their flowers are at once beautiful, welcome for blooming as they do at the worst time of the year, and narcotic.

Their fragrance is nauseating to some but not to me. Closed up in the basement greenhouse as they are, their fragrance saturates the air awaiting such time as I open the basement door to flood the upstairs with an overwhelming sweet, springlike fragrance. By January I need some drug to see me through to March and April. Paper-whites are that drug. I do not care if I am branded a thug by those who support plants' rights. I will continue to force those poor, innocent bulbs to do my brutish bidding, and I shall enjoy it.

Now, to more bulbs. In addition to the paper-whites, I repotted three bulbs of *Lilium* 'Casa Blanca' that I grew last year in a ten-inch pot. I don't know how, or if, they will repeat their performance of last

July, but it's worth a try. A year ago at this time, I potted up the newly purchased bulbs and kept them cool and damp in the greenhouse. I put a few *Anemone blanda* tubers in the upper inch of soil and then did what most gardeners do best: waited. In February the anemones flowered and the lilies sprouted but stayed low. As soon as the last frost passed, I put the pot outside on the terrace and waited.

And waited.

And waited some more. Obviously, these bulbs weren't about to be forced into anything!

Sometime in July my wait ended. 'Casa Blanca' bloomed with six-inch flowers of the purest white. Absolutely no yellow speckles. (I don't like yellow dots in flowers. Yellow washes, OK. Yellow stripes, OK, sort of. Yellow dots, never! It's one of those personal gardening quirks one picks up for no apparent reason—like a fear of pansies or an irrational fondness for dahlias. Who can say where they come from or how long they will last? Next year I might even like yellow dots. But not this one.) The three bulbs produced fifteen to twenty flowers that lasted almost three weeks. I brought the pot in at the least hint of rain, and this helped the flowers last longer than if they had gotten wet. A secondary reward for saving the flowers from the rain was that they flooded the house with fragrance. The bulbs were a great investment, but I shall be very much surprised if they bloom as well the second year in a pot as the first. It is not the natural state of affairs for these sorts of bulbs. However, if they bloom half as well, I will be amply rewarded. If they don't, I can still plant the bulbs in the ground and eventually they may recover.

Whatever the three old bulbs do, I took out an insurance policy on them. I bought three new ones, this time of 'Sterling Star', another robust, purportedly white beauty. When it comes to the garden, you can never have enough insurance.

I raked leaves for the second time this season. The wet kind. It was so cold and windy that there was little else I could do. Then, too, raking should be done before the heavy, wet, soggy leaves form a crust over what few plants still remain above ground, especially the very small alpine plants and the newly emergent self-sown seedlings. Yes, there are seeds sprouting at this time of the year, some incredibly thickly.

A chartreuse green film has formed over one spot in a gravel path where *Tanacetum parthenium* 'Aureum' seedlings are sprouting by the bucketful. This plant may be found under many names, including *Chrysanthemum parthenium*, *Parthenium matricaria*, and *Pyrethrum parthenium*, and is sometimes sold in seed catalogs as yellow-leaved matricaria or feverfew. For years I have admired this descendent of some pretty weedy stock, but in my garden I've had to coddle it as if it were a rare gem of the tundra. At first I started new plants from seed each year as scarcely any survived over winter in the garden. Then a few survived but looked so awful the second year that I renewed them from cuttings. Then a few seeded themselves about, but with great reservation. And now there are hundreds of seedlings in one square yard of pathway. This does not bother me a bit. This week I'll pot up a couple of dozen seedlings for the flower show (more about this later) and for next year's garden. I'll let the rest go to spring. Winter will take out a few, and I will take out whatever else remains—they are shallow-rooted. Some I will move and some I will leave in the path; I like plants in a pathway.

This yellow-leaved form of feverfew grows about six inches tall (twelve inches with flowers) and has self-illuminating ferny foliage. It calls out from darkened corners and demands to be appreciated. It is especially gorgeous in early spring, its pristine foliage pulsating with neon-chartreuse vulgarity. It is devastatingly beautiful before a thundershower when the black, bumbling clouds turn the air itself green. With a little sunlight straining through a hole in the clouds, but especially when backlit, the plants explode with a highlighted intensity that verges on the heavenly erotic.

Although essentially a full-sun plant, I find that its foliage stays a bit softer and the effect more intense in shade. It even does well in deep shade if planted out from potted stock (it doesn't seem to reproduce itself in the shade, much preferring the hot, dry gravel of the pathways). The plants tolerate heat and dryness and have no insect problems at all. More importantly, slugs don't touch them.

This feverfew does have one or two (or even three) possible drawbacks, but they shouldn't put anyone off growing it. The worst of these,

I'm sorry to say, is its flowers. They are attractive small white buttons that anyone would like, but they detract greatly from the foliage, which, in my opinion, is the only reason to grow the plant. I frequently cut the flowers off, but this is time-consuming and brings us to their second drawback. The foliage is extremely aromatic and might be considered unacceptable by those, for instance, who don't like the smell of marigold leaves. I like the odor in moderation, but when clipping off flowers I am overcome by it. The third drawback is that it can become weedy under the right circumstance. So far I have not seen this, but I have witnessed the ordinary dark green species take over large areas of disturbed fields. Fortunately, 'Aureum' comes true from seed and does not revert back to the form typical of the species.

Well, as I was saying before I got sidetracked, it is best to rake the leaves off seedlings because they are easily smothered. In addition to the feverfew, there are large numbers of single-flowered hollyhock seedlings, of sweet williams, of Shasta daisies, and purple toadflax. It is better that these be blasted by the cold winds of winter rather than squashed flat and left sunless for four months. It is a little late, I think, for them to be sprouting, but we had a long dry period in August, September, and October when seeds couldn't sprout, then we had five inches of rain in fourteen days. The seeds, knowing full well how to govern themselves, took advantage of the situation and sprouted like grass. Not all will survive, and it's a good thing, too. Come next spring there would be no room for me in the garden.

Week Three

Rain fell all night and most of this cool November day . . . two inches, and needed at that. I am not much of a rain-person and seldom venture out into it without good reason. Perhaps I have seen the Wicked Witch of the West melt one too many times.

But today my friend Dee Wilder has driven three hours in the rain to visit the garden and spend the day in garden chitchat. It is a great day for chitchat—but gardens? Not only is it raining, but the wind is blowing and the temperature is in the bottom fifties. At first we talk of rain, then of new bulbs, and eventually of garden well-being. Here I have had plenty of rain and have not watered much; there she has had no rain and has watered often. It is no fun spending endless hours watering when, in fact, rain is supposed to do the job.

Dee was at one time a colleague at the Museum of Natural History. We both worked for the U.S. Department of Agriculture as members of the Systematic Entomology Laboratory. As two of nearly twenty-five researchers, we provided identifications and information about insects that were submitted to us from people in the United States and around the world. We backed up our information with hands-on research. Whereas Dee studied the world of parasitic flies, my interests lay in the more fascinating world (to me) of parasitic wasps. But, as the adventurous among us are wont to do, she gave up insects to pursue her alternate passion of wildlife photography. Eventually, she became equally passionate about gardening and now devotes much of her free time to a two-acre retreat west of Richmond, Virginia.

Dee is what I would call the saintly sort of gardener: she saves plants from the evils of humankind. She just returned from a week's worth of plant salvation and horticulturizing in Michigan where she rescued a few hundred odds and ends from abandoned farms, roadside ditches, and her folk's farm. Before the trip she'd buried hundreds of bulbs beneath her garden's quilt of soil. Bulbs that I, ever the wicked gardener, had earlier uprooted and tossed in the compost heap to make way for "better" sorts.

The bulbs were all 'Ice Follies', a daffodil that is beautiful in its paleness yet pallid in its spunk. It has no backbone and cannot stand up to a drop of rain. For years I've grown the variety and for years it has spent its entire blooming period face down in the mud. And it multiplied copiously. So much, in fact, that it was beginning to not bloom at all. I'm not certain what is worse, having a daffodil that doesn't bloom or one that blooms horizontally on the ground. It takes me a long time to decide that something will not work in the garden. I am tenacious in that respect, giving a plant more chances than it has a right to expect. Then I do something drastic. That time had come for 'Ice Follies', so out it came from nearly everywhere in the garden and straight it went into the compost pile.

On a previous visit, when the subject of discarded bulbs arose, I was severely chastised and reminded that all plants deserve a life and that any discarded plant material would be gratefully received, regardless of pedigree. I rummaged through the compost heap as ordered and retrieved the maligned bulbs none the worse for the months they'd spent buried beneath its surface.

I made the mistake again this morning of mentioning another discarded plant, this one a dreaded yet beautiful monster that had eaten all the plants around it and was insinuating its underground tentacles into yet more distant reaches of the garden. The plant, *Lysimachia clethroides*, began as a well-behaved, upright citizen of the border. The first year its roots spread out a bit farther than I thought they ought to, so I cut them back a foot. This year the plant retook that foot and expanded out in all directions. I became suspicious when I noticed large, snakelike creeping roots erupting from the ground. Then, too, a number of plants around it had died or declined substantially. A vigorous boltonia that last year was two feet across and four feet high was nearly gone. A solidago was dead, itself no slouch when it comes to spreading. *Phlox* 'Elizabeth Arden' had been strangled to death and was being absorbed by the roots of *Lysimachia*.

I did not hesitate, at this final sight, to remove the savage. Or try. There were pounds and pounds of pink, fleshy, wormlike roots for a four-foot diameter and a depth of six inches. I suspect the plant will come back next year from pieces of root, but I will be on the lookout. Then again, I've probably made a grave mistake by putting the roots on top of the compost pile where I hope winter freezing will kill them (it probably won't).

Needless to say, Dee wanted to resurrect those roots immediately. In all candor, not wishing to spread the dreaded plant-eating plant throughout the universe, I did what we evil gardeners do best, I confused her with distracting tactics until she forgot about the roots. I never claimed to be a saint myself, but keeping a real saint on the straight and narrow path ought to earn me at least a good crop of cosmos next year.

Not only does Dee save plants, regardless of their social behavior, but she is also an "R-rated" person. That is, she has no fear of the rain; it has no hold over her; when wet she does not melt. It came as no surprise, then, that after a few hours of gardening gossip, she wanted to go out and look at plants . . . in the rain, naturally. I suggested the local, and fabulou;, Brookside Gardens, knowing full well that it has a conservatory and that once therein I could hide the shame that I *do* melt in the rain.

We proceeded to Brookside where, naturally, we spent the first hour freezing our wet hindquarters off in the windy, rainy outdoors. (Well, truthfully, I was the only one who froze; saints have antifreeze.) Interestingly, the garden ponds were so overflowing of their banks that steps had turned into waterfalls and drains were themselves ponds. The normally placid little trickle that flows down the west side of the garden was a nightmare of white-water havoc gnawing away at its channel. I begged, nay pleaded, to be taken to the conservatory where it would be safe and warm and certainly dry.

As it turned out, the conservatory was basically safe and dry. Warm it was not. The main displays of seasonal chrysanthemums were outstanding in their topiary corsets. With months of intensive training on frames, these plants had been shaped to resemble tall pillars and trees in full bloom from top to bottom. Then, too, there were hanging baskets of cascading flowers—but not your garden-variety baskets. These were four feet in diameter draped with three-foot sheets of flowers. The football mums, too, were impressively garish in their cabbagey way. But the most outstanding display was the banked mounds of spoon-type pink chrysanthemums interplanted with the wispy, arching lavender-and-white flowers of the Mexican bush sage, *Salvia leucantha*. The upstanding branches of salvia made the otherwise dull, static bank of pink into a nodding, bustling collage of motion without any real movement. It was one of those plantings destined to be emulated, somehow, in my own garden, maybe even next year.

A gardener can learn a lot from observations made at opportune times. That is one reason for visiting public and private gardens, nurseries, and even public buildings. Not to copy—though there is no harm in it, and it is nearly impossible, given the vagaries of gardening—but to envision. Even on an otherwise bad day (such as today), some bit of wisdom may be gleaned from even a casual study of the work of others. Then, if one is somewhat creative, s/he can begin to embellish these thoughts. I find it is no big crime to take an idea and try to make it better. Eventually, I might even create a new thought. Or at least think I have, which is just about the same—as long as you don't get caught!

Ever so gradually, after several circuits of the conservatory, all thoughts of rain, cold, winter, freezing winds, snow, sleet, ice, and other upcoming winter distractions were laid to rest. Short visits to paradise now and again but especially in winter can overcome bad thoughts—maybe even metamorphose them into next year's garden. And being in the presence of a fellow gardener doesn't hurt either; it does wonders for the spirit. If we gardeners are famous for anything, it is the company we keep.

This week I ordered 996 new perennial plants for the garden and it didn't cost a cent. The plants are on loan from a cooperating nurseryman to be used in the display garden several friends and I are designing for the Maryland Home and Flower Show next March. How this came about is a long, involved story, the gist of which is that a colleague of mine, Bill Gimpel, who is in charge of the Maryland Department of Agriculture, was asked several years ago to represent the state in a display garden. Bill then asked Dug to help. Dug, who is not only a long-time friend, but just as important, my boss, then asked me to help. Does a picture emerge here?

The exhibit is nonprofit and unjudged, and the three of us have been working nights and weekends on it (actually I just work weekends, I'm not *that* stupid). You might call this a labor of love, or of charity. This will be the third garden that the three of us have designed and helped put together, with the cooperation of dozens of dedicated colleagues, in the past four years. Our only qualification for doing so is a certain bravura that comes from not knowing what we've gotten ourselves into. After four years you'd think we might have an inkling, but we're just simple-minded government workers, after all.

You might imagine after the first show, which went remarkably well in a panicky sort of way, that our inclination would be to rest on our laurels. But since we had no laurels (I think it was too early for them), we did a second, larger garden. It went well also, so naturally we were asked to do yet another—next year's garden at sixty by eighty feet. Not only will it be the biggest garden in the show, it will also be the first garden to be seen upon entering—a so-called "Entrance Garden." The general consensus among us is that somehow, somewhere, something went terribly wrong. We didn't mean for it to go this far.

Our first display garden was placed safely at the back of the flower show—way back in one corner (but still in the same building as the rest of the show). It was a seaside garden, complete with dock, boat, and sea. This, we knew, would be our first and last garden display, so we decided to do a professional job with an amateur's enthusiasm. If not good, at least something to talk about. The display turned out quite well, and we were encouraged to think that, yes, even amateurs might have their day.

The second exhibit was an informal garden backing up to a natural area complete with "stone" outcropping, walk-under waterfall, and babbling brook. At the time we didn't realize just how much babbling we were in for. We made the stone outcropping and waterfall from a material called hypertufa, a mixture of peat moss, perlite, and portland cement. It took many, many weekends of work to build everything, but in the end it was a successful exhibit and one we never expected to surpass.

Now comes next year's show, and everyone will expect us to outdo ourselves. Does this spell disaster or what? We're not certain our last garden can be surpassed for showmanship, so five months from now we will be stressing education, plantsmanship, home garden ideas, plant combinations, and underused plants. My job, for now, is to select and organize some of the perennials to be forced in greenhouses for next March's show. Since forcing any plants (except a few paper-whites) to do nearly anything they don't want to do is beyond my known abilities, we may have some interesting (read "disastrous") results.

Week Four

Today was finger-raking day. I did not plan it that way, it just happened. The air was warm, nearly 60 degrees, which is quite warm for a Thanksgiving Day. With winter coming, it is always wise to take advantage of the last few balmy days of the year. I had some time to kill before dashing off to dinner, so while boiling my contribution to the event (onions and sweet potatoes, but not together, of course), I decided to get in a little finger-raking. This is not as gruesome as you might imagine, for I don't actually rake up loose fingers that happen to be lying about, I simply use my fingers as rakes to clean up the rockery plants.

I know it is not wise to have a rockery near trees, but when one is surrounded by trees on all sides, wisdom has very little to do with it. Actually, wisdom has nothing to do with anything, since the most offending tree, *Taxodium distichum*, is one I planted myself eight years before I made the large rock garden at the back of the property. It is situated perfectly so that the northwest wind (our basic wind around here) blows most of the leafage directly on top of the rockery. In spite of which, I have no inclination to cut it down.

The cultivar of *Taxodium distichum* that I grow is a slightly pendulous form of the native southeastern bald cypress. I bought it some years ago and have not seen it for sale since. As the species is beautiful beyond belief to begin with, a little weeping simply glorifies it. It has grown over twenty feet in ten years, but at the same time it is open and ferny and acts as a fine filter for hot afternoon sun. I built this rockery in its lee on purpose. Our Maryland sun is pitiless by two o'clock in the afternoon, and combined with a nearly saturated atmosphere, it tends to reduce rock garden plants to quivering mush if something isn't done.

The only slight drawback to *Taxodium* lies in its branchlets and leaves, which drop in great heaps in the fall. Unlike other, more rotund leaves that simply blow off the rockery, those of bald cypress catch onto the slightest obstruction. *Dianthus erinaceus*, with its fistful of needles towering at less than an inch, gins the air for every strand of cypress leaf. *Veronica prostrata*, also at less than an inch, and even *Lysimachia japonica*, essentially a two-dimensional plant, act like velcro in catching and holding *Taxodium* leaves. And once a bald cypress leaf is stuck in something, it acts like a lodestone, drawing the entire tree down upon itself. Even so, I would not cut it down.

And so today, the day of Thanksgiving, was spent on my knees giving thanks (that I have only the one bald cypress) and finger-raking each tiny rockery plant until it was picked clean for the winter. It is better, I believe, to uncover plants for the winter than to leave mounds of duff all about the rockery. For one thing, slugs love to hide beneath the cool, damp leaves, and ground cover makes it easier for them to travel from plant to plant. As most of the rockery is covered in gravel, with great distances between plants, I think leaving the surface uncovered tends to keep slugs slightly at bay. I also believe that the smaller evergreen plants suffer greatly from soggy, decaying vegetable matter piled on top of them. Fortunately, *Taxodium* leaves are light and feathery, but even so, when piled two to three inches deep they eventually become matted. In fact, *Taxodium* leaves become so intertwined so quickly that they can be rolled off plants nearly like a blanket. It is much easier (and kinder) to take the leaves off with a slight raking motion of the fingers than with a garden rake.

Not only does finger-raking relieve the plants of their burden, but also I receive a tactile, visual, and olfactory sense of them that would be impossible to gain otherwise. Today I was especially glad for sensory inputs into my winter-adapting body. A few more weeks and the outdoor gardening season will be coming to a crashing, freezing, mushy, blackened finale—along with my psyche. I was glad to partake while I still could.

There is much to be said for plants with texture, especially when you're finger-raking. Unfortunately, not all of it is good. When your hands are cold, spiny plants grab your fingers long before the sensation actually reaches the brain. In this respect, we differ little from the thick-skinned, small-brained dinosaurs. *Erinacea pungens*, for example, is the great finger grabber. It would, I think, drag the unwary gardener to his or her death if s/he had not the greatest amount of patience to start with. Compared to this porcupine, some of the more delicate creatures of the rockery are much more subtle in their attack. *Dianthus petraeus* ssp.

noeanus, *D. hungaricus*, and *D. erinaceus* are mere finger ticklers. It is still a cautious little game to rake the leaves off without gaining a few "ouches" for the trouble. Even *Minuartia circassica*, so innocent in its slightness, is not above lashing out when the fingers get too close or too ham-handed.

Jasminum parkeri is not so much prickly as it is wiry. To reach down into the plant is like threading your fingers through a pile of twisted coat hangers looking for just that special one. It is tough enough when you have full balance, but to get at my *J. parkeri*, I have to straddle the small pond with both legs, balance with one hand on a suitable outcropping, and imitate, for all intents, a wobbling tripod about to take a dunking. Much easier picking is the skeletal *Betula nana*. Raking leaves out of that pile of twigs is like picking meat off a bone—easy once you develop a taste for it.

Much to be preferred to those angular sorts of plants is raking leaves from among subjects with pliable, velvety leaves or buds or a fragrance that recalls the better times of last summer, now but a distant memory. Grooming *Teucrium aroanium*, with its soft leaves and slightly pungent aroma, is a pleasant affair. And the furry leaves of the diminutive *Verbascum* 'Letitia' have their tactually explicit rewards. But slipping the duff off *Marrubium rotundifolium* is damn near immoral: the leaves are of the finest, silkiest cashmere. That is why it takes me so long to finish up the one small plant I have.

And if the leaves are both woolly *and* fragrant, then perhaps the less said the better. *Nepeta phyllochlamys*, *Teucrium cussonii*, and *Calamintha cretica* fall into this category. Merely brushing their foliage starts an onslaught of memories of the highest, hottest days of summer, which, by the way, I infinitely prefer to these sissy fall days and the despicable winter ones to come—days when the blast of Maryland's humidity mixes with the song of its crickets. Heat always steeps the garden's fragrance and its music, especially at eventide, one of my favorite times to be in the garden.

Some plants, such as the dwarf form of *Origanum vulgare* 'Compacta', are raked primarily for their fragrance and only incidentally to remove the fallen leaves. Slow to grow at first, my plant is now three square feet of intensely sweet scent. I wish I could roll around and around in it much as my cat, Bruno, does in his patch of *Nepeta mussinii*. After a few minutes of such intoxicating behavior, he feels no pain, as I am certain I wouldn't either.

Some odors are not so exotically nice. Interesting perhaps, clean perhaps, aromatic perhaps, but not the sort of thing that calls for rolling around in. *Teucrium marum*, for example, has a bitter odor. Not too pleasant, but faintly attractive in small quantities.

The many forms of *Thymus*, some with so many parents in their begettings as to raise eyebrows, are all attractively scented in their ways, and each is a challenge to interpret. A few years back a friend gave me several different "fragrances" of thyme—lemon, caraway, mint—and these are always well worth raking.

Most of these plants are common, probably even dreary, subjects for the rockery. Many do not bloom with any degree of enthusiasm, and even if they did, would not generate much enthusiasm in the gardener. But they are in good foliage the entire growing season and provide a reward for anyone willing to lower him- or herself for a quick caress. In early spring, late fall, or even midsummer, this attribute is not to be sneezed at (unless, of course, one is allergic). Many other rock garden plants are so abysmal-looking after they bloom that you quite wish they could be buried beneath leaves starting some time in June.

It does not bother me that once (or at most twice) a year I must go to work, fingers akimbo, tidying up each of my fragrant or furry friends. Even the spiny and wiry ones aren't ignored at this time of year. In fact, at any time of the year, I am likely to be seen on all fours feeling or smelling some plant or other. Fall is not necessarily a prerequisite for such behavior. My neighbors find it a bit odd, and when pressed for an explanation, I simply say to them, "Tidying things up a bit you see. It's these damn bifocals . . . can't see a thing." They go away amused, and I don't have to explain exactly what I'm doing. I would rather they consider me nearsighted than odd.

I have one of the world's largest collections of small cardboard boxes stored away in my basement. In them have come chrysanthemums from Ohio; dahlia tubers, rare alpines, and hydrangeas from Oregon; narcissi, tulips, and crocuses from Holland (via Wisconsin and New Jersey); thalictrums from North Carolina; caladiums from South Carolina; lilies from California and Connecticut. I keep all these boxes (and the packing material) for three reasons: (1) I hate to waste stuff, (2) each box is the perfect size for making troughs, and (3) I might need one someday to send plants off to another gardener. Today my supply was diminished by one box—someone else will have to store it for a while.

The box, weighing two pounds four ounces, was stuffed with garden pinks and sent to my brother on the other side of the continent. Technically, this is not entirely legal, but they were small rooted cuttings from which I had washed all the sand and then packed in damp peat. If I am thrown in jail, so be it. I could use the writing time. I am certainly no worse than the person who introduced tree of heaven or kudzu (and who should be hanged by his own vine). I struck the cuttings in July and August in my six-by-two-foot sand bed with the broken heating cable. (It is important to have a broken cable because it gives off metallic trace elements that are good for cuttings.) Then, as usual, finding that I had overproduced in the cuttings department, I opted to start my brother along the pink pathway to abundance.

But to return to the boxes. I feel much better now that I've sent one of them off because it justifies the rest of them. You never know when you might need a box. In fact, if any of you ever needs an empty box for some reason or other, just send me the cost of shipping and it'll be off to you in the next mail.

Week Five _____

I can tell that spring has finally arrived because the first seed catalog was just delivered to my door. To others the laying down of bulbs is spring's gentle precursor. But for me it is when the seed catalogs arrive that I begin to think—no, to dream—about spring, and more important, about next year's garden. No matter how enticing bulbs might be in spring, they are not the backbone of the garden and play, in my opinion, only a brief introductory (but necessary) function.

As a gardener, growing things from seed has always been one of my favorite gardening pastimes. I have done it since childhood and still cannot believe what wonders arise from a ten-cent packet of paper (though, of course, packets now cost anywhere from one to five dollars and may be plastic or foil). The catalog that came today was from Thompson & Morgan, the first mail-order company from which I ever bought seeds. It is an English firm, established in 1855, that only recently began selling seeds directly in the United States. As a young teenager in the late fifties, I would pool a seed order with my friend Virginia Stewart, who converted all those strange currencies of one shilling and six pence (then about twenty cents), or two and six, into nickels and dimes, then send off the princely sums in pounds sterling. Today it is much simpler because Thompson & Morgan maintains a U.S. distribution system with prices in dollars (long gone are the cents!).

The old T & M catalogs (spelled "catalogues," of course) were severe in the extreme. After a few listings and descriptions of "Best Novelties," the catalog launched into alphabetical listings of species followed by catalog numbers in precise numerical sequence and price per packet. Each variety had one or, rarely, two lines of description. (Can you imagine one line of description in a modern catalog?) For example T & M's 1964 catalog started at *Abies concolor*, catalog no. 1, "highly decorative, shoots green, globose," one shilling, six pence, and ended at *Zizyphus jujuba*, catalog no. 4049, again one shilling and six, "an attractive small tree, hardy in milder parts, dark red fruits, turning black, edible." Then followed the ornamental grasses (to catalog no. 4085), and finally, several hundred sorts of vegetable seeds by common name only and without catalog numbers.

The 1991 catalog (at least the U.S. edition) is now heavily laden with color pictures of many offerings and expanded descriptions of all. There is still an introductory section of new things, including "Exclusive World Firsts" and "Newest and Best," but the main sequence remains alphabetical. It starts with *Abelmoschus moschatus* 'Mischief', catalog no. 2730, at a dollar ninety-five for eighteen seeds, with "scores of Hibiscus-like rich cherry red and white bicoloured blooms 2½–4 in. across, from July until the first frost," and ending with *Zinnia* 'Old Mexico', catalog no. 6809, at two sixty-five for thirty seeds. The vegetables still follow, but now with numbers.

It is somewhat startling to compare these catalogs, separated as they are by over twenty-five years. The most obvious differences—glitz and price—are not really unexpected. Consumerism demands pretty pictures, color, superlatives. Prices, we understand, rise over the years. A package of sweet william 'Harlequin' cost fourteen cents then, a dollar forty-nine now; florist's cyclamen (improved) about two and a half cents a seed then, now about twenty cents a seed for a comparable variety. Prices have increased tenfold, which isn't unreasonable it seems to me. Inflation or not, the return from a packet of seed at ten cents, or even ten times that amount, is still a damn good return for the money.

Of somewhat more concern than either glitz or price, however, is that the number of seed offerings has dropped significantly from 1964 to 1991. The drop is at least one-third, though the calculation is admittedly approximate. Comparing some of my favorite groups, I see that in 1964 T & M offered fifty-nine different varieties of *Campanula* (now thirty-two), ninety-four varieties of *Dianthus* (now forty-eight), and ninety-four varieties of *Primula* (now fifty-one). Certainly fifty-one varieties of primroses would be enough for anyone—about fifty varieties too many judging by most gardens. Yet it does indicate a more general falling off of diversity than might be apparent at first glance. Of the primroses, for example, the 1964 offerings included forty-four different species of *Primula*, the newer one only nineteen. Thus, if one were interested in growing different species of primroses, there has been a more than 50-percent loss in diversity in the last twenty-five or so years, at least in the Thompson & Morgan catalog.

This loss of diversity bothers me, but not from my viewpoint as a gardener—most likely I will never grow all those species anyway, though I once thought I would. The loss bothers me, instead, in my role as a naturalist and as a human being. I view this as another measure of the way humankind reduces biological diversity to biological monotony and, equally likely, to economic simplicity suited to our basically unembellished minds. Take the case of the American lawn, for example. We have destroyed 50,000 square miles (an area the size of Alabama) of native living, breathing space with introduced and engineered lawn grasses, foreign weeds, and millions of gallons of chemicals and fuels and created unimagined amounts of air, soil, and ground-water pollution. Those who condemn the destruction of South American rain forests for immediate gain are merely condemning their own behaviors. For years we have been eroding and toxicating our own soil and water and life. In the name of agriculture we have simplified the entire center of our country—our tall-grass prairies—to virtual extinction (less than one tenth of 1 percent remains). In our gardens we transform what could be a rich biological potpourri into a near monoculture. And not content with that, we then pour chemicals upon everything to insure that it stays simple. Those who imagine this will have no effect upon forthcoming generations are worse than shortsighted. They are, unfortunately, human.

It's not often that the last week of November presents an Indian summer like this. Today was balmy and clear . . . too good to be real and almost certainly too good to last. A leisurely stroll about the garden was the first order of the morning, followed by an inspiration to do something worthwhile to honor fall's magnificent coda. A good day to start a project, and as a matter of fact, nearly finish it, too. But then I nearly finished myself off as well, due to my back, which gave out under the onslaught of heavy work.

The job was to start a new walkway and to begin a new garden. This sounds grand on paper, only proving that the printed word is mightier than reality. The new walkway is only about twenty square feet and the new garden about the same. And to make things even less grandiose-sounding, neither project is really new: the walkway is an expansion of the front walk, while the garden is an expansion of an old garden. The only new part, actually, is digging out the lawn to do both, but since I've been digging out grass for ten years, even that can't, strictly speaking, be called new. I guess I'm just doing the same old job I've always done, just in a new place. Well, at least something is new.

Removing lawn requires two tools: a spade and a spading fork. If you count yourself, it takes three. Many people would use a high-powered gasoline-engined cultivator to get this job done, but not me. It is entirely too simple (and disagreeable) that way. In the past twelve years or so, I've taken out about 8000 square feet of sod by hand and it's too late to think about a cultivator. Way too late—there's scarcely any lawn left to take out. And besides, I'm not certain that if I'd had a cultivator I'd have used it.

Mechanical things go too fast for me; I can't keep up with them physically or mentally. Twelve years ago, if I'd used a cultivator, I would most likely have chewed up the whole lawn in two hours' time and not had the faintest idea what to do next. When I take sod out by hand, I have plenty of time to plan and worry about what I'm going to do with the space when I finish tearing it up. Why last year, for example, I made a new garden by taking out 200 square feet of lawn. I started in November and was still taking out sod this past June, long after my seeds had sprouted, been transplanted to market packs, started flowering, and died—all still in the market packs. Now that's what I like about digging out lawn by hand. It gives you plenty of time to plan ahead.

This morning I took out enough sod to lay an expanded walk at the entrance of the house. I have never liked the walk up to my front door. It is a dull, narrow strip of unattractive concrete that cuts diagonally across the front lawn then runs starkly to a little stoop at the front door. The walk is so narrow that even one person must walk single file, and that is narrow, indeed. I decided to cut off part of the diagonal and to expand the walk where it meets the stoop. That way if several people come to the door at once they won't have to stand in a line halfway back to the street. They can at least bunch up at the new waiting area just before the stoop.

After digging out the lawn for the path, all the while pondering what sort of expanded garden I would make, I decided I didn't need to make elaborate plans for the laying of the path itself. I would just wing it. This is totally unlike me. I scarcely wing anything, and certainly not a scheme that has heavy-duty stone moving in it. The paving for the new path is some flagstone left over from building the terrace at the rear of the house. For the terrace I planned everything out to the last minute detail on graph paper (including some alternate patterns that required extra flags). Moving 800 square feet and several tons of stone once seemed like more than enough to me, so I made all the major moves on paper before I touched a stone. Today, seeing that I needed only twenty square feet of paving, I imagined I could lay it out as I needed to—no need for diagrams.

As usual, when I don't plan (and sometimes even when I do), I had to move and remove, lay and relay, groan and regroan every stone at least five times before it found its correct resting place. It is amazing how heavy stone can be, especially when it weighs a lot. After the stone laying I collapsed. Digging the new garden would have to wait until another good day.

Sometime next May should be about right.

2

DECEMBER

_____

On this first day of December there were still cleanup chores to finish. Lots of them. They would have to wait. Instead, I wanted to return to the lawn-removal project in the expanded front garden while the soil could still be worked. Even though the temperature was supposed to stay around 40 degrees, it thundered into the sixties without difficulty. The jacket came off first thing after starting the job. A flannel shirt is fine for digging in 55-degree weather.

First came the outline by spade, then removal of the sod. In the past sod removal was accomplished by undercutting with a spade and then skimming off the top two inches of grass. This is expedient when the grass is actually grass and the root mass is too thick to shake off the soil. In today's section, the grass was mostly weeds with little root mass. After cutting the outline, I used a spading fork to coax the soil off the roots. It is hard work and slower than simply stripping a roll of sod off the subsoil.

The spading itself was uneventful for a while, with the exception of banging into a few rocks, nails, and gutter ferrules. (You never know what you might hit during these excavations. I found a dime today, dated 1974; a friend of mine once found a ten-foot piece of aluminum siding at his place.) I also found a little patch of Japanese honeysuckle that had seeded itself into the lawn and been mown repeatedly for who knows how long. It had a rather chunky stem and an artistic above-ground root mass, so instead of throwing it in the compost, I potted it up to see what sort of top growth could be coaxed out of it. (This shouldn't be the least bit difficult with a honeysuckle.) With its gnarled root top exposed it could make an interesting pseudobonsai.

At other times, also in the front lawn, I have seen similar flat-topped plants of multiflora rose, privet, and native aster. As you might imagine from previous comments, I am not overly fussy about the lawn, or as it might better be called, the mowed weed patch. At least I don't put chemicals on it. It is safe to roll around on if one is into that sort of thing (the roses are too shorn to have thorns, but you'd still have to watch out for the rocks).

With the exception of the shortened honeysuckle, the spading went without hitch for two mindless hours, so I had plenty of time to catch up on my thinking. I spent most of that time dwelling on what sort of garden I might make when the time comes.

The front of my house faces almost due south, receiving nearly full sun. The new garden will be partially protected from the wind by the left side of the house, which forms a backdrop. Where the house ends is a small rockery (not to be confused with the large rockery, the terrace rockery, or the pond rockery). This falls rapidly down a steep embankment toward the lean-to greenhouse that is built onto the lower room of an addition that I added to the main house some years ago. The new garden will have two views: as you walk up the front path it will look like a ten-foot strip backed by the house except for where the rockery falls away behind it; from the bottom of the rockery and the greenhouse, the new garden simply looks like the top of a hill.

Because the garden will be viewed from the two aspects, its planning needs to be rather precise. From below, the plants at the top of the hill should not appear too tall, certainly not over one foot and preferably shorter, or else they will be out of scale with the smaller plants in the rockery. The plants in front of the house should be about three feet tall —four feet tops—so as not to obliterate the living room windows.

The height and shape of the new garden was coming into focus, but now the plants and color needed attention. (To hark back a week or two, I would never have had the time to think this through if I were using a power tool. I'd have hacked out enough lawn in minutes to start a turf farm and had no idea what I was supposed to do next.) Left of the new garden there has long been a hedge of pink *Rhododendron* 'English Roseum' underplanted with nearly a hundred white *Iberis sempervirens* 'Snowflake'. The left side, then, is entirely white and pink, and I decided to play upon this theme by adding more white flowers to the new garden.

Last year I created a much larger garden on the east (right) side of the walkway, facing the house. That garden is predominated by shades of pink and lavender with a little white thrown in. This garden was an endless amount of planning and planting that, in all honesty, will need a good deal of rethinking this winter. Enough rethinking, in fact, that I really won't have much left to think with, so I was not at all anxious to take on the planning of a new white garden.

Then it occurred to me that the problem was not a problem at all and that I'd already solved it. I'd ordered the garden, lock, stock, and seed packet, from Thompson & Morgan.

Two weeks ago, I had finished my order to T & M and was perusing the catalog for any important item I might have missed, when I began to study a stunning picture called "The White Flower Area." For some reason I first thought this was an advert for a book or garden magazine and passed it by at least a half dozen times. Finally, after reading and rereading the description, I discovered I was drooling—not a good sign at my age, at least. I was entranced by the simplicity of the prepackaged garden: the seeds for at least ninety varieties of white annuals were in three groupings by heights three to ten inches, ten to twenty inches, and twenty-one to forty-eight inches. Just scatter the seeds and wonderful things happen. Normally, I don't go for collections, but the picture was so enticing, and the idea of tossing out seed and recapturing an unknown mass of white flowers for the effort seemed irresistible.

At the time I ordered the seeds I had no idea where I would plant them, or even if I would. Sometimes, when you just have to have something, what you do with it really isn't so important. It never consciously occurred to me to create a special garden just for the seed collection. But somehow the "white garden" must have seeded into my subconscious. As with many gardening plans, only next year's growing season will confirm its success or failure. I can scarcely wait to see what happens.

I am always on the lookout for new places to publish my writing, mostly because it doesn't fit in most of the old places. I ought to know because I've tried them all. Most garden magazines want some sort of how-to, hard facts angle in their articles. Unfortunately, my writing does not readily fit into this market. It's not that I don't have facts, you know, it's mostly that I don't remember them for very long. About six minutes is my maximum fact-retention period. After that the edges start to fray, and I can't remember if what I'm remembering is a fact, a half truth, a lie, a line from Shakespeare, or something I read on a cereal box.

That is why I write more about the "whys" of gardening rather than the "hows." And it is also why I was overjoyed to find a new-to-me gardening journal devoted to garden design, notable gardens, people, and books. It is a literary garden magazine called *Hortus* and is published at a very mysterious-sounding place called The Neuadd in Rhayader, Powys, Wales. The subscription price is a bit steep, about sixty dollars for four quarterly issues, but each is a nicely bound 128-page volume. The illustrations are exceptionally rich black-and-white woodcuts or pen-and-ink drawings. No glitzy "colour" here. With great fear and trepidation I sent off a short piece to them yesterday, outlining my view of gardening experts and my first visit to England some years ago. It will be interesting to see if British rejection slips are different from our own.

On the home front, there was some good news for a change. Last month I submitted an essay to the year-old American journal called *GreenPrints*, whose goal is to "chase the soul of gardening." The essay, entitled "The Fall of Winter," is a subversive piece deriding the concept of fall. The way I see it, there are three seasons: spring when the weather is fickle, summer when it isn't, and winter when the weather is even more fickle. Fall is a verb, not a noun, and describes what happens in the first week of winter. As in, "All the leaves fall down." It's a concept created by New England chambers of commerce as tourist propaganda. It's the signal that death is around the corner waiting in a Mack truck for me to step off the curb. Need I go on? Amazingly, the essay was accepted today.

Although not yet as polished as *Hortus, GreenPrints* is the first periodical of its kind in our nearly gardening-illiterate country. It is also a quarterly, though much shorter at thirty or forty pages an issue, and correspondingly less dear at a mere ten dollars a year (though this is bound to inflate somewhat by the time this book is published). The mix of writing is a good one, including thoughts on inner city gardens, humor in the garden (we need more), and garden-people relationships. Also, some of each issue is gleaned from old garden writing—from a fourth-century retired Chinese magistrate to the Czechoslovakian science fiction writer Karel Čapek, whose *The Gardener's Year* is one of the most insightful, amusing garden books ever.

Because it has been well over a year since an editor has published anything of mine, today should be a red-letter day on the writing front. Oddly, it isn't. After any number of rejections, I become a little concerned that the odd acceptance or two is a cruel hoax. Recently an editor accepted a piece for publication, then six months later sent it back saying they'd made a mistake. In writing, it ain't published 'til it's published.

For me, every new piece of writing is like a battle, with little reinforcement from the past. Unlike in the garden, where even I occasionally learn from past mistakes, I find that writing is a forward-oriented struggle. I have only the future to look forward to, and even that is by no means guaranteed. I write and strive to improve, but no matter how good (or even how bad) the writing, my future is always in someone else's hands. In the garden we gardeners are in charge, or at least believe we are, and except for acts of nature, we cannot blame anyone else for our own inabilities. From that point of view, writing looks a lot better. There is always someone else upon whom to pin our failures.

The temperature didn't rise over 45 degrees today, but at least the sun stayed out. That meant I could work in the greenhouse without freezing anything important off. Mine is a cold house as opposed to a warm one, as I provide no direct heat to it. This twelve-by-fifteen-foot lean-to affair is sunk three feet into the ground and is embraced by the protecting west wing and southwest corner of the house. A small fan, sitting in the window of the east wall, runs continuously to move air internally and, I hope, to pull a little warm air out of the furnace room that lies on the other side of the window. Standing in the greenhouse at night one realizes there is no sensation of warmth coming from anywhere—it is just cold, and the fan makes it drafty as well. In five years of operation, the greenhouse has not fallen below 30 degrees at bench level in spite of outside temperatures of − 5 degrees. I haven't lost much except some extremely tender impatiens that were growing in flower pots with the geraniums. A five-foot dracaena, a hanging stapelia, and the pony-tail palm, beaucarnea, have not suffered in the least.

On cold December days the greenhouse comes to room temperature with the least amount of sunshine, and I can idle about feeling warm and comfortable. My favorite pastime is listening to Garrison Keillor's illuminating descriptions of life in Lake Wobegon while I putter around the greenhouse and potting room (a basement room leading to the greenhouse), transplanting, cleaning, pruning, preening, taking cuttings, repotting, and generally thermoregulating in the warm, humid atmosphere.

Today's primary chore was attending to the tropical night-blooming water lily that I mentioned earlier. I had planned to let it go dormant and dry out. But looking at the drying plant today, I could tell the outlook was not favorable. The top of the plant was obviously rotting off, not drying as any respectable plant might. So I dumped the planting container out on a tarp and took a closer look at the root ball. As I suspected, rot was spreading rapidly throughout the two gallons of snake-like roots.

The books are fairly ambiguous about what to do with these plants with the exception of a nearly unanimous "toss them out." Well, anything is worth a try at that rate, so I've fallen back on some instructions given by both Lilypons and Henry Mitchell. It seems that as a tropical waterlily goes into dormancy, it produces nodules at its crown. And sure enough, when I examined my plant, it had seven of them. These were as hard as walnuts and looked like them as well. When forced with extreme pressure, each one snapped off the crown, leaving a crater at its previous point of attachment. The clean break from the old plant appears to be an abscission point. Each of the seven nuggets was the same size, approximately one and a half inches in oblong diameter, with one end rather pointy and the other flat where it had been attached.

After removing the nodules, I placed them on top of moistened sand in a half-filled flower pot and covered the pot with a piece of plastic wrap held in place with a rubber band. Now I must wait and see—the gardener's official motto.

Week Two

My brother, Dee (not to be confused with my friend Dee), earned his revenge, and it took him only two weeks. It wasn't so long ago that I decimated my substantial collection of cardboard boxes by shipping one off to him. At that time it gave me a sense of satisfaction to put a box back into circulation. But now it has returned, this time filled with an assortment of exotic plants. They'll have to stay in the greenhouse, I'm afraid, because they are too young to plant out at this time of year and the weather is proof of that. It has just taken its big headfirst dive into winter. (This a.m. the temperature was over 50 degrees and this evening it is 32 degrees and falling, accompanied by howling winds.) Some of the plants he sent are marginally hardy here, anyway, so they would have to stay indoors no matter what the weather was like.

Before discussing the plants, however, first let me make a few comments about my brother. There is an eight-year difference between us, he being the younger. Professionally, he is a horticulturist, and avocationally, as well. It's not as if he didn't have enough to do working at gardening all day. Now when he comes home, he can play at it, too. Perhaps play is the wrong word. His life is full enough as it is with half a dozen goats, three kids (of his own), a wife, a fruit orchard, and a vegetable patch as big as my entire property. Not enough. He just built a 2500-square-foot greenhouse and started a custom propagating business in his spare time. And, as anyone who loves propagating knows, if you're not careful you can create enough plants in a few weeks' time to plant up an entire country (and I'm sure he isn't and I'm sure he has).

That is why I got a box of plants today. It's called spreading the wealth, cleaning-out-the-greenhouse-so-I-can-plant-more, plantsupmanship, making room, and a number of other such terms all translatable as, "What am I ever going to do with all these damn plants?" It would never occur to someone like Dee not to start all of them in the first place!

Now to the plants. They almost all cause problems for me in one way or another. Most are not reliably hardy and so need to be propagated anew each fall for overwintering. And some I haven't the foggiest idea what they might be. Questions immediately spring to mind such as: How tall (wide) will they grow? What exposure do they want? What color is the flower? Are they hardy? Will they survive once planted out? Will I ever be able to eradicate them once they're established? Since I am an older brother and since Dee unfairly credits me with some intelligence, I generally do not bother him with these trivial questions. First I try to find the answers, then, if necessary, I call him to find out what he has inflicted on me. (The old adage, "never talk to a sibling if you don't have to," also plays a large part here.)

In the case of the unreliably hardy plants, I have some basic idea of what to expect and won't need reference books (mostly because they are different cultivars of species Dee's sent before, and I've already done the reference work on them). Two dwarf *Penstemon* and *Phlox* cultivars will go to the rock garden in spring. They are known to be hardy. Nine plants of various cultivars of *Penstemon hartwegii* (and its hybrids) will be kept over winter in the greenhouse then set out in spring to be treated as annuals, and cuttings will be taken next fall to repeat the process. Actually, I've already begun some "experiments" (too grandiose a word, really) on cultivars of *P. hartwegii* from an earlier spring shipment. I've left the old mother plants out to brave the winter and rooted up some progeny to ensure survival for next year. A perennial *Helichrysum*, also included in the shipment, will have to be treated similarly.

The remaining five plants fall into the "surprise me" category. I have found out a little about *Barbarea vulgaris* 'Variegata', a mustard, commonly grown in England and called common winter-cress. The un-variegated form is cultivated for salad but is also a roadside weed in America. (Just what I need brother dear!) Apparently, the variegated form is nicer and is often grown in the border for its foliage, according to my sources. I will give my brother the benefit of the doubt—he may be playing a little gardening joke on me. (Maybe he finally figured out who threw that handful of kudzu seeds in his lower forty.) This plant can stand a little close inspection for a few years (if it lives that long).

Another plant he sent was *Sanguisorba tenuifolia* var. *purpurea.* According to Dee, who volunteered the information without my even asking, the plant grows three to seven feet tall and would look good next to my pond. Well, maybe. I have *S. obtusa*, the Japanese burnet, and it is quite a charming plant. It has gray-green fernlike leaves with caterpillarlike, long pinkish-red arching flowers. (Perhaps I should have said it is charming if you like caterpillars.) The most I can turn up in my reference books is that *S. tenuifolia* is more delicate than *S. obtusa* and flowers in spires. For *S. tenuifolia* var. *purpurea* the flowers are purple as the varietal name suggests.

Another plant is one I tried to buy seeds of last year without success. The plant, *Azorina vidalii* 'Rosea', does not appear in any of my books (even under its older name *Campanula vidalii*) but fortunately is described in my latest Thompson & Morgan seed catalog. Although the height is not stated, it appears to be two to three feet tall in bloom with Canterbury-bell-like flowers. Again, it is not hardy, but it does look like quite a show-stopper. It supposedly blooms sporadically at any time of the year, and that's always good for a surprise.

The last two plants, *Corydalis saxicola* and *C. cheilanthifolia*, are also scarcely mentioned in my books. They both grow to about a foot and have yellow flowers. The former species has blue-gray ruelike leaves; the latter fernlike green foliage. Both seem suitable for the rockery (according to Reginald Farrer, the well-known British plant explorer and authority on the rock garden), and that is where I suppose I shall put them.

All in all, I have Dee to thank for many splendid gifts. Not only for the surprise of the plants themselves but also for the bonus of knowledge and for the dreams of next summer's warmth. As the freezing wind filters through every crack around every window casement and through every crevice in every door frame, I am warmed by thoughts of next year. I have had to pour over many a book and catalog to ferret out even the few facts I have found, and in so doing the knowledge has been more deeply imprinted than if it had been handed to me directly.

These plants may well prove doubly surprising in the end, for I shall be surprised if I can persuade half of them to grow more than a year. And very pleased, indeed, if they should do so.

Sometimes it is hard to believe how little information there is in books. To write the last few paragraphs I perused six books and two seed catalogs, and they provided barely any information at all. This does not take into account the other half dozen books I looked at but found devoid of information. Nor does it count the dictionary that I must use to write anything because I can't spell worth a damn.

It really isn't that there is so little information in books, it's just that there is an incredible amount of information, and one book can only treat one sort of information in detail or a lot of details in general if it is to be a manageable book. For example, *The Genus Cyclamen* by Christopher Grey-Wilson (Portland, Oregon: Timber Press, 1988) treats nineteen species in its 150 pages, while my most recent book on perennials, *Perennials for American Gardens* by Ruth Rogers Clausen and Nicolas Ekstrom (New York: Random House, 1989), treats several thousand species, cultivars, and hybrids in its 630 pages. Each book attempts to do something different. The fact is that even two books on the same subject won't necessarily overlap. I have another recent book, *Herbaceous Perennial Plants* by Allan Armitage (Athens, Georgia: Varsity Press, 1989), also treating several thousand plants in its 672 pages. It is not precisely the same as the one by Clausen and Ekstrom. Then again, I have the 1946 edition of *The New Garden Encyclopedia* (edited by E. L. D. Seymour [New York: Wm. H. Wise & Co., Inc.]) that treats the whole subject of gardening in 1380 pages.

The first assumption might be that the last-named moldy old know-it-all encyclopedia would be outdated. Not in the least! It was the only book among those listed above that discussed *Barbarea*. Even my copy of *The Illustrated Dictionary of Gardening* from 1884–87 (edited by George Nicholson [London: Upcott Gill]) discussed *Barbarea*. In gardening, old information does not mean worthless information, not by a long shot (except, obviously, for plant nomenclature, which is perennially out of date no matter what year it is).

Nor does new necessarily mean up to date. Take the case of *Azorina*. The dearth of information indicates that the plant is either newly discovered, newly rediscovered by the trade, nomenclaturally mixed-up with some other name, rarely grown, or generally not worth growing. To solve this question I will most likely visit the botany library at the Smithsonian Institution's Museum of Natural History and check up on the genus in a few more books. It never hurts to be too thorough. Then, all else failing, I'll just have to roll up my sleeves, grow the damn thing, and see what it's all about. Either that or kill it because I'll have no idea what I'm doing.

But to return to comparisons. The two newer perennial books differ between themselves even though they treat the same topics. On the subject of *Sanguisorba*, for example, Armitage discusses two species at length while Clausen and Ekstrom discuss four species and one variety very briefly. In this case, since I am interested in *Sanguisorba tenuifolia* var. *purpurea*, the latter book is more helpful. For *Corydalis*, the Clausen and Ekstrom is only marginally more helpful, but neither book really hits the information mark.

Lysimachia clethroides, which I wrote about last month, is an interesting example of the differences that can be found between books treating the same subject. In this instance, Armitage's book is clearly the winner simply because he has personally grown the plant under three strikingly different conditions. He writes about its peculiar behavior from personal experience (rather than from research on someone else's experience). Now *that* is the stuff that separates the gardeners from the writers. At one time Armitage considered this plant one of his favorites. That was when he lived in Montreal. There the plant was "not difficult to control." Later, in Michigan, however, he spent much of his time wondering how plants suddenly appeared in areas where he knew they had not been planted. Then in Georgia the plant "explored" every square inch of his garden. In Montreal the plants were covered in "fine foliage and . . . handsome white, arching" flowers; in Georgia they become "weedy" with small flower heads. Not often does one learn of such geographic diversity in a single plant based solely upon the experience of the author. And that is one reason why books on the same subject can be so different.

Another reason books differ is because of their personality, and, as you might guess, a book's personality is defined by its author. Armitage, as the sole author of his book, has the luxury of being pithy, human, and idiosyncratic; Clausen and Ekstrom's book is, as you might expect from a collaboration, somewhat straight-laced. Facts yes, personality no. I suspect, after reading the biographical pieces on all three authors, that I would get along better with Armitage than the others, but the written word is not always the best test of a person's character (as you might find out if you met me).

I find that the more books I have the better I like it. You can never have enough books I say, except when you have to move them. My gardening library numbers some 250 books, 300 horticultural magazines, and dozens of catalogs dating back a hundred years. There is plenty of information at hand, but still it is not enough! Often I consult books in the botany library or sometimes in the horticultural library at the Smithsonian. And even with these resources I often find little more than passing mention of the plant for which I seek information. There is an awful lot we don't know.

When you take the genetic and geographic variability of plants and combine this with nutrient requirements, substrates, climate, moisture, and temperature, and then combine all this with the gardener's fallibility, inaccuracy, and just plain bad luck, there's an awful lot of stuff to think about when you plant a petunia. It's always good practice to hit the books first, but few books have all the answers (or even some of them, for that matter). The lesson is either to own or have access to a library full of books, or failing that, make it up as you go along. I usually end up doing both!

Week Three _____

There often comes a time in the garden when one must do penance. Today was such a day. Penance for planting the wrong plant in the wrong place, penance for not moving it when I could, and penance for lacking the gumption to remove it completely. And the odd thing was that I did do all these things for its twin without the least bit of conscience. But let me begin at the beginning.

Many years ago, just after I'd moved to this garden, I bought two dwarf conifers. *Chamaecyparis obtusa* 'Crippsii' they were, Cripps' golden cypress. As I had a plan of how the garden would eventually look, I simply planted these trees according to the plan. As most of us who make plans know, this is almost always the wrong way to do things.

After about five years I knew that most likely I'd managed to put both trees in the wrong places. At that time one of them had grown to about eight feet tall and the other to about five feet. The latter tree was obviously stunted from root competition created by a gigantic silver maple (since logged off the property). Not only was it stunted in growth, it was unthrifty and threadbare in habit. Its sister tree, however, was full and lush with glossy green inner and golden yellow outer foliage—in every way a perfect specimen. Perfect, that is, except for the slight problem that it was planted between two paths and now threatened to overgrow both.

At first I thought about moving the less thrifty tree and giving it a second chance somewhere else in the garden. One attempt at excavating it from the root zone of the maple, however, convinced me to abandon that prospect. The area was, at the time, being converted to the newly created large rockery, so I simply cut the cypress off at ground level (enough to insure death in itself) and then mounded two feet of earth over it. One tree down.

When it came to the second tree, I knew I could not move it and would never purposely kill it. I have often admired a beautiful specimen of this tree in the Gotelli Collection of dwarf conifers at the National Arboretum. This plant is about fifteen or twenty feet tall, perfectly pyramidal, and lush. My specimen is a little less lush, mostly because it has its back to the shade. But I could imagine what my tree would look like in ten or twenty years. This vision precluded any thought of permanent removal, even though the tree was obviously outgrowing its allotted space.

The only logical way out was to trim the tree as judiciously as possible—something I don't like to do with conifers. It seems to me they pretty much know how to grow by themselves, and any helping hand I might provide would be more likely the hand of the antigardener. But one does what one must, and about five years ago I started trimming the tree with hand pruners. Hedging shears would not do. I did not want a tightly sculpted gumdrop or artifice of any kind. So each year I endeavor to cut back only the outreaching tips in the late fall. This way the new spring growth flushes out strongly yellow and stays that way until the next fall. In winter the tree is drab anyway, losing much of its color naturally. To prune it in fall is no great loss to the garden.

The system seems to work well except that the tree is now about ten feet tall, and in addition to hand pruners I now must use a pole pruner to get at the top branches. I have to do it every year if the tree is not to outgrow its space, so I am bound to do my penance until either the tree or I die. I do not think it is much of a contest.

The weather has gone quite berserk. Last week it went from the midseventies to the midtwenties overnight. This week it went from the midsixties to the teens with wind blown in for all it was worth (which isn't much, by the way). The high was 40 degrees. The wind whipped unraked leaves to a frenzy and made the windows rattle (the inside ones, not the storm windows). To make it all worse, it is Saturday! I was going to tidy up the large rock garden (again), but no such luck. Instead, I fed the wood stove all day, drank lots of boiling hot coffee and tea, and read the latest *Bulletin of the Alpine Garden Society.* This inspired me to place my first order for next spring's plants. Not seeds, mind you, but plants. These normally small and often temperamental plants ship without difficulty.

Some of these plants I have had no experience in growing. There's a species of *Astragalus*, a genus known to me in my professional capacity as a wasp researcher. These are often pungent, subshrubby plants whose flowers are extremely attractive to a large variety of wasps. (As an entomologist who specializes in wasps, especially parasitic ones, I am always delighted to introduce wasp-attracting plants into the garden.) Also on order are *Oxytropis lambertii* and *Polemonium viscosum*, described respectively with endearing catalog restraint as "one of the most beautiful Rocky Mountain wildflowers" and "one of the gems of the Rockies." Then there's *Pterocephalus perennis* from Greece, which the catalog describes as a prostrate plant with furry foliage and pink bachelor-button flowers. I ordered these plants along with *Alyssum, Erigeron, Mimulus, Penstemon,* and *Primula*. Though I could not clean the rock garden, or even step outside without becoming two inches shorter, I could begin envisioning my new plants of spring as if winter were almost over.

By coincidence, I visited the National Arboretum today and had a chance to reexamine *Chamaecyparis obtusa* 'Crippsii'. Something has happened to the tree. I had not seen it in perhaps four years, and it has become threadbare. It is open, with foliage mostly at the tips, and with long, naked branches. Not at all what I had expected. It is not the location because the tree is in full sun, nor does it look diseased. Perhaps it is age, but I don't believe the tree could be much more than thirty years old. I saw the site at the time of its original construction and planting in the early 1960s, and I base my estimate on that. None of the trees was much taller than I at the time (about six feet). It is possible that this variety opens up naturally as it ages. Whatever the problem of the arboretum's specimen, the continual shearing given my tree encourages more compact, branched growth so that, theoretically, it should not become as open. Either that or the denser growth may eventually choke itself out. I guess only time will tell. I'll just have to wait another twenty years and see.

My reason for visiting the arboretum was that I had received a call last week asking if I'd be willing to give some advice (free, of course) on the site preparation for a small screelike streambed being built in a new section of the Asian Collection. The site, called "China Valley," is to be landscaped with plants from China.

The fact that I am neither an expert on screes nor on Chinese plants might give one pause, but it has little bearing on this story. The term "expert" is a relative one. It is possible to know only slightly more than someone else on a subject and, for all purposes, be considered an expert. Or at least a relative expert. Sometimes the person seeking advice does so much of the talking that by merely nodding or shaking your head at the appropriate times you can establish your reputation as an expert.

The designer, Larry Lee, asked four of us from the Potomac Valley Chapter of the American Rock Garden Society to offer our opinions and answer questions on the building of this streambed feature. With four people you will most likely have four opinions, but today everyone fairly much agreed on certain basic factors, such as that the streambed should run downhill. This made sense to us, but if the committee had had a few more members, we might have made an even better suggestion.

Mr. Lee asked us a variety of good questions for which we had a variety of good answers—no two of us agreeing completely on anything. And that is probably as it should be, for each of us approaches a problem differently or has a different goal in mind. Also, no two of us have exactly similar garden situations. Our soils are different, our rocks, our shade/sun ratios, our patterns of light, our root and overhead competition. No two of us have the same patience or past gardening experience or knowledge of plants or even the same parents, at least to my knowledge. So we were bound to bring different perspectives to the problem, and we did. Whether we brought Mr. Lee any solutions is another matter entirely.

A gardener gardens where he has to but dreams wherever he can. If he should happen to be at 37,000 feet, hurtling through the sky in a metallic hull, so be it. If he should be surrounded by 200 strange people, so be it. I am on Christmas leave, returning to my childhood home near San Francisco. My mother, brother, sister-in-law, two nieces, nephew, and assorted old-time friends will be there. My gardening mentor, Virginia Stewart, will be there. Much of the time will be spent in talking of gardens and gardening, of books and reading, of seeds and sowing, of weather or whether, of past times and future—idle chitchat that springs to mind as we muddle through winter in the best way possible.

At present, however, I have just finished reading the Park Seed Company catalog for the tenth time. It arrived yesterday and I am glad it did, for I would not want to wait until January to place a seed order. The late order is the "substitute" or "out-of-stock" order. I always check the no-substitute box myself, because if I wanted substitutes, I would have ordered them in the first place. I try to order seed in a well-thought-out, planned, organized manner. I try, but like most gardeners, I end up ordering what I think I want, not necessarily just what I need. It is difficult to anticipate one's mood six months in advance.

The "need" plants are specific items for specific purposes: for the pink garden, *Gomphrena* 'Lavender Lady', *Lobularia* 'Easter Bonnet', and some single and double petunias with appropriate names like 'Think Pink', 'Cherry Pink', and 'Apple Blossom'; for the rock gardens, *Aethionema coridifolium* and *Gentiana septemfida*; for the purple-leaved garden, *Lychnis* × *arkwrightii* 'Vesuvius'; for the balcony garden, geranium 'Orbit White'. The "want" plants are three varieties of pansies, including rose ('Majestic Red/Rose') and blue ('Maxim Marina Hybrids' and 'Moody Blues') and a huge woolly rosetted plant called *Verbascum* 'Arctic Summer'. And for good measure I always throw in something new to me. Sometimes the plants are virtually worthless, such as *Silene* (*Viscaria*) 'Blue Angel', a variety I bought at Butchart Gardens in Victoria, B.C., and planted out earlier this year. The plants were scantily clad and scarcely flowered, though such flowers as there were were a beautiful shade of blue. In my garden the subject was scarcely worth growing, though I admit it must have its merits. Perhaps in cooler climates, such as those found in the Pacific Northwest, it is more attractive, but I do not know, as I have never seen it growing. Many normally beautiful annuals, here in our hot, humid climate, simply collapse.

Occasionally one makes a real find when purchasing seeds of plants previously unknown to oneself. Year before last the "new" plant was *Patrinia scabiosifolia* 'Nagoya', a tall, umbelliferlike herbaceous perennial with airy yellow flowers. This is well worth growing, in my opinion, but not easy to find. I purchased my seeds from Park's. This year's find may be *Polygonella americana*. It sounds like a twin of *Patrinia* except that the flowers are white. There is always a chance that such a newcomer will be a successful addition to the garden repertoire. At two dollars twenty-five cents a packet it is a much better gamble than the state lottery. Even if the choice ends up to be a loss, I will still have gained a little new knowledge.

So my list is made up, my order transferred to the blank form, and I have salvaged a really worthless time (all air travel time is worthless, as far as I can tell) to some productive end. The day, a total loss of nerve-wracking plane schedules and transfers, has served its purpose. Still, I'd rather have my fingers in the ground than my brains 37,000 feet above it. Man was meant to garden, not to fly.

Week Four_____

Traveling has its good points, to be certain, but being forced to entrust the garden to the care of others leaves me a bit queasy. True, at this time of year, little can happen outside (at least over which anyone has control). Inside, however, in the greenhouse, there are years of labor invested that can all be lost in a day. One does not face this prospect with great joy.

Among the normal cache of a few hundred pots, there is a special batch of over a hundred small plants that will be used in the plant sales and giveaway by our chapter of the American Rock Garden Society. The chapter is sponsoring a "winter study weekend" in late January with an emphasis on China. Most of the small plants on my benches have been around since last July, when I struck the first cuttings of *Dianthus erinaceus*, a ground-hugging mound of stiff, prickly leaves. Unlike most pinks, this one is grown more for itself than for its flowers. Since July I've added several cultivars of *Phlox douglasii, Frankenia, Thymus, Vitaliana, Verbascum,* and even dwarf *Opuntia.*

While these are the plants of most immediate concern to this traveler, there are still a number of other plants I do not easily abandon. I would not want to lose them to over- or underwatering. A number of small pots of alpines, cyclamens, pseudobonsai (like the Japanese honeysuckle), and all overwintering cuttings (geraniums, penstemons, salvias, rues, dusty millers, etc.) are susceptible to overwet soil conditions combined with cold. Then, too, there are a half-dozen pots of paper-whites, some in bloom, and some awaiting my return, that I would just as soon not forsake, given the choice.

Fortunately, I have two saving graces in this instance. The first is Dug Miller, with whom I have a reciprocal plant-sitting agreement, and the second is that I can't generally think about two things at once. If I'm far away and in a confused enough state, I tend to forget that I have a greenhouse full of labor-intensive plants that could die at any second. It really is a good thing to have a bad memory.

I did not expect the greeting I received upon arrival in San Anselmo: "The Arctic Express." It's come all the way from northern Canada and brought death and destruction with it. So far, three days of all-time record low temperatures have settled into this Mediterraneanlike area just north of the San Francisco Bay where, normally, frost barely takes a nibble at the edge of the tenderest plants. Now hanging geraniums do not hang so much as ooze over the edges of their pots. Fuchsias and hydrangeas are downcast in blackened mourning for their kind. Impatiens are puddles of broken cells. It will all get back to normal, of course, but this will henceforth be known as the "Year of the Record Freeze."

In San Anselmo, as elsewhere in the area, neither plants nor people are prepared for 13-degree temperatures. Neighbors on all sides of this house where I grew up awoke to broken water pipes—some flooding and then freezing driveways, garages, laundry rooms, yards. All water wasted in a county where drought has reigned supreme for over ten years and where prospects for summer rationing appear more likely as each rainless day passes. Water is the commodity most gardeners—most humans—take for granted. Today it is being wasted in record gallons.

As a Westerner transplanted to the East I am well-watered. Our rainfall is properly spaced and we scarcely rely on artificial irrigation in the open garden except for a few odd dry weeks in July or August. Potted plants may need water more often, but that is not much of a task compared to the garden proper. Here, however, rain does not fall from May until November, the air is dry, and the sun warm. Most plants must be watered or they will die. I know! For many years as a lad in these parts, I had a job watering a garden two hours a day, three days a week. This included watering by sprinklers and hand watering the hundreds of pots and odd places the sprinklers did not reach. Nowadays, the authorities do not approve of sprinklers, and water costs so much that their use is voluntarily curtailed. It is all rather discouraging to the gardeners of the past, like me, who knew how splendid gardens could be with a little work, a little water, and a little care. Those days will probably never be seen again in this region, and water rationing will become more and more commonplace as the population of the West increases.

The currently accepted technologies provide ways of decreasing water use: drip irrigation systems, careful hand watering, and xeric gardening. All fine, of course, but each has its problems. Drip systems are technological fixes that, like all fixes, require expensive outlays for previously unnecessary equipment that have previously untested parts. Parts that clog easily or are easily disturbed by animals or kids or that just plain fall apart at the most inconvenient and inappropriate places. Hand watering is necessary, of course, but overhead sprinklers provide a more even distribution of water to the soil, provide a humid atmosphere for foliage during heat stress, and are not labor intensive. Xeric gardening is fine if you like arid-adapted plants, and I most certainly do. But I have seen few examples of well-designed gardens that demonstrate their artistic use. As currently used, they are not yet my idea of a garden. Which, I suppose, most water-savers would say is the main problem. Many of us gardeners have only one idea of what a garden should be, and that is the quintessential English garden.

Growing up in the region as I did, I was unaware that our gardening was abnormally wasteful of water or that it was anything but typical.

We grew colorful plants that liked warm weather and had to be watered every other day: fuchsias, dahlias, marigolds, petunias, zinnias, delphiniums, larkspurs, begonias, columbine, roses, pinks, cactus, succulents, plumbago, alyssum, impatiens, calendulas, and so on *ad infinitum*. Almost anything grew if you gave it water. Now the authorities proclaim that it is wrong to grow plants that require water—or at least too much water. It is now politically correct to grow only drought-adapted plants, if you must have a garden at all, that is. What the authorities really mean, but do not say, is that people need the water more than plants do. Well, to this I say "hogwash." (I say this because what I really think is not fit to print.)

The number of gardeners—people who place their gardens before all else—is so few, judging by the number of even modestly planted and tended gardens, that if you gave them all the water they wanted for free, it would scarcely amount to a drop in the proverbial bucket. I am not talking here about the great societal sod farmers who surround their houses with endless lawn or build their mansions next to evergreen golf courses. I speak, instead, of those who have flower beds and a few vegetables that they respect and wish to see make it through the season. For my part, I would not oppose an allocation scheme wherein these gardeners received all the water they needed before the real water-wasters got a drop.

Who are these wasters, you might ask? They are our own ever-increasing, overabundant, biologically procreative selves, I would reply. The too many people who want too much water to wash too many clothes, too many cars, and too many dishes. Who take too many showers and flush too many toilets. Too many people who take water for granted and see no connection between themselves and the necessity of siphoning (a polite word for stealing) water from a river in one state or possibly two states over to grow heavily populated cities in arid places where water shouldn't be taken in the first place.

To say that California is suffering from a drought is only to admit that there is uncertainty in our natural environment, nothing more. Much of California is a dry place. Droughts happen. We know this from historic records, just as we know that floods happen in other states. Still, in spite of our knowledge of floodplains, we build buildings where they will flood. It is not surprising, given human nature, that we build cities where there is no water or where there is not enough water for more than a handful of people—not surprising and certainly not smart.

I do not think that droughts or floods or even volcanoes, for that matter, constitute problems. It is people who are the problem, not nature. Instead of planning populations to fit the environment, we populate the environment and then think we can force it to adapt to us. Ask the residents around Mount Vesuvius or Mount St. Helens how well this works. Droughts and floods are no different. Until we accept the idea that the natural world is the starting point from which to populate the earth, we will make no progress toward finding solutions.

Solutions require some degree of planning *before* a situation arises, not reliance on some happy ending predicated on imagined technological fixes: building pipelines from remote natural areas, draining age-old aquifers, floating icebergs down from the Arctic. What happens to these ageless and environmentally altered areas is not so important, society argues, as long as society gets its water—and right now. When it comes down to the bitter and thirsty end, we are going to let our descendants pay the price as best they can.

I can speak of these water dilemmas, smug in my Eastern excesses, but I believe that the eastern population, as massive as it already is, will eventually outstrip its supply of water or, even worse, completely foul it before this point is reached. Whether either eastern or western water dries up or is destroyed by human hands, my own fear is that gardening, at least as we've known it, will become less feasible as the country fills with people. Water prices have risen continuously during my lifetime, and the summer water bills are often rather dear. Soon will it be only the water lords who can afford a garden? In the end, will water be reserved only for the necessities—such as the Sunday car wash? Will the gardener be reduced to dripping pipes and a few xeric plants? Will plastic plants be the final solution? Will those few of us anarchists found watering our foxgloves and Canterbury bells be forced to wear a scarlet *W* emblazoned on our chests as the sign of the Water-Waster?

Earlier this year, I visited the old homestead right after my mother underwent some serious surgery. During that visit I planted out a small section of the back garden so that there might be some semblance of color and renewal for the difficult times ahead. In a long, narrow section visible from the house, I put up a fifteen-foot section of net trellis upon which to plant sweet peas, my mother's favorite flower. At that time, in June, it was too late in the season to plant the seeds and yet too early for a fall sowing. With the trellis in place, at least the seeds could be put in later. In front of the trellis I planted cosmos, dusty miller, alyssum, and dwarf, red-foliaged dahlias—all common, everyday plants, heat tolerant, and none particularly water-wasting.

The attempt didn't last long. It was eaten by deer and uprooted by cats. A gardener's life is hell. The deer in this area are voracious. My mother has seen eight at one time feeding in her backyard. Without predators, they, too, have overpopulated their range and come down from the dry, parched hills to browse on whatever strikes their fancy: tasty violets, tangy geraniums, tart tomatoes. They spare no buds, no twigs, no leaves. No greenery of any kind. Even now, in December, when the hills are somewhat greener, they feed on whatever they like down in the suburbs. Yesterday I walked to within an arm's length of two deer feeding in a neighbor's yard. They checked me over not out of fear but as a potential food item. Fortunately, I was not wearing green.

Some people try to combat the deer, as they can decimate a garden in mere minutes. Some place small-mesh black netting over select plants, while others put tall wire cages around such plants, and still others build eight-foot-high fences around entire sections of their gardens. My gardening friend Virginia has an acre surrounded by such a fence, and it is to this garden that I make as many pilgrimages as possible during my visits out West.

Readers may recall from my previous book that Virginia and Coulter Stewart are my gardening mentors, a relationship dating back to 1958 when my family moved to the neighborhood and I started high school. For many years I served my apprenticeship in their garden learning to do those jobs that are basic: watering, weeding, cleaning, transplanting, and growing plants from seed, divisions, and cuttings. More importantly, I learned about plants, nurseries, plantspeople, books, magazines, and seed companies. All necessary steps in the gardening life. I could not have learned from two more avid gardeners.

The Stewarts' garden is surely a rarity—in cultivation by the original creators for over fifty years. Although Coulter passed away some years ago, Virginia still maintains the hillside garden much as it has been since our early acquaintance. The details change, of course, but certainly not the spirit of the place. When I visit at Christmas, I make many excursions up the short hill that separates my mother's house from the Stewarts'. Virginia and I talk of many things, mostly related to gardening or books or, more than likely, books on gardening.

On a particularly adventurous day, the two of us might travel farther afield, nursery-hopping with one of Virginia's other long-time gardening cronies: Steve Parlee, my replacement when I left for college, or Larry McDougald, a buyer for the local nursery called Sunnyside. At least three and often all four of us end up making half a dozen trips to Lone Pine Nursery and Miniature Plant Kingdom in Sebastopol or Western Hills Nursery in Occidental or Ed Carman's nursery in Los Gatos or Smith & Hawken's gardening emporium in Mill Valley or to any of the other decent establishments that admit itinerant gardeners from off the street. By the end of the day, we have filled the car well beyond California's legal plant limit (seven tons in any single vehicle) and wend our way homeward, disappointed that we didn't buy more.

Some of the local residents, including my mother, hire so-called garden and lawn services to perform routine yard maintenance. I do not know what qualifications or experience many of these crews have, but I suspect it isn't any. Quite possibly the possession of a truck qualifies one to provide quality garden services (at exorbitant prices). When I gaze upon the work done in my mother's yard, it is difficult to imagine, really, what constitutes the garden aesthetic in these individuals.

It is obvious that their favorite tool is the weed-whacker. It is used as a weeding substitute, and every nonshrub in the garden is scalped monthly to within an inch of the ground. If a little tuft of grass emerges from between two pinks or in a patch of oxalis, everything is shaved to the same height. If Bermuda grass creeps across a border, a good crop-ping is the answer. After five years of this, there are no more borders—just tightly trimmed Bermuda grass with tightly trimmed irises for added color. No errant foliage is allowed to disturb the Zenlike patterns of chopped vegetation on the ground.

The worker's other tools, all power, also maintain a certain degree of order in the garden. Anything not lower than an inch is trimmed with electric hedge clippers into some object of a globular nature: privets, ju-nipers, roses, euryops, chain link fences. Anything. All loose organic matter is blown away with a leaf blower. This not only accentuates the shaved organic patterns on the ground but gives the various globular shrubs a coastal, windswept look.

As a final, universal tool, the lawn mower is used to chop, shave, scalp, dice, trim, and blow. The lawn is the primary object of this atten-tion, but since everything else is so wonderfully attenuated, it doesn't matter too much if the mower strays from time to time into "garden" ter-ritory. In truth, it is becoming difficult to tell the garden from the lawn; everything is blurring into pattern.

Perhaps this will become the newest trend in gardening: the low-cropped, low-maintenance, water-saving, geometric-design garden—maintained entirely by machine-wielding maintenance crews. Or, if one can't afford the help, then the natural look created by browsing deer might be the next best thing. Well, it's a thought anyway. And I give it away freely to the newest generation of landscrape designers. No charge.

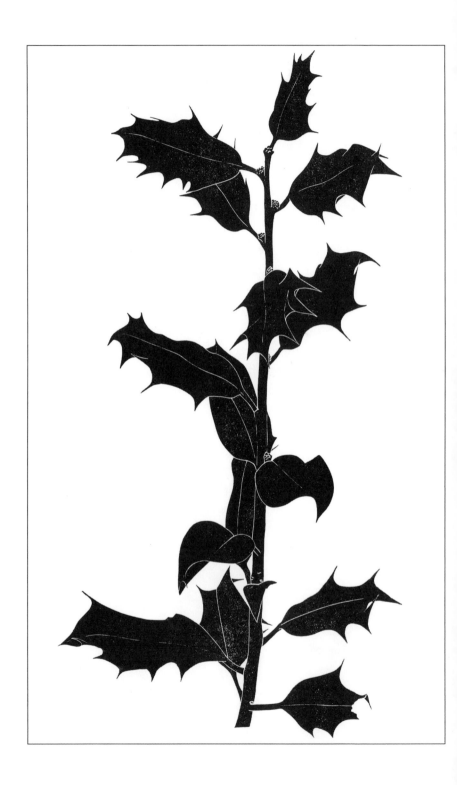

3

JANUARY

Week One _____

Today begins another year. Most gardeners began the new year some months back, maybe even last spring, with their orders for fall bulbs that will be blooming in a month or two—or three, around these parts. Or maybe the new year got off to a start in November with the first seed orders. Whatever today's date might be, it is the first of the new year in name only—the calendar first, not the gardening first.

Whatever may befall us this year, whether good or bad, joyful or sad, we have little ability to predict the outcome. In fact, if I might be so bold, we have absolutely no ability to predict the outcome—any outcome. Not one of us knows when our best laid plans might be spoiled: the roof might cave in just as we sit down to Eldred's sixth birthday party; Uncle Jack might back the car over Aunt Ethel; or Grandpa Seth might trip over a rake and fall headfirst into a den of poisonous vipers . . . killing all the vipers. These things happen, you know, and I for one do not think anyone can predict them, including the fabled tabloid psychics.

Fortunately, gardeners have one refuge, one respite, from the chilling thought that nothing is ever really predictable. We have the garden, and although we will never predict all its idiosyncrasies, at least we have the vague notion that if we work hard enough it will be almost as we expect it to be . . . eventually . . . maybe . . . perhaps . . . someday. Show me a gardener that does not believe this and I will show you a . . . a . . . well, an undertaker, I suppose.

We gardeners stand upon the backbone called "garden," often underestimating or not aware of the strength it imparts to us. In a world where we have control over scarcely anything, the garden is worth more than tomatoes or marigolds or even a dozen long-stemmed roses, for that matter.

Even though it may not be totally predictable, it is still about the surest vantage point from which to view life: any port in a storm, as long as it's the garden. Here we are able to think clearly, calmly, while the ocean crashes all about us. Or perhaps, even better, we will not think at all . . . merely *be.* Exalting in the sun's calming rays, accepting the woodland's soothing shade, meditating on the border's rolling waves—lulling our inner selves with color and shape and fragrance and texture. On the slightest of movements. On the quietest of sounds.

Hypnotized, we gradually become one with the garden. Even with our bodies working at a furious pace, our minds slow down to a rhythm, to a cadence. Situations that seemed incomprehensible—or worse, too comprehensible—now start to lose their grip. They become so much chaff muddling the mind. A little breeze and they are gone. The boss turns from an ogre to a strawman and, poof, is gone; the innumerable car bills become leaves easily removed; Uncle Jack and his nearsightedness fade into so many grains of sand as the soil is lovingly smoothed and groomed.

All the hostilities have drained from our minds, through our arms, down the fingers, into the soil—there to lie entombed in a tidied, neatened piece of garden. But it would be wise for all the bosses and auto mechanics of the world to remember one thing: it is they who inspired our gardening efforts in the first place. It is they who have caused us to hack and scratch and rip and tear and slash—to create a garden that looks as if it were a paradise. And we, the innocent gardeners, appear as caring angels in this paradise. No one but us, the gardeners, is the wiser for our thoughts, and any bedeviler from the real world would be advised not to confront the gardener on his or her own territory—for there would surely be hell to pay.

Well, I must apologize for that last little outburst. Too much gin and tonic last night, and you see what happens. I started thinking about how this new year might turn out and imagined the worst parts before it even began. Certainly the first of the year is an appropriate time to reflect, but perhaps it is best to begin with the positive rather than with my normal life.

Like many other people, I begin the new year with a self inventory designed to focus my attention on directions, perspectives, accomplishments, resolutions, predictions, life (another year survived), and death (another year to survive). Generally, after about two days—or as many hangovers—all this is promptly forgotten. It is best to get this reflective stuff over quickly and then get on with the mindless humdrum of the remaining 363 days of the year—the coming onslaught, as I fondly refer to it.

To this end, then, I am going to objectively review the past gardening year as well as make arresting predictions (just like the tabloids) for the coming year.

First, the year in review:

- After careful analysis, I've calculated that I planted enough seeds and produced enough transplants to cover Rhode Island, Ohio, and eastern Texas. Still, it wasn't enough to make the garden look anything more than threadbare. Be it resolved, therefore, to buy enough seeds to cover Alaska and parts of central Nebraska.

- Upon removing piles of sand, gravel, and mulch from the driveway, I finally made enough room to order more truckloads of sand, gravel, and mulch. You can never have too much work to do, I always say (just for once I wish I'd stop saying that).

- After twelve years of removing lawn to make gardens, I finished the job last year. The trouble now is that the remaining lawn appears so shabby that it detracts from the garden. The only solution, I reckon, is to remove the remaining sod and replace it with new. This seems like the classic definition of a public works project. And they claim perpetual motion is impossible. Gardeners are always in a state of perpetual motion.

- The best section of the garden was the pink garden I created early in the year based upon Monet's garden in Giverny. By mere chance it was also the worst. I don't know exactly how this happened, but I think it has to do with selective pride: some parts of the design were good, some bad. Next year perhaps I will practice the gardener's second basic rule: improve upon the bad and retain the good. (The first is: wait and see.)

- You know that you've been at the same garden too long when you have to start taking out plants you paid good money to put in. Last year I took out five hollies that refused to grow an inch in all the time I had them. I gave them to my friend Dee, who claims that they've grown six inches since she put them in. It's just as well, eventually they would have outgrown the space I gave them—say in 300 years.

- The old apple tree, the last of four, was chopped down. Not only did it cost a lot of money to remove, I then had to refinance my house to plant the area with new subjects. And they weren't even big specimens—just expensive. I have resolved not to remove anything else until the mortgage is paid off.

- Now, back to piles of things. When I took out the apple tree, I decided to move most of the compost heap, which had grown enormously in ten years, to the new garden that I built where the apple once stood. The problem was that where the apple tree had stood was the location of my ten-year-old-brush pile, so I had to move it first. I moved the brush pile to the compost heap and the compost heap to the brush pile. Don't ask me how, but they both nearly disappeared. It's a good gardening trick if you can figure it out. I haven't yet.

- I added a new water feature to the garden, a small, terra-cotta dolphin fountain surrounded by an arched trellis. Everything worked as planned. This was an absolutely unique day in the history of my garden.

In overall terms, last year was not particularly noteworthy, but I must say if I had it all to do over again I'd think twice, or even three times, before I installed another fountain. Being a gardener I'm not sure how to handle anything that goes right.

Now to my startling garden predictions for the coming year:

- At the beginning of the year the garden will be twice as wonderful as anyone could ever imagine; by the end, half as good as it might have been.

- Everything you plant will be either in the wrong place at the wrong time, in the wrong place at the right time, or in the right place at the wrong time. Any plant in the right place at the right time is in someone else's garden.

- This will be the best year ever for weather—except for where you garden.

- In any one year you will correct only enough old gardening mistakes to balance the new ones. Many new mistakes will just be old ones with new names.

- You will grow three types of plants: those that live, those that die, and those that you wish would die. Of these, the plants that live will be the plants you wish would die.

- When the garden is at its absolute peak of perfection, you will be on vacation; when at its absolute worst, you will have company.

- There will be only three things you can be certain of: death, taxes, and weeds. The former two are preferred.

- There will be at least one variety of plant you must have. If you can't have it you will go mad.

- Any variety of plant you desperately want will be out of stock. You will go mad, but find it an improvement.

- You will need the garden more than it needs you.

Week Two

For gardening activity, this January week has been about as busy as any two Junes I've known. First was the visit to Cheltenham. No, not a quaint English village but a state-owned greenhouse. This was a hard-headed planning session to ward off Disaster in March—our code name for The Maryland Home and Flower Show.

The big event is nearly upon us—just seven weeks away—and Dug, Bill, and I, three amateurs (in every sense of the word), are getting set to produce the show of our four-year career. We are testing our collective panic and anxiety at the medium level, leaving plenty of room on the dial for the time when maximum panic sets in. One eventually reaches the point, after all the necessary planning, where fear overcomes thought and the job gets done subconsciously in spite of oneself. We have not yet reached that point. Medium panic is the level for the day.

About 1000 plants awaited us this Saturday in the Cheltenham greenhouse, a facility owned by the Maryland Department of Agriculture, which is sponsoring the exhibit. These plants were purchased some weeks back as winter dormant stock and were placed in an air temperature of about 60 degrees. Many are still dormant or are just starting to break the soil's surface. These plants include astilbes, hostas, lilies, various grasses and sedges, liriope, daylilies, peonies, phloxes, rudbeckias, Shasta daisies, and numerous ferns whose names I can never remember. A few plants were up and blooming, most noticeably forget-me-nots and a wood anemone. A few other varieties, such as veronicas and violas, were getting mighty anxious to join them.

Since we do not exactly know what we are doing and since forcing perennials is not the sort of treatment most books recommend, we are very much on our own when it comes to slowing down some plants while speeding up others. We came to assess the situation (always a good ploy when one is learning). And assess it we did. The late-blooming sorts of plants (for example, daylilies and lilies) and anything grown for foliage (grasses, ferns, hostas) are being placed under lights for added day length (and some heat from the lights). Anything that has a hint of bloom will be put in the warehouse, where the temperature hovers just above freezing, to discourage haste. (The warehouse has barely enough natural light from skylights to keep plants from growing spindly.) Fortunately, only *Anemone sylvestris* has bolted in the greenhouse, so it will be eliminated from the show. We can be mean when we have to be.

We pored over each bench, noting which plants to push with heat and light, which to slow with cold and limited light, and which to retire because they were already too far over the hill for the show. Then we made notes on weeding and general cleanup. Next we adjourned to the inside offices for a thought-kicking session.

Earlier we had thrown a plan on paper, but the plan was now obliterated by so many marks representing imaginary trees, lawns, hills, valleys, streams, sunrooms, rock gardens, perennial beds, greenhouses, vegetable gardens, orchards, compost bins, terraces, courtyards, and annual beds that we were faced with a nearly black piece of paper. Time to regroup, recount, refigure, and hopefully retire. After several hours of refinements (most for the better) we finished off the morning's work at about one o'clock in the afternoon.

Then it was off to Annapolis thirty miles distant to inspect more plants being forced in another greenhouse. There was no lunch, I might add, and I was beginning to get grumpy. It may be that, since I wake up grumpy, food had nothing to do with it. Again we inspected plant material, this time annuals, vegetables, and bulbs. There were dwarf marigolds in bloom as well as cosmos, lobelia (in three colors), and vincas. Vegetables included corn (what chance to grow this to some height in six weeks?), onions, carrots, and tomatoes. I can't say that I surveyed the vegetables too well, because by this time I dared not look at anything resembling food. And besides, vegetables were not my job. My job was to help design the garden and make sense of the perennials. This I had done. Highly qualified state personnel were taking care of the vegetable end of things.

Next came the bulb-forcing chambers, which were walk-in refrigerators. Forcing is perhaps the wrong word, as the bulbs were doing whatever they wanted to do, and there was little force of any kind being brought to the workplace. The crocuses and bulbous irises had all broken ground, the daffodils were trying, and the tulips were dying. So much for forcing bulbs.

By the time the bulb consortium had adjourned, I was really hungry and grumpy, so naturally we drove another thirty miles to a place where we could continue to work on the plans. Fortunately, this was Bill's house, where I could at least get something to drink. There's nothing that can take the place of three glasses of wine on an empty stomach—except maybe a stomach pump. Finally, however, there were turkey sandwiches to be inhaled in one bite, and I realized I wasn't nearly as hungry as I'd thought.

Then it was back to the plans for a few more rollicking hours of fun.

Then to dinner.

Then a movie.

Then to bed. Perchance to dream of gardens and garden shows.

The day ended as it began. In the dead of winter; in the life of spring.

I said the week was a gardening week, so here goes "Plant Shows: Part II." Well, not a show, actually, so much as a "show and tell." In two weeks the Potomac Valley Chapter of the American Rock Garden Society will have its Eastern Winter Study Weekend. Since I've never been to one, I can't say very much about it. I do know that it lasts three days, that there will be a lot of plant persons talking about plants (mostly alpines, one would hope), that the main theme is "Plants of China," and that lots of plants will be given away as registration and reception gifts and table favors. They will also be sold at the plant auction. As some 200 enthusiasts will be present, we will need a lot of plants.

To make plants you need one of two things: seeds or plants from which to take vegetative matter for propagation. Although I grow a lot of material from seeds, this time I stuck to cuttings. They are more reliable, and the end results are what you expect. Seeds, on the con, can often be totally unpredictable in germination and end product.

Starting last July I began nipping and whacking at my own plants to provide material for rooting. Since many alpine plants are prostrate and have wiry little stems (if you can see the stems at all), you end up working with fairly small pieces of plant material. A little patience is all that is required . . . and a strong will. The hardest part is the removal process. Taking a few inch-long pieces off a plant that is only three inches across takes a great deal of nerve and self-confidence. You never know when a little is too much, but the plant does. Generally, taking cuttings doesn't harm the plant, and there is always the belief that you will end up with two or three or a dozen new plants where before you had but a single plant. Sometimes it is only a belief. There are no guarantees with plants.

When it comes to gardening, I am not a technical sort of person, so my operation might best be summarized like this: I cut, I stick, they root, or they die. It is simple enough. I prefer coarse builder's sand as a rooting medium, about three inches deep. I use hormone powder on the cuttings, but I cannot say I really believe it helps. It is an offering— just in case it might have some effect. I have a cheap heating cable under the sand, and it used to work very well. I cut the cable in half, however, so it doesn't heat up at all (the electricity just leaks out the end). I can see the benefit of replacing it, but I don't like the idea of taking out the cuttings, the sand, the old cable, and then replacing everything. Just lazy I guess.

At first I was going to put in a really fancy automatic misting device to keep the cuttings moist. After reading about solenoid valves, pipe saddles, GPH ratings, and monel screens I decided I didn't want to go back to college for a degree in engineering—I'd rather grow plants. So now, once a day, I get out the old tubular H_2O compressor (that's a hose to you) and put on the H_2O diverter-strainer attachment (what we pros call a nozzle), and I moisturize the plants until they think they're in the professional-type place where they ought to be growing. It works.

I have just over a hundred good plants rooted up for the study weekend. Additionally, there are a number of so-so specimens I wouldn't give to a stranger let alone a gardening compatriot, and I'm keeping these (come time for the society's spring plant exchange, they might actually look alive). The job now, after getting them this far on their journey, is to spruce them up a bit. I cleaned the soil surface of each pot and put a layer of granite chips on top. Then I washed the pots and arranged them by genus in flats. Finally, I made new, permanent labels to replace the cryptic half-abbreviations I'd used for some species. I checked the names in the various books and catalogs at my disposal. One name, in particular, gave me trouble: *Paxistima* or *Pachistima*. This is a native American dwarf evergreen that looks like a prostrate boxwood (at least from a few feet away). I've seen it spelled both ways, but I spelled it yet a third—*Paxistema*—another nomenclatural hybrid. Fortunately, I caught the mistake after writing only half of the labels.

Today I took the plants to the holding area in Virginia. Here they are being assembled in a heated greenhouse for a final tally. A sort of preemptive review, as it were, just to make certain the volunteers really bring what they said they would and to counter any potential and unexpected disasters.

It was questionable most of the week as to whether the roads would be passable when the time came. First, four inches of snow on Monday. Then frozen, icy streets. Then another three inches of snow on Thursday, followed by cold rain, sleet, and more rain on Friday. Today, more rain. All the while the temperature hovered at 32 degrees. Luckily, fate dealt plain rain; the freezing sort would have been more than any gardener could bear. The snows earlier this week were wet, and heavy snow caked a lot of plants, especially conifers, bending them precariously low. Broken branches were in evidence everywhere, and in a few places quantities of saplings were bent to the ground like rows of archers' bows.

My garden was not immune to the damage. Two large, old junipers in front of the house took on such a load that one toppled over, pulling its roots out of the overly wet soil. This happened once before to the same plant, and I wedged a chunk of concrete and an old broken shovel under it to prop it up. Later I corseted it with stakes and rubber hose. This time it will just have to grow where it fell. (These junipers are a monument to plant life. Once, many years ago, the front gutter dammed up with ice, ripped off the house, and gave them both a jolly good thrashing. I came home at the end of a singularly gruesome day [Washington gets that way when it snows, and even when it doesn't, for that matter] to find the perfect reason to live elsewhere.)

But that was then. Today there is still snow on the house, the gutters might be dammed (but I won't know until they fall off), the backyard is covered in snow, and the pond is frozen. It was a perfect day for a drive. The roads were passable, so damn the slush, full speed ahead. I had people to see, plants to share, and I was off with a carload of *Phlox, Calamintha, Dianthus, Erinus, Frankenia, Nepeta, Opuntia, Origanum, Pachistima, Saponaria, Teucrium, Vitaliana, Gypsophila, Verbascum, Jasminum, Arenaria, Iberis,* and *Thymus.* A carload of spring and summer to share with my fellow gardeners.

Week Three

Finding a small, insignificant flower attempting to bloom in the cold, seemingly hostile environment of mid-January was the high point of the day for me. Having just arrived home from work in the rain, but with enough light to see, I took my first garden tour in several weeks. I was amazed, delighted, and overjoyed to see not just one but several small bulbs attempting to bloom—their barely colored tips pointing the charge to spring. There was *Crocus tomasinianus* 'Taplow Ruby', *C. sieberi* 'Violet Queen', and *C. ancyrensis* 'Golden Bunch'. Theirs is an untimely debut considering that ofttimes these crocuses don't bloom until late February or early March. They've just emerged from the five inches of snow under which they'd lain for the better part of a week. Perhaps they are a bit too eager to get the show on the road, not knowing that anything can (and likely will) happen along the weather front in the next few months.

Nor do they know that not too far south of their ancestral homeland another show has begun along much different fronts. A show not of

life but of death and destruction. Their compatriots are not that far removed from the hostility that has awakened this evening in Iraq. Who
knows what path this season's despot will lead us down? Certainly not a
primrose one.

There are times to garden and times to reflect on gardening; often
one cancels the other. For me the physical act of gardening initiates re-
flections on almost any other subject, whereas thinking about gardening
is best done while walking or driving or even watching the news. This
week I have not felt much like thinking about anything, especially while
watching the news. Perspective can be sobering.

January, even in a good year, can sap the determination of the
strongest of us. Coming, as it does, right after the joyful gluttony of the
Christmas season, it is almost a guaranteed sump for the spirit. The
weather, at least in this area, is often overcast, dark, wet, dank: the tran-
sient beauty of snow and sun overcome by the uncertainty of ice, can-
cellations, fallen trees and branches, and now fallen people, too. The
winds can be cold, and the winds of war colder still, causing our bodies
and souls to shrivel.

Although we personally may not bear arms, if there is any humanity in us, we feel for those who do. And, if I am not mistaken, we feel
for the people on both sides. In truth, there are few of us who could
harm another person in a face-to-face confrontation without feeling
some remorse, some guilt, some sense that no matter how deserved, ag-
gression is not the best solution to the problem. Rational thought, however, is not the same as the self-generated madness found in individuals
who follow pathways of brutality. I would be very much surprised, indeed, to learn that any such individuals had ever been gardeners. Personally, I cannot conceive the "gardener/warrior," but I am told by a reliable source that Bābur, first Mogul emperor, devoted his life to making
war and gardens. I would suggest that such a person was gardener in
name only, certainly not in spirit. Such a person would be the type to
have others pull weeds, prune, plant, and otherwise garden for them.

This is not to suggest that we gardeners are immune to the waging
of wars within our gardens. We do it all the time with those whose lives

we deem of lesser value than our own. We are continually at war with insects, either by chemical, biological, or physical means (a simple snap of the finger with the pest between them). We drive out the moles, voles, gophers, squirrels, rabbits, dogs, cats, and deer within the limited abilities of our arsenal. We kill weeds without a single thought as to their right to life. The only good weed is a dead weed. We chop, lop, and amputate with nary a sidelong glance. We can be cold-blooded to the core if something must go: a forgotten *Forsythia* suddenly found to be in the way becomes expendable; a silver maple taking up too much space *will* be liquidated.

We can be ruthless, but I do not believe we prefer to be ruthless. It is an attitude we adopt out of necessity. It is part of the job. We do these things in the name of order. We do them in the privacy of the garden, but that is our limit. Perhaps the best thing about gardeners is that we know our limits. Too bad the politicians and generals of the world could not all be gardeners.

The week rounds out a bit better than it began, at least for this gardener, though barely so. One cannot blame oneself for every madman in the world—whether dictator or president—nor even be quite sure that one is not mad oneself (at least when viewed from another's perspective). Calm returns in its own way, in its own style, shall we say, and though the feelings are nearer the surface than usual and though one is subject to fits and starts at the sound of the news, one adapts too quickly to the current notion of reality. To speak of gardens and war in the same breath accentuates the absurdity of both life and death. Although both are real, I know which is my preference at least for the moment.

I spent this day, the nineteenth of the year, gardening. There was no snow, no ice (except on the pond), no howling wind. The temperature was about 55 degrees, and it seemed like a good day to work outside, but as often happens, my plans changed. I was committed to working inside for the good of THE FLOWER SHOW. Yes, the day approaches. Only six more weeks, and we are now slightly more than waist-deep in panic.

The plans have been altered yet again, the enormousness of the space has been realized (sixty by eighty feet), and the quantity of plants involved has grown to unimagined proportions. We now have plants spread out in four greenhouses, both public and private, safe and condemned, and all at least thirty miles from where they will need to be in six weeks. We have donated plants, loaned plants, bought plants, seed-grown plants, and dug-up plants; we have dormant plants, half-up plants, half-dead plants, all-dead plants, blooming plants, finished-blooming plants, and plants that wouldn't bloom even if they had another year.

Today's job was to go over the plant material, clean it up, and inventory its stage of growth. Plants too far ahead of schedule are being moved to the warehouse. The peonies, for example, which last week were mere points above the soil, now have flower buds swelled with color. This should not happen in only a week's time, should it? They will never last at this rate, so they will be banished to the cold for their imprudence. *Potentilla crautzii* var. *nana*, a ground-hugging yellow-flowered little gem, is now too tragically beautiful for its own good. It, too, is banished from its idyllic 65-degree greenhouse. Even with cold it will probably not make the show. Jack-in-the-pulpit and Shasta daisies, just pushing buds, also will go. These are all one-time bloomers—once flowered, they are likely not to see the show, although we will reconsider their use as foliage textures as the date of the show approaches.

Some of the continuous bloomers were also too far along to suit us, so we took the guillotine to them (so to speak). Veronicas, violas, and yarrows had their heads removed. They will also, most likely, be moved to the cold. This may be the wrong treatment, but since we do not know what else to do and have received little advice from the trade, we have to make things up as we go along.

Many plants are growing about as we expected them to. This shocks us to some degree because we are not used to matters going as planned. There is something unnatural about it, even unsettling. Materials that fall into this category are the grasses, sedges, ophiopogons, liriopes, daylilies, sedums, lilies, artemisias, santolinas, rudbeckias, hostas, and cannas. These are either foliage plants or late bloomers. Some, for example, the daylilies, may not bloom at all. We thought this would be true of the lilies as well, but they are determined to bloom as soon as they can.

That was unexpected. The rudbeckias and cannas are such really late bloomers that we thought there was no chance of their flowering at all. Now we are not certain. After reassessment, they may be the only plants left blooming by early March.

Week Four

The catalogs begin to inundate in anticipation of spring planting. Not the seed catalogs—those are long gone—but the ones featuring herbaceous perennials and shrubs in pots. The catalogs range from the down-to-earth, down home, newsprint sorts with homespun prices to the upscale, laid-back-but-uptight, glossy sorts with uppity prices. There is something to be said for each and every one of them, I'm certain, but I don't suppose I'll be the one to say it. From time to time I think that I would like to meet the minds behind these catalogs, to see what the writers are like as real people. But, then again, some of life is best stored in the imagination, where reality doesn't spoil it so quickly.

Some catalogs are obviously the result of a corporate intelligence (an oxymoron that screams the meaning of the word). Corporate catalogs are the ones with scarcely any humanity in them at all. If you read the phrases "our growers have selected" or "available in many rainbow varieties," you know you are consorting with a boardroom catalog. What is a "rainbow variety" anyway? One that has all the colors of the rainbow? Not too likely, I think. Probably the catalog writers have never seen the plants in the field, so they use the term rainbow in the sense of "I don't know what colors there are, but there sure are lots of them." These writers leave the fieldwork to some jobber or distributor who also has never seen the plants in the field. There may actually be someone in the firm who once saw a growing plant of some kind, but my guess is that most of the boardmembers live in luxurious New York highrises. It's just a feeling I have, nothing scientific. I hope I'm wrong. I seldom purchase anything from these sorts of catalogs.

The extreme opposite of the corporate catalog may be found in the hand-typed, photocopied, hand-folded, hand-stamped sort. The tops of the *o*'s or left arm of the *t*'s are missing, the bottoms of the letters don't line up, and some letters are darker than others. The effect is a chockablock roller coaster patchwork of a page. There is probably also some suspicious-looking nomenclature such as *Chrysanthemummaximum* or *Oenotheramexicana*—obviously hybridized at the typewriter. There are treasures to be found in such catalogs, however, perhaps local varieties, such as a violet from "the hills of Scioto, Ohio," or "back of Maysville, Ky." There's no telling what gem might be found out back of Maysville. Somebody (and the key word here is "somebody"—not some committee) thinks enough of the plant to propagate and sell it, so it must have something going for it. The opportunity arises to obtain plants of historic interest or maybe just some old fashioned cottage-garden plants that grandma might have grown. It would be worthwhile, I think, to make a collection of these antiques.

Some catalogs are so darn slick it's a problem just holding on to them. You'd almost think the pictures would slip right off the paper, it's so glossy. I was about to say that it is we gardeners who pay for this extravagance—who pay, say, one hundred fifty dollars for a new peony that differs in some inscrutable way from one that costs five dollars. But it's probably the avid collector who pays that sum or an estate-owner who has more dollars than sense. They may choose these plants, but the gardener generally doesn't. Obviously, someone pays for the slick catalog. I admit that in the past I've contributed a small share to such outfits, but lately it's been less and less. Often the catalog hype loses its appeal in the reality of the ground, or the company doesn't even send the highly touted gem in the first place.

As an example, I can resurrect my quest for *Sambucus racemosa* 'Plumosa Aurea'. This shrub is handsome in its five to eight feet of dissected yellow leaves. I ordered it for a goodly price from a prestigious firm because I was under the impression that it was the only firm on earth that sold it. That is the sort of impression they wished to give, of course. What I received, however, was entirely different from what I had ordered. After some time, the company sent a correct replacement for the bogus plant. Then, not long after that, I was visiting a local, rather chaotic nursery and found the same *Sambucus* at twice the size, one-third the price, and, most importantly, triple the vigor. It is informative to have these high-roller sorts of catalogs, but I keep them mostly for research value and the overly glamorous photographs. I can almost always find the same plant at a better price from some other firm.

A catalog that starts out "Dear Friends" or begins with a description of "our business" or "our family business" tells me a lot more than one that opens with the boast of being "the complete garden catalog" or "America's only mail-order source" (for a plant that no one would want in the first place). To suppose that a company is complete in any way, shape, or form is the height of arrogance.

Then there are specialist catalogs. These come in two varieties, those that specialize in a few plant species and their cultivars, for example, in chrysanthemums, dahlias, or irises, and those that specialize in a single category such as shade plants, rock garden plants, shrubs, aquatic plants, or orchids. The distinction sometimes is not all that clear, but in general, specialist catalogs offer more of one thing than you ever thought you'd need and certainly more than you can afford. I must admit that I'm a sucker for such catalogs.

Many of us go through gardening phases, and whether we are collectors of single plant groups or advocates of theme gardens, we are easily caught up in the conflict between collecting one of everything and having too much of a good thing. Take bearded irises, for example. One of the biggest U.S. catalogs lists 400 to 500 cultivars of the bearded sorts. This is too many. This form of temptation should be made illegal. I find when ordering from such a list that the four or five varieties I need for the garden quickly grows to three dozen. Every one sounds better than the last, and they are so cheap that it doesn't seem right to deny myself the pleasure of their company just because I have no room in the garden. Surely I could fit six dozen irises somewhere.

The problem is, and I ought to know, a collection of irises (or dahlias or daylilies) is not a garden, it is a monotony. Everything is generally of the same height, nearly the same bloom time, and the same structure. It is impossible, I think, to make a collection of bearded irises look like anything more than a collection of bearded irises. And they will look good only for a few weeks at that. It might be possible to combine bearded irises with Siberian irises, Japanese irises, Pacific Coast irises, and Louisiana irises, but even then their appearance will be fairly uniformly irislike. In terms of cultural requirements, I don't believe such a garden would work anyway. Each requires slightly (to vastly) different treatments. It is better, in my opinion, to mix collections, if one must collect, to produce a collage effect rather than an expanse of sameness.

If one collects by theme, for example, aquatic plants, rock garden plants, or conifers, one is cutting across plant families, genera, and species with a much greater possibility for variety. Any one of these groups would make an interesting garden in itself; when combined, the effect can be inspirational. Here, again, the catalogs of specialist nurseries are enough to drive one mad with indecision and bankrupt with desire. It is difficult to remain calm when surrounded by dozens of catalogs offering hundreds or thousands of plants one wants to try in the garden.

But we must be realistic, mustn't we. For example, there is no more room in my garden for conifers and that, as they say, should be that. But I am still tempted by nearly every conifer I see or read about, and some are actually quite small, really. They could fit just about anywhere. I know I could make a space if only I had the plant in hand. And there is always bonsai. I mean if the Japanese can fit a whole forest in a pot, surely I can fit one more conifer in my garden . . . somewhere.

The variety of plant material available to the gardener appears to be infinite. There is always some new cultivar, something slightly different, one that blooms later or is shorter or has variegated foliage or twice as many petals. As a biologist, I am fascinated by the seemingly endless varieties of life that exist on this planet, and I am also amazed at the life forms that humankind creates. I know that I step on some very serious toes when I say that we create these forms, but we do, and I see no point in attributing the success to any force other than ourselves.

In their book *Your Kitchen Garden* (New York: Simon and Schuster, 1978), G. Seddon and H. Radecka remark about the onion, for example, that "no wild form . . . as we know it now survives." Have we eaten every last wild ancestor of the cultivated onion in the world? It is certainly possible, given humankind's propensity for overdoing everything. In fact, Seddon and Radecka state matter-of-factly that the staple diet of ordinary ancient Egyptians was "onions, washed down with beer." I suppose it is possible that these folks, as gassy as they must have been, finished off the wild onions, but I think it more likely that over the millennia we humans have selected for bigger and bigger onions until we have created them in the image we wanted. And now we no longer know what they originally looked like.

I believe that God would never have created brussels sprouts if left on his or her own. Only some fiendishly perverted humanoid life form could have taken the cabbage (itself highly suspect as a creation) and turned it into brussels sprouts, broccoli, kohlrabi, and cauliflower. And the same for beets—surely a vegetable created straight from dirt. At least they taste like it. But I digress.

That modern plant catalogs offer so much innovation is attributable in large part to humankind. Historians claim that we began as hunter gatherers, then graduated to hunter cultivators, agriculturists, and medicinal (and magic) plant growers—all extending from about 8000 to 2000 B.C. as gauged by development in different parts of the world. It was not until surplus agricultural crops were abundant that wealth and urbanization became possible and that strictly ornamental gardens arose, probably some time from 2000 to 1500 B.C. (although exact dates appear to be open to scholarly debate).

After several thousands of years we now ought to have a large enough selection of vegetables, flowering plants, shrubs, and trees to satisfy every taste on earth, but that is not the human way. Even as I write, hundreds of researchers, horticulturists, and amateurs alike are rearranging plant genes to suit our never-ending hunger for variety. Some of this work, such as gene splicing, is ultrasophisticated, but it can be as simple as gathering seed and selecting for desired traits. Whatever the level of sophistication, the gardener (and the diner, too) benefits from all this mixing up of the earth's life forces.

Unfortunately, as one small group of workers is building up an artificial and innovative variety of organic life, a very large group is tearing down the world's natural diversity as fast as it possibly can. Soon it will become painfully clear that to create innovation we must first start with natural diversity. The correlation is not too difficult to make that the more diversity to be found in the natural world, the more diversity humankind will have to work with in its quest for the perfect iris, the perfect potato, and maybe even an edible brussels sprout. Perhaps if we fully understood the extent of the world's natural riches, if we really knew what wonders were available naturally, we would not be in such a hurry to bury it beneath tons of garbage, to pave it over, to damn it up, to strip-mine it, to cut it down, or to burn it up. Or even to wage war over it.

I would like to believe so.

Week Five

The Eastern Winter Study Weekend began on late Friday afternoon and went through Sunday midday. I attended, sort of. The meeting was held about twenty-five miles away on the other side of Washington, D.C., and I thought it would be simple enough to drive over and take in the festivities. It wasn't.

Friday night the meetings began with a banquet, after which a talk, "Traveling in Central Asia for Alpines," was given. I would have liked to have heard the talk, but I was not interested in the banquet, nor did I especially feel like driving fifty miles round-trip to hear a fifty-minute talk that began at nine o'clock. By Friday night I usually feel like collapsing on the floor and pulling a blanket over my head.

On Saturday, as I discovered rather late, there were to be five talks presented in two different locations separated by about fifteen city miles (that equals about 106 country miles, or 211 freeway miles). Due to a misunderstanding on my part, I missed out on the bus transportation to one of the locations, so I decided just to stay for the talks at the place where I actually was located (this seemed the most logical thing to do). I didn't want to jump in my car and chase over to a place that I would have gone to in the first place if I'd known that that was the place I should have been. (When life becomes too complicated, especially on a Saturday, I tend to ignore it and hope it goes away.)

I attended two talks in the afternoon (which, to confuse the picture even more, were repeats of the talks that had been given in the morning for those people who had caught the bus), which were very good. One was "Rock Gardening in Washington, D.C.," and the other "Rock Gardening Possibilities with Plants of the Southeastern United States and the Orient." Another talk, "Rhododendrons from China," was of little interest to me, not because I don't like rhododendrons or China (I like both as a matter of record, having grown rhodies and been to China), but because I have given up on both for now. Another talk, which began at nine, again after a banquet, was distant enough in time to lose its appeal.

Instead of talks, I wandered over to the book salesroom and perused the few books that were for sale. My being a day late didn't improve the selection. I did find a particularly nice work on auriculas to add to my library. These are absolutely stunning members of the genus *Primula* with thick, succulent leaves. I've grown several dozen exhibition-type named varieties for three or four years in my greenhouse, and I've also grown nearly a hundred garden-type plants from seed. Unfortunately, almost none of either of these types bloomed for me. The few that did overwhelmed the senses, but mostly the plants were zombies: neither fully alive nor dead. With few exceptions, I have ruthlessly dismissed them from the property. No sense in investing any more time in a plant than it deserves . . . even if it is devastatingly beautiful. Better to move on to some primroses that might like it here. (I have yet to fully succeed in this goal.) In the meantime, I can read up on how one is supposed to grow them, so that the next time I try (yes, there will be a *next* time), maybe I will know how to do it.

After looking at gardening books I walked over to the plant-viewing room. There were some hushed comments about this choice of words to describe the room because it was feared that perhaps there was a roomful of dead plants on display. But this was not the case. The plants, several hundred, including many small planted troughs, were in fine condition and were the subjects of both a raffle and auction to be held the next day. I noted with a slight bit of pride, that my contribution of *Opuntia microdasys* 'Desert Gem' was placed on the table reserved for especially choice auction items. This is a dwarf cultivar of the species, its pads less than an inch long and russet in color. (At home, in a small trough, I've combined this eight-inch cactus with sempervivums that look like agaves to create a miniature desert scene.)

A majority of the plants propagated by other members of the chapter, a few nurseries, and myself, were used as giveaways to attendees as they registered for the event. Attendance numbered about 200 participants, most of them from the eastern United States but also from across the country and across the Atlantic. Enthusiasts came from Toronto to Atlanta, from San Francisco and Seattle to Denver, from London and Horach, Czechoslovakia. There was no doubt about the keen interest of these attendees. The speakers were world travelers and included plantspeople, nurserypeople, plant researchers, organic chemists, and civil engineers. They all spoke of subjects near to their lives, and whether they were chemists or professional plantspeople, you could tell that plants were at the forefront of their thoughts. The same was obviously true of the attendees, who ate, drank, and talked plants for two nights and the better part of three days. It was easy to imagine that no one "slept" plants because they were too busy enjoying themselves to sleep. Such is the power of plants.

I try diligently to be charitable toward my fellow gardeners. For the most part we are all good sports who put up with a lot of eccentric behavior that might pass as merely incompetent in the real world. Today, however, is the last straw. I am dumbfounded by the idiocy practiced by the so-called municipal garden planners in our town.

To say that the planting scheme of our fair city, which sits next to the capital of the entire known United States and is not, therefore, lacking in any social or artistic graces, is revolting, is possibly to damn with faint ridicule. In short, the plantings must be the result of a committee, no one person could be *that* incompetent.

Every day on my way home from work, I have the privilege of carpooling past what euphemistically might be called a streetside planting. Many years ago, the street sides and medians were either concrete or grass. This was never taken care of, so often it ended up as grass growing out of broken concrete or broken concrete on top of grass. Either way, it did not seem possible to further debeautify the situation. Then about four or five years ago, a great flurry of activity took place: cement was removed then repoured, the ground dug up, and hundreds of bales of peat moss and great mounds of sand incorporated into the soil.

The sides of the road were furnished—in high summer—with about a hundred yews on two-foot centers. This was a daring concept, I suppose, but even *I* could have thought of it, given a few weeks' time. Within a few years the planting turned into a weed-choked, unwatered, untended mass of vegetation with every sixth plant dead and others begging to be allowed to die. Sticking up through the yews were elm seedlings and locust suckers that were a good two or three feet taller than the yews themselves.

It had looked horrid enough, lo these many years, but today they came in and chopped everything off at the two-foot level! Obviously with a mechanical hedging device because no human hand could butcher plants in that manner. The effect, as you might imagine, was breathtaking—in somewhat the same way that a ride in a free-falling elevator might be. All the weeds are there, shortened to be certain; all the tree seedlings, too, but now with the advantage of much-shortened yews that can never keep pace. Ah, the beauty of it all. The thought.

The median strips provide further evidence of the desecration, though here one never knows if the plants are merely dead or are being used as an artistic statement. Maybe to the effect that life mirrors life; that is, all passengers on the road of life are simply dead, shallow beings in a sea of concrete . . . or something symbolic like that. When the medians were renovated, an underground sprinkling system was also laid before planting, so someone must have had some knowledge of what they were doing. Here, I could see, was some forethought, some indication of a planning process.

The sprinklers were broken within two months of construction, the water squirting on passing cars while the trees died. The trees were crab apples and oaks, many of which did not survive the first month of planting. Even the underplantings of juniper and euonymus began dying in short order. I suppose when you set plants in the ground in July and then water the streets and cars for long periods, death is almost certain. Not being a city planner, however, I don't know that for sure.

4

FEBRUARY

Week One

The week begins auspiciously . . . well, heatedly might be a better word. Yesterday in the sixties and today a hundred-year record high of 70 degrees. Not bad for the first week of February and for us humans (as I fondly refer to my kind), as well. Perhaps not so good for the plants, however. All sorts of false hopes rise with the temperature: daffodils and Dutch crocuses spring from their beds; azaleas show color in the bud; aubrietas try yet again to bloom (they've been practicing since November); pansies struggle to get their flowers unfurled; poppy anemones, a gamble even in warm winters, barely pop their parsley-mop of leaves through the mulch, knowing full-well the penalty for such indiscretion.

Intuitively, you would think that early reaction to warmth is bad. Yet to come we still have the potential for great disasters, such as the nearly two feet of snow we had in late February of 1979 or the 2 degrees we had a few Februaries back. You might imagine that such changes as we've been having, whether abrupt or gradual, would wrack plant growth fiercely. And it does occasionally, but rarely. Last year, for example, in early March, the temperature rose to 90 degrees for two days just as the daffodils were in full force, turning them to near mush. That is to say, the leaves and flowers keeled over and never recovered. On the other hand, almost every year the nation's capital goes through a sudden cold snap just as the hundreds of plants of *Magnolia* × *soulangiana* are about to bloom. These trees are covered from top to bottom with goblet-shaped pinkish white flowers that usually collapse just as they open up their cups of color. Tens of thousands (maybe hundreds of thousands) of buds and half-open flowers turn to brown, dreary death—an insult to spring and to those of us who hold our breath waiting to see if just such a scene will happen . . . again. Ah, but when the flowers are not damaged, every few years or so, the sight is such that it is worth waiting for. In fact, one should be ecstatic merely to see such a show once in a lifetime and learn not to take so much for granted.

I haven't said much about THE SHOW lately, mostly because it has reached the wait-and-see stage. While fingernails are being slowly gnawed to the elbow and panic rises to neck height, we salute ourselves for our outward appearance of serenity. Inwardly, we are beginning to waver, and it shows in various ways. The primary debate is do we let the plants develop to the swollen-bud stage and then hold them back with cold, or conversely, do we keep the plants from developing at all until just a few weeks before showtime and then heat them up fast. We are babbling in the dark on this one. Two of us, including me, say to hold first, the third says let them go. Already a quince has bolted and spent its savings. Several Japanese cherries are also bolting, as is a twelve-foot-tall ornamental pear. These plants will not be of any floral use for the show. It's a pity, too, because they are (were) nice plants. Hopefully, we have protected our backsides, somewhat, with plants in four or five different greenhouses.

The basic argument over plant policies belies a further problem in our methodologies. I like to identify the work, organize it, get in, get it done, and get out. My compatriots Bill and Dug are what might be called—and I hope they will forgive me for this—dawdlers. They seem to take great enjoyment in what they are doing, at least judging by the time they take to do it (and by their enthusiasm). I, on the other hand, often take greater enjoyment in planning to do things than in actually doing them. You'd think we would be a perfect team—but not always.

Last week, for example, I, ever the placid, level-headed sort, lost my temper while standing outside in 20-degree weather trying to stay warm. Dug and Bill (the principal coconspirators) were discussing whether to put a pencil mark three inches to the left or right of an erasure smudge on the master plan while the wind moved the pencil an extra inch or two at every gust. I was not amused, shall we say, and expressed some opinions about their sanity (and silently about the sanity of all the cousins in their families who'd married each other). It was enough to break up the gang (my goal) and send us heading back inside.

As in all relationships, however, where the sum of the parts is greater than the parts themselves, we never stay peeved for long. None of us could afford it. We've had several more meetings to discuss plans and plants, and one day we met at a great, empty warehouse where the garden was chalked out, life-size (sixty by eighty feet) on the concrete floor. Again it was cold. I had on a down jacket, gloves, wool scarf, and wool hat pulled down well over my ears. Somehow, in spite of myself, I could envision the garden in all its imaginary glory. I walked the paths, looked at the greenhouse, the sunroom, the woodland creek, and the rockery. I could also envision the daunting amount of work required to bring this into existence and thought to myself, "If a fool is born every minute, then there isn't three minutes' worth of brains among the lot of us." If fools rush in, then we were traveling at the speed of sound.

There is something to be said for structure in a garden. Not just in having the garden structured into a plan or scheme but in having an actual structure. I have often longed for a nice sculpture or a massive, huge stone to serve as a feature in my garden. Today I saw structure with a vengeance—somewhat along the lines of Stonehenge and equally evocative. It is at the U.S. National Arboretum and is available for all to see. For those who revel in the theatrical, who delight in the dramatic, who adore the grandiose, it is just the thing: the National Capitol Columns.

Darkened, unstable clouds roiled overhead as I pulled into the empty parking lot near the bonsai pavilion. I changed my normal office shoes for the snug, warm, dry duck boots I always use when the misty, liquid air brings a dampness to everything it touches. The walk is about 200 yards across a rolling landscape that might be called lawn but is more accurately mowed weeds (just like mine). Across this landscape on a distant knoll, the columns held up nothing except, perhaps, the sky, which could have fallen at any moment with no surprise. The columns are of a massive scale even at 200 yards. On this brooding day they were all mine.

There was no one in sight save for a dozen or so crows that were agitated by my presence. In their raucous cretching they called out to each other or to no one. Or to me, perhaps. They circled overhead for a moment, then flew off. It was an eerie feeling walking across the moorlike, undulating swales: the monoliths, the ominous clouds, the darkness, the crows circling overhead. Garden high drama.

The columns, twenty-two of which once stood at the east central portico of the United States Capitol from 1826 to 1958, have been moved to the arboretum for permanent safekeeping. They are massive in stature and girth and not the sort of thing one thinks of as a typical garden ornament. Here, however, essentially alone on a hilltop, they capture the romantic element of the English landscape garden of the late eighteenth and early nineteenth centuries. They stand as a stark but welcomed contrast to the remainder of the arboretum.

The National Arboretum is a fine place to visit if you ever have the chance. Spread over 450 gently rolling, wooded, and open acres, it is delimited on the southeast by the Anacostia River and everywhere else by the city of Washington, D.C. Although technically a research facility of the U.S. Department of Agriculture, the arboretum displays much of its research as well. There are ornamental garden settings such as the National Herb Garden, the Gotelli Collection of dwarf conifers, and the developing National Bonsai and Penjing Museum. These are gardens as we know them, that is, landscaped. My favorites are the Gotelli Collection, composed of about 2000 dwarf and slow-growing conifers, and the walled Japanese garden adjacent to the bonsai pavilion.

The Gotelli Collection had just been planted when I first saw it in about 1961 or '62. My family was on a visit from California, and about all I can remember was the open vastness of the planting. None of the trees was large, and they had plenty of room to grow. Now the collection is an intricate maze of foliage color, form, and texture. Without a single flower (if you don't count grasses), the planting is a complete garden within itself. If only gardeners could learn to harness this diversity to replace the barrenness of the traditional lawn around their homes, how much more interesting yards and gardens could be.

The walled oriental garden once served as the primary entrance to the bonsai pavilion, which houses many examples of the art of bonsai (tree dwarfing) and penjing (landscape dwarfing). New construction is changing that, but you still have to go through the garden to get to the pavilion. The walled garden is a small area, perhaps thirty by thirty feet surrounded by an eight-foot stucco-and-wood wall. By using a wandering path, short-distance focal points, sculpted, flowing azaleas, and a few upright shrubs and trees, the area seems far larger than it really is. It is a quiet garden, if no one is about, and contemplative. Much as with the conifer garden, the essence of the space is shape, texture, and design. Flowers are unnecessary; though the azaleas do bloom in the spring, their flowers are irrelevant. This garden demonstrates grandly the illusion of space. In so doing, it should serve as a model for city gardens everywhere. Unfortunately, this will most likely never be the case.

The Bonsai and Penjing Museum is now undergoing a great renovation. Eventually, the area will encompass two acres with a pond. Already available to view are some fifty bonsai (up to 350 years old) and thirty penjing (up to 200 years old). A number of viewing stones, once housed in the administration building, eventually will be moved to more appropriate quarters better suited to contemplation. These rather small, individual stones capture the great architecture and soul of the earth's landscape.

In addition to the ornamental gardens, the arboretum has many collections of plants that are grown as much by genus as by design. Here you can study the plants themselves and discover their colors, heights, spreads, good points, and bad points. In this respect, there are plantings of hollies, magnolias, viburnums, crape myrtles, lilacs, crab apples (over 300 kinds), dogwoods, and azaleas. The major azalea area is said to contain about 70,000 plants. (About 69,995 too many for my taste.) Then, too, there are great plantings of daylilies, peonies, daffodils, irises, and ferns. (Kew Gardens in England has a similar plant library divided by families. If you like composites, for example, you can go to that section of the garden and see dozens to hundreds of species arranged by height.)

Arranging plants by groups is a pleasant way to learn about them and brings me to one of the primary functions of any arboretum: education. This is straightforward education, as you learn about plants directly from themselves. To see thousands of varieties growing in one area is to see a condensed version of the world's flora. We can't help but learn from observation. The National Arboretum also has lecture series, demonstrations, flower exhibits, flower-art exhibits, short courses in horticulture, introductions to gardening for children, and probably a lot more activities that I don't know about.

Research, too, is a form of education for the professional botanist, horticulturist, and landscape architect. All those plants are not just sitting there waiting for you or me to visit them (although at peak azalea season there can be upwards of 20,000 visitors a day on weekends). There are researchers constantly working the collection over for some reason or other. Not all research ends in dry, dull papers. Research in plant breeding and selection has led to the introduction of at least 150 plant varieties into commercial production. Even nonplantspersons do research at the arboretum. As an entomologist I was interested in the parasites of some small flies that damage holly berries. I found a good infestation (for me, of course, not for the hollies) to study in the holly collection at the arboretum.

The administration building houses some 600,000 prepared specimens of both cultivated varieties and wild plants. Botanical and horticultural researchers from all over the world study these to help identify unknown specimens. Even researchers from related fields rely on the specimens and expertise at the National Arboretum. On a recent trip to Florida, for example, I collected several dozen specimens of native hollies that needed to be identified in relation to my study of a newly discovered holly-seed-feeding wasp. With the aid of the arboretum's collection and one of its holly experts, Dr. Theodore Dudley, the hollies were identified, and this material, in turn, became part of the collection for future reference.

Eventually, when all nature has been subdued, controlled, and obliterated by the hand of humans, the plants left growing in the arboretum and the collections of flattened, pressed specimens may be our prized legacy to our grandchildren. Although arboretums may act as nature's conservators and benefactors, these institutions can't serve as nature's replacement, nor should they. Far better that they serve as nature's reminders of our enlightened stewardship of the natural world.

Week Two

Last week's abnormal extravagance of warmth has been interrupted by winter's reality. A typical ploy to upset the gardener. I, too, vacillate with winter's moods. Even a half-week's worth of warmth breaks the cold-adapted body, and now I must start all over again to build up my cold resistance. The weather-guesser is calling for single digits by week's end. That is one reason I am writing this as I sit next to the wood-burning stove in a room near 80 degrees rather than at my desk where it is scarcely 70 degrees.

I am not alone in this predicament. Many plants were of the opinion, given last week's record-breaking warmth, that spring had arrived. A few daffodils here on the property have either opened (*Narcissus asturiensis*) or are trying ('Dutch Master'). Along Rock Creek Park, my normal and somewhat scenic commute route home, a few dozen clumps of miscellaneous daffodils were open yesterday (when it was 55 degrees), but today (at 35 degrees) it is obvious they are thinking better of it. Normally they wouldn't be blooming for three or four more weeks, and if this return to normal winter temperatures holds sway, they will be right on schedule. A slight miscalculation of a few weeks doesn't seem to matter; unlike me, a little cold never hurt a daffodil, even in flower. They do much better, as I pointed out last week, than when a 90-degree day befalls them. No, spring bulbs were made for the cold—they would laugh in winter's face if they had a sense of humor (and winter had a face).

Coincidental with the cold and adding to its insult, I am facing an old dilemma. In a few days I will be giving two short talks to the local chapter of the American Rock Garden Society. I don't much like giving talks: it is a difficult task for a shy person. I have spoken to groups of up to 500 people as part of my profession, but that is not the same as venturing into the unknown territory of an avocation. It should be no problem. Technically, I know what I'm talking about (within reason, anyway), and I don't particularly fear the audience (within reason, anyway). It is just an experience I do not find comfortable until it actually begins, and then I generally forget the preliminary agonies. This week, just the thought of having to do it has nearly crippled my normal garden writing.

One of my talks deals with propagation, which, as I pointed out before, is a simple matter: either something propagates or it doesn't. As a basis for a talk, this is not much to go on. If the techniques were incredibly complicated, I could dwell at length upon that aspect. They're not. You take a piece of plant and stick it in something that holds it. I use sand for this purpose, but each propagator usually has his or her own favorite medium. So far I think I have about thirty seconds' worth of material to talk about.

When I first planned my propagation bed it was going to be the very best and most expensive that money could buy. That was until I figured out how much it would cost. After that I just built a box in my greenhouse and filled it with sand. It was a big box to be certain, two by six feet by four inches deep. It was a big box filled with sharp builder's sand. Need I say more? It took only a day for Bruno to put the box to good use. I was forced to ban him from the greenhouse for a goodly period of time. Eventually, he wheedled his way back in, and it was not uncommon for a while to find all my cuttings mashed flat where he had slept on them. Life would be simpler without cats.

As far as I can tell, plant propagation requires two basic attributes—patience and experience—neither of which is teachable. Of the two, experience is the less important because it is easy to gain experience, but one is always losing patience. The only secret to propagation that I know of is moisture. Moisture at the point of cutting (i.e., the bottom of the plant) and moisture at the point of growth (i.e., the top). If a cutting runs out of moisture in its tissues then it is dead. Having a large bed of sand stabilizes moisture to a great degree, and a single watering a day is enough to keep it wet. The sand, in turn, keeps the air humid around the tops of the plants. A warm root zone seems to expedite root growth but is not absolutely necessary. That's a fairly simple secret, I suppose, but it's the best I can offer. Somehow I will wrap this information into a more presentable package by next Saturday.

The other talk is about pinks (*Dianthus*) and how to grow them. It is slide-prompted and thus will be easier to present. It is always preferable to stand in the dark while people look at something on a screen. It's a good hiding mechanism while still being in plain view. Although giving this talk may be easier, it presents more of a problem beforehand. To put it candidly, I do not have a good system for organizing slides. Often I have tried to organize them and just as often I've failed. For that reason it is possible to find slides of flower subjects, let us say, in about fourteen different places. Well, not places so much as piles. This is actually a very good word to describe the way I organize slides. I have slides in piles in two drawers in the living-room wall unit, in the cubbyholes and drawers of my desk, a drawer in the guest room, a cabinet under the computer, between the pages of my address book (not many there), in a bedroom cabinet, in the china cabinet, and in a paper bag in another cabinet. It's an awful system, but I usually can remember where to find specific slides—except for the one I need.

Pointless to say, I suppose, that it will take me longer to find the slides I want than it will take to talk about them. Ah well, it will be over with shortly and then it will all have been great fun.

As long as I've brought up the subject of slides, I might as well continue on the subject of art. I know this is a garden book, but if gardening is not art, then what is? In my last book the publisher advised me to supply illustrations with the final revised manuscript. I was not expecting this, but I did as I was told, and it was a last-minute, mad-dash affair. One of my coworkers, Taina Litwak, is a professional scientific illustrator and free-lance artist, so it seemed expedient to work with her to furnish the work with illustrations. And this Taina did with splendid vignettes taken from my garden (her vignettes actually were much more splendid than the garden). Her illustrations added much to the book, judging by the comments of various readers.

Now, however, I am faced with a dilemma. I would like Taina to illustrate this book, but I would also savor the opportunity to have it illustrated by a long-time favorite artist of mine whose work I admire greatly. His name is Henry Evans, and he does linocut prints of his own plant portraitures. It is best, perhaps, to describe his work, if it can be described at all, as "simple elegance."

I have just written a letter to Mr. Evans inquiring whether or not something could be worked out. You will know the results of my request as soon as you have looked at the title page of this book. But that point is still many months away for me.

Week Three _____

What I call the spring yo-yo effect is starting. Last Saturday it was 12 degrees when I arose and the temperature barely broke 20 degrees all day. A wind of fifteen to twenty miles per hour did not help matters in the least. Today, four days later, it was 58 degrees when I went to work (6:30 a.m.)—and humid, too. A summery sort of feeling. All this is relative, of course, because 60 degrees is a warm day when you're used to cold, but in summer 60 degrees is a cold day.

Last Saturday was the winter meeting of the local chapter of the American Rock Garden Society, and it was to this body of rather keen gardeners that I presented the talks referred to last week. There were forty to fifty members in attendance, and the room was filled to just about overflowing—one more person and it would have been. Normally we meet at the National Arboretum for our winter talks, but this time the meeting was held at Green Spring Farm Park in Arlington, Virginia.

My first talk, on propagation, was all planned out and scripted to cards. I knew what I was going to say. But as the first speaker rambled on, I began to rewrite my cards. It wasn't so much that he was saying everything I was going to say, it was more that what I was going to say was not worth saying after listening to him speak. I had prepared a general talk, and the first speaker was dwelling on some highly detailed aspects of potting mixes, seed-starting temperatures, starting and stopping times, lighting needs, and so forth.

Then came the second and third speakers, and by my turn the cards were virtually useless. They were twisted and folded and damp, the ink was smudged, they were out of sequence, and there were so many notes to myself that I could no longer read the writing. Not only that, but the session was running late—it was ten minutes after noon, and the audience was about to grill the speaker for lunch. It was not a good position to be in—virtually no talk and surrounded by a hungry mob. And believe me, I was no more enthralled with the situation than they were. Probably less so, because I bruise easily. Not to mention that I, too, was hungry, and there were two more speakers after me before we were scheduled to break for lunch!

I cannot say that I gave anything approaching a coherent account of myself. I really don't know what I said for the most part (except for one good retort about buttermilk that would be out of context if I repeated it). The basic point I tried to make was that, as those who had gone before me had just demonstrated, everyone has a different system of propagating plants and they all work about equally well for 99 percent of what we want to grow. Therefore, it is not the system or technique itself that is always so important but rather the fact that anyone can propagate plant material if he or she puts the effort into it. It took me about fifteen minutes to say this, so I must have left something out of my recapitulation. The point is still valid.

When I first moved to this garden, my seed-growing operation consisted of half a dozen recycled and stacked moving boxes for benches, four shop lights hung from floor joists in the furnace room, some plastic flats and market packs (or cells), and a lot of faith in seeds. For five years I raised thousands of plants using this set-up, and it worked just fine. Better, in fact, than the system I've been using for the last five years since I built the greenhouse. I've recently rigged up some new shelving in the potting room next to the greenhouse, and I'm going back to growing seeds under lights just as soon as I can clear a path through the used flower pots, heaps of potting soil, buckets, firewood, and bags of dormant summer bulbs.

I think conditions are more stable in the potting room (essentially a basement room) than in the unheated greenhouse, where temperatures can drop into the low thirties at night and up to the seventies or eighties in the daytime (if the sun is out). This may be a good stimulus for some seeds to germinate, but they don't seem to do as well after germination as they did when they were in the basement. Here they received a twelve-hour light-and-dark cycle with the lights on timers, and the air temperature fluctuated less wildly (about 55–65 degrees). This sort of treatment is certainly better for annuals and probably for perennials in general. Rock garden plants are a lot trickier than most things, so I will probably plant them in the greenhouse and leave them there. Sometimes it takes a year or two of heat, cold, drying, and wetting to get them to germinate.

After lunch I also gave the talk on pinks. These are among my favorite flowers dating back to my second childhood garden in San Anselmo, where my interest began with a border of garden pinks. These were, I learned later, hybrids of *Dianthus plumarius*. From these pinks I gradually developed an interest in seed-grown carnations and just as gradually lost it. Carnations produce flowers as positively wonderful as their plant structure is detestably floppy. I soon returned again to the much more garden-worthy pinks as a focal point of interest. Many of these make evergreen mounds of gray-green or blue-green foliage that is attractive throughout the year. *Dianthus erinaceus*, for example, forms a slow-growing, rock-hugging mat that molds itself over any object in its path. Although scarcely ever producing flowers, it is wondrous in its fur-like overcoating of the rockery. *Dianthus plumarius* forms hedgehog mounds of gray foliage that define any border with undulating precision. Other dianthus are grown for their flowers, having relatively undistinguished foliage. Who could live without sweet william, *Dianthus barbatus*, and its forms? Or *Dianthus chinensis*, a typically annual pink that often survives its first winter to bloom again the next summer? This species is painted in reds, whites, and pinks and is so incredibly gaudy that it ought to be sown where it can't be seen. I plant it right out front, though, just to irritate the garden and wake it up a bit.

There are between 250 and 300 species of *Dianthus* in the world, which is a good enough figure to begin any lifetime of interest. But this number belies the high degree of innate promiscuity and human tampering that caused Reginald Farrer to comment that in "no race is there more confusion." The *International Dianthus Register*, Second Edition (London: The Royal Horticultural Society, 1986), lists about 27,000 registered cultivar names, a staggering load, indeed, for any humble genus to bear. Or mere mortal for that matter.

At one time I grew every pink species I could lay my hands on from seed offered in the various annual lists of the Alpine Garden Society, the Royal Horticultural Society, and the American Rock Garden Society. This proved rather disappointing in the end, however, because a lot of species all appeared the same to me and were not worth growing in the first place. It is difficult to identify species of *Dianthus*, and I imagine many mistakes in naming plants are made and then perpetuated by people who harvest the seed and distribute it through the various seed exchanges. Additionally, pinks hybridize readily so that flowers producing seed must be isolated to prevent contamination with pollen from some nearby pink. Few growers have the time to be so precise.

I still grow pinks from seed, especially the variants of *Dianthus plumarius* and *D. gratianopolitanus*, from which I select the most interesting growth forms. To be acceptable, the plant must look good in foliage all year long, and attractive flowers are not scoffed at. Unfortunately, here in the East, pinks tend to succumb to our high humidity and acidic soil, but if you grow enough of them from seed, every fiftieth plant might be a survivor and actually contribute form and grace to the garden. A dry atmosphere and alkaline soil are certainly preferable, but pinks are worth fighting for even in my climate.

If I had any fortitude at all, I would attempt a book on the subject of these fine plants, but it would be one of those projects that could lead to an early grave: complex, convoluted, technically demanding, arduous, formidable, and a lot of other words of a synonymous nature. In fact, just thinking about the difficulties makes me hyperventilate.

Right after the rock garden society meeting I dropped by one of the greenhouses where a large amount of plant material for the garden show is sitting and doing one of two things: either blooming its head off or beginning to green up in anticipation of blooming. Show set-up starts in just ten days, and the actual show itself starts six days after that. Time is running out.

Unfortunately, I don't think there is any way to hold back the plants that are blooming. The worst (or best) offenders are five large apple trees that were rescued from the woodsman's axe (or chainsaw) and that will be used in the exhibit to make up a backyard orchard. They are in full bloom now and will never last long enough to make the show. These were orchard trees, about eight to ten feet tall, that were removed from the ground with a tree spade. The root balls are bigger than all outdoors, and even if we could put them in cold storage for a few weeks, the process of moving them to the show would most likely knock all the flowers off anyway. When the time comes the trees will go as is because they are all we have for the orchard. It's not all that easy to find an orchard that's being cleared—especially when you need one.

Half of our azaleas also are in total bloom. These were dug, in part, from a nursery that is going out of business. The plants, possibly Glendales or Kurumes, were stuck out in a woodlot some years back, judging by their growth. They are tall and lanky with scarcely any foliage. In spite of this, they are certainly lovely, blooming as they are in pastel profusion. But they've missed the point entirely. What a shame that only two or three of us will see these plants and not the tens of thousands who might have otherwise done so. It is painful to see them miss their cues by a mere two weeks. Let us hope that the other half will hold themselves in abeyance for just the right time. Let us hope.

In normal years, whatever those might be, I've usually got five or six flats of seedlings sprouted and transplanted by this time and as many more coming on in seed pots. This year, however, being entirely abnormal, I've only just begun the planting today. In fact, I've just sent off another order of seeds. I stagger the seed planting over three or four weeks because if I planted them all in one session, I'd never be able to keep up with them when they sprouted. This way, instead of one incredibly busy month of transplanting, I spread the work evenly over nearly forever. It works out better that way, you see, because there is never enough time to do massive gardening jobs, but always enough to work endlessly at the small ones.

Often, when I plant seeds, my thoughts drift to the more technical aspects of planting. But today's seeds were quite diverse in appearance, and I paid more attention to their shapes than is normally the case. The first batch actually began the process, for they were the most unusual seeds I'd ever seen. In *Polygonella americana*, a native of the southeastern United States, each seed is three-dimensionally diamond-shaped, with the tips sharply pointed, almost daggerlike. The color is a rich enameled red. Either of these attributes would have been noticeable, but taken together they were exceptional. Another seed, *Myosotis sylvestris*, was just the opposite: a smoothly polished ebony disk. Also disk-shaped but entirely different is *Lunaria annua* 'Variegata Stella'. Here the disk is swollen in the middle, and the thin edge appears like the brim of a well-worn straw hat: wavering and undulating, rough, coarse. It is a big seed, nearly a quarter of an inch across. *Anchusa azurea* 'Dropmore' also is a large, coarse seed, but its shape is more like a shrunken, wrinkled kernel of corn. *Anemone rivularis* has an elongated seed resembling a flattened banana with its ends curving in opposite directions. *Lychnis* × *arkwrightii* 'Vesuvius' appears like a tiny bean. And finally, *Verbascum bombyciferum* 'Arctic Summer' scarcely appears at all. It is a fine powder that could easily be sneezed away if you weren't paying attention. The truly amazing thing about this *Verbascum* is that the seed is so very, very tiny and the plant is so very, very big—easily five feet or taller.

All these seeds are different, yet all serve exactly one common purpose: to perpetuate a plant species. Why, then, if they all do the same thing, are there so many different-looking seeds? The only credible explanation is that seeds assume the shape that serves the goal of reproduction best. That is, the seed shape is adapted to insure survival of the species.

The sharply pointed seeds of *Polygonella*, for example, might stick in the fur of animals and be transported for long distances, thus increasing both the spread and the range of this plant. Alternatively, and completely at odds with this explanation, is that perhaps the seed simply falls to the ground and because it is so angular will not be blown or moved too far from where the mother plant grew. After all, if the area is good for the mother, it would be wise to keep the kids close at hand as well. If I were a botanist, I might be able to speculate upon two dozen different possible explanations (or hypotheses) as to why a particular seed looks the way it does. In most cases, I would be willing to wager that no one has studied the biology of these particular seeds in any detail. My guess would be that if they did, each type of seed morphology would be found to serve its biological purpose. Such research takes much time and patience and is not the sort of undertaking that normally receives high-priority funding unless associated with endangered species.

So it is left to the common seed sower to marvel at the apparently simple yet undeniably complicated structure of seeds and to ponder the reasons for their diversity. The more we gardeners know about the needs of the seed, the more likely we will succeed at fulfilling them. Much of gardening is like this, after all, a form of applied botany in which the gardener attempts to make the plant happy in artificial surroundings. The more we know about the natural history of a plant, the more likely we are to duplicate its natural environment in the unnatural thing we call a garden.

Week Four_____

I write this while sitting in a small gazebo on the eve of the second day of construction for the garden show. Bill, the leader of the loonies, drills merrily away as he constructs a mountain out of a molehill of two-by-fours and plywood. It does not sound like the foundation for the most natural area of our garden, and it looks like the jungle gym on Monkey Island, but it will be brought to life. Bart Smith, one of Bill's volunteers, is on the other side of the garden doing some finely detailed work on the house and sunroom that form another element of the garden. It is nearly 9:00 p.m. and generally quiet. We all await the arrival of another truckload of plants to be used in greening up the garden. Dinner is also on that truck, and I await this eagerly as it is four hours past my dinnertime. A particularly nice piece of redwood has definite possibilities for dessert.

As is usual (at least based on the previous two shows), what I came to do today could scarcely be started (let alone finished) because I must wait to build the rock garden until after someone else has built the pathway through it. The path is being built by a fellow who has donated his time and materials for the good of the garden, so we dare not push him for fear of alienating him. Thus I started a few bits and pieces of the rockery, then turned to helping out elsewhere. The path layer would not let me (or anyone) touch his pavers, so I made myself useful by holding lumber, stacking stone to be used for walls, sweeping up, sorting and watering plants, moving balled and burlapped material to berms of mulch to help keep them moist, and finally by writing. Not this writing, but a descriptive tract on rock gardens to be included with some informational literature to be passed out during the show. When asked to write more, I regretfully declined and started on the present chronicle. Otherwise, I would have no record of our progress until it was too late to remember. (In retrospect, I am glad I declined because Dug was up until 4:00 a.m. writing the document.)

As I said, I am sitting in the gazebo awaiting plants and dinner. That piece of redwood is looking better at every passing minute. It is the finial on top of the cupola, which is temporarily propped up outside the gazebo. Actually, the cedar shingles might not be too bad either . . . maybe with a touch of garlic. They smell good enough to eat. The gazebo, as it turns out, is too big for the garden. It was going to be placed at the base of the mountain, but it took up too much space, so it was moved to the concession area immediately behind our garden. It was on loan from a builder who wanted some free publicity. I am glad it is now out of the picture because there is too much planned for the garden already.

Dinner has just arrived, and I am off to enjoy some sort of greasy repast that will, no doubt, make my day complete and my sleep miserable. Such is the life of an itinerant gardener.

Two days and one night have passed. It is now Friday night and I'm safe at home. I came down with a cold yesterday, and on top of that, I am taking three days of vacation and a weekend to work on the show. I should have stayed at home in bed on sick leave, but this endeavor has more to do with lack of sense than common sense.

The pace of construction has been hectic. Because the garden site is fifty miles from where anyone lives (it is just north of Baltimore) and because this is a seven-day project (not unlike the first gardening project ever undertaken), Bill has rented rooms at a local motel for anyone who wants to stay. Actually, for anyone who doesn't want to drive home is a better way of putting it. I did not want to drive home, but since I am taking care of my neighbor's house plants while she is gone and since no one is taking care of Bruno, I went home this evening. I also had to water my greenhouse, and since Dug lives nearby, I watered his as well. It is good to be home and to rest up from the garden construction.

By the time I left there was still little evidence that a garden was being built. The mountain looks like a pile of sticks and chicken wire. The pathways, some 1000 to 1200 square feet of interlocking pavers, are still not finished. The house and sunroom are in good shape. The greenhouse awaits construction tomorrow. Another compatriot, Bob Trumbule, and I constructed a partial rock garden using straw bales for contour and mulch to conceal them. We've installed the rocks but few plants. The two of us also built a decorative block wall across the front of the garden and laid in a large number of six-foot cannas in two-gallon pots behind it.

During the months of preparation for this construction, I've purposefully avoided writing about its specific design. This has been so for several reasons. For one thing, we changed the design every time we looked at it, so to describe it in any detail would have required endless revisions. Another reason is that I do not like to write (nor usually to read) descriptions of how a garden is laid out. Now that it is almost finished (however, we still retain the right to improvise as we go along), I can at least begin to firm up the design.

The overall theme of the garden is to emphasize the diversity of garden-making and to be somewhat educational but not overly pedantic on the subject. To this end we combined the following elements into our assigned sixty-by-eighty-foot space: a house with a sunroom and deck, greenhouse (with biological insect controls), container garden (demonstrating troughs, planters, trellises, and living wreaths), composting and potting area, natural area in the form of the ten-foot mountain with waterfalls, raised vegetable beds, orchard (with bee-keeping materials), herb garden, annual beds, perennial beds, rockery with dwarf conifers, ornamental grasses, hosta bed, and lawn surrounded by bedding plants and groundcovers. One of the primary features of the garden (though this was mostly by necessity) was to show what can be done with foliage color and texture as opposed to flower color. We also used the device of surprise and elevation to give the illusion of greater space than was actually available.

This is an incredible amount of variety for such a small area. But we now have, I believe, a good design that is amenable to impromptu planting schemes as we go along. This sentiment is not based solely upon our own conceits. It was corroborated by a judge of the recent Washington, D.C., Flower Show, who, upon walking through the unfinished exhibit, complimented us on the quality of our design and use of plant material.

Ours has been labeled the "Entrance Garden" because it is the first obstacle beyond the ticket booth. You either go through it or around it. From the front, purposely little can be seen. The right two-thirds is a screen of the cannas I mentioned earlier. This is a purple-leaved variety of great stature. We overlapped them three deep as a screen so that visitors could not see immediately into the garden, but it is possible to see the top of the mountain at the back right of the exhibit. A small observation deck, two steps high, breeches the canna wall to provide an overview of the garden. The cannas follow the deck contour, and when you surmount the deck they reach knee-high to act as a railing. The entrance to the garden is immediately to the left and will be the hosta area.

I will discuss the planting of the garden when it is finished. For now, the design is mostly indicated by piles of things. In the case of the rock garden, it is mostly a mulch pile. Mulch is one of the fillers that give height and topography to the garden. Unlike the mountain, which is constructed of wood and wire, about the only way to achieve elevation is with walls or heaps of mulch or piles of things such as straw bales, rocks, bags of leaves, or overturned flats covered with mulch. Show-garden building is pretty much a job of heavy cosmetics.

The ornamental grass garden is largely piles of rocks waiting to be moved or constructed into low stone walls to retain the mulch. We cannot move the rocks yet, because most of them go to the container garden, which will shortly be the piles of glass and tools used to construct the greenhouse. The orchard is indicated at present by a power saw, heaps of wood, and piles of sawdust. The vegetable garden is visible as a thin layer of mulch.

All the plants, or the vast majority at least, are in the back of the hall where the concession stands and eating area eventually will be placed. In effect, then, the entire backbone of the garden is being constructed and will be covered with living materials when we have made enough progress in the framework department to apply the fur, so to speak. At the present rate it could be weeks or even months. Of course we have only days—slightly over four to be exact.

It is with great reluctance that I head for an almost deserved rest. Tomorrow I must drive the fifty miles back and begin my gardening duties in earnest. The pathway through the rockery will have been finished, and the greenhouse people will have done their job. Then we will have room to work and create the walls necessary to hold the rock garden in place and to move the rocks out of the ornamental grass area to begin the work there. This garden is almost like my own . . . a pile for everything and everything in the wrong pile.

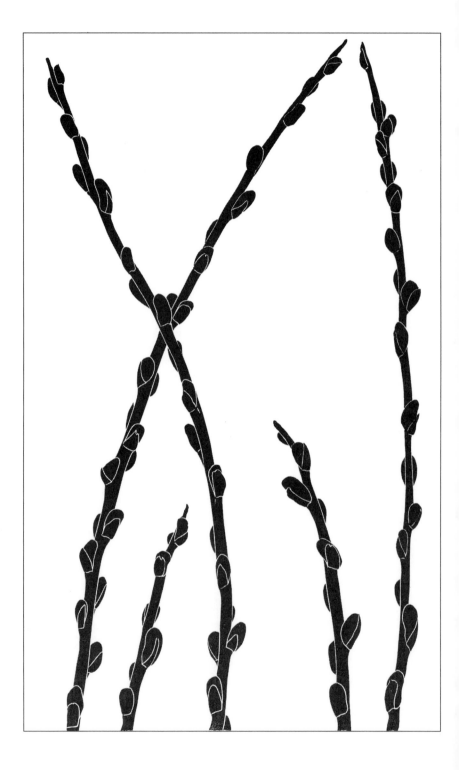

5

MARCH

Week One _____

    The past five days have been a solid blur of activity: of people, pain, pleasure, panic, pots, plans, plants, pitchforks, pavers, and pizza. Of forklifts, fences, flats, falls (both water-and prat-), and filthy clothes. Of rocks, rakes, rapport, repartee, and writing. Of brooms and ball-dollies. Of mulch (ninety cubic yards) and "Magic Mountain," of headaches and houses, glasshouses, sunrooms, compost bins, and concrete. In the course of five days I've put in seventy-five hours of labor (not to mention thinking at the same time—nearly impossible for me), and I was the shirker of the party. Others worked two days more and put in longer hours at that. I cannot imagine how they did it. Food, such as it was, was eaten at the site on the run. (This time I was smart and brought much of my own—no more redwood nibbling for me.)

    Somehow a garden was built, but it is not readily apparent at this time just how it happened, nor can it be easily explained in rational terms. As I said, it was a blur, all happening so quickly. What follows is a reconstruction based upon recollections and finished reality. I don't even know when I had time to write it!

Magic Mountain, the largest, most grandiose part of the garden, was built from about a hundred two-by-fours, sheets of plywood, twenty-five pounds of screws alone, nails, plastic sheeting, chicken wire, foam insulation, paint, roofing rubber, plastic tubing, water pumps, and rocks. This, the most artificial pile of materials imaginable became our natural mountain waterfall. The structure alone took two to three men working full time for seven days. Fortunately, with the exception of a few minutes' work, I was not one of them.

I had some serious doubts all along about how this would work, but I kept them to myself. Good thing, too, because it turned out to be an absolutely miraculous piece of flimflam that looked for all intents like a mountain rising up out of the garden. About ten feet high, it had an additional height of five or six feet in arborescent azaleas in full bloom. Two waterfalls cascaded off the top down two rock faces and formed a small stream flowing around the mountain into an underground cavern. Well, it was supposed to be a cavern for dramatic purposes. It actually disappeared into a hole in some rocks where it was captured in a rubber-lined sump for reuse. The entire wooden-rubber-plastic-chicken-wire mountain was covered in azaleas, rhododendrons, hemlocks, white pines, ferns, Jack-in-the-pulpits, grasses, irises, and other plants. A final coat of mulch and dried leaves camouflaged the framework as well as could be expected. Anything that remained showing after that was hit with a spritz of black paint. It's amazing what a little paint will hide. The entire project suggested to me what a Hollywood soundstage must be like—reality blurred with fantasy at the flick of a wrist. I have absolutely no doubt, now, that Magic Mountain (as I called it, along with some other appropriate names) will be the hit of the garden show. It will be remembered for years to come.

The falls themselves started at ten feet above ground level and fell seven feet before hitting the catch basin. Late, on the third night of construction, before any plant life was placed upon the mountain, the waterfalls were tested. The pumps were fired up, the yell "Water in the hole!" was given, and water started coursing down the vertical, three-tiered face constructed of hundreds of inch-thick, flat stones stacked one atop another. The falls were about four feet wide. At first the water splashed off the stones in all directions, but after twenty minutes' worth of fiddling, this was corrected. The sound of falling water was pleasant for a while, but then an ominous rumbling began, and the bottom section of the rock face came crashing to the ground . . . sort of a rockfall, you might say. It was not a good sign, and spirits were immediately dampened. But in spite of the disaster, the lateness of the evening, and the tired, worn-out state of all present, the waterfall-rock-man, Dug, began immediately rebuilding the wall. Our anxiety lessened by example, we all went back to our chosen chores grateful that no catastrophes as major as this would likely result from our efforts. It was not much to be thankful for, but it was something. We all needed something at this point.

Magic Mountain, being at the rear of the exhibit, thus saves the best for last. Wisely, perhaps, I was relegated to working up the entrance at the left of the canna wall. As a visitor walks toward the entrance to the garden, s/he must walk past a barrier composed of dark-leaved *Canna indica* 'Purpurea'. Embedded in the canna wall is the observation deck, and just beyond this is the garden entryway with a massive bed of hostas to its left. The hostas, arranged by height and color, are dominated by 'August Moon', an expanse of two-foot-high chartreuse yellow foliage that sweeps down to a six-inch-high bed of 'Kabitan', a dwarf, yellow-leaved variety. This forms quite a contrast to the purple foliage of the canna walls. The bed is framed in back by a solid snow white fence and a collection of dark-leaved hollies. For height, *Betula nigra* is planted at the most distant corner, and the twelve-foot-tall ornamental pear (long since beyond bloom) stands over all. The more subdued, green-leaved *Hosta plantaginea* helps tone down 'August Moon' a bit, as do a few grey-green-and-white-foliated plants of *Hosta* 'Frances Williams' and a ground cover of *Lamium* 'Beacon Silver'. This bed, which has virtually no flowers, is strikingly colorful in a garish sort of way. In a darkened woodland situation, the foliage of 'August Moon' glows like the sun. In fact, 'August Sun' would be a much more appropriate name; I can't imagine where the notion of moon came from.

Once the entrance is breached, the eye is directed diagonally across the garden by the path and an extended sweep of red, white, and pink astilbes on the right that lead from ground level up the bank to the natural area at the mountain's base, then up the mountain itself. The sunroom and house to the left are also visible, as is part of the greenhouse to the right. Not until you are half a dozen steps into the garden do you see the ornamental grass area and rock garden off to the right. The grass area is backed by the canna hedge and is composed of grasses (naturally) and grasslike plants such as *Ophiopogon* and *Liriope* in various cultivars. At the front is the four-inch *Ophiopogon japonicus* backed by both *Ophiopogon nigra* and *Liriope muscari* 'Variegata' (each about twelve inches). To one side is a large patch of *Carex buchananii*, a dead-looking sedge that is handsome in a straw-yellow-and-red sort of way. Behind these smaller grasses and grasslike plants is an assemblage of taller grasses, including *Miscanthus sinensis* 'Gracillimus', 'Variegatus', and 'Zebrinus'.

A small swale with a stone footpath that disappears off to the left separates the grasses on the right from the rock garden on the left. This rock garden contains at least fifty species of plants of low stature, including cultivars of *Dianthus, Arenaria, Armeria, Iberis, Aubrieta, Aurinia, Viola, Helianthemum, Arabis, Thymus, Carex, Festuca, Deschampsia,* and the like. Interspersed among these are dozens of choice borrowed dwarf conifers with endless combinations of cultivar names. (Why such small plants should have such big names is beyond me.) The rockery was built to resemble several ridge outcroppings that are traversed by the path to the greenhouse.

Between the greenhouse on the left and the rock garden on the right, we built a container garden with a few boxes holding trellises and climbing plants. In addition, there were living wreaths, living pictures, and troughs. The living wreaths are constructed of two wreath rings (obtainable from craft shops), each of which is a three-dimensional wire topiary frame shaped like half a sliced bagel. The two halves are lined with sphagnum moss, then filled with soilless mix, and placed back-to-back to produce a whole wreath. These can be planted with cacti, succulents, ivy, hens and chickens, sedums, bromeliads, or almost anything that will take semidry conditions. Plantings should be made on a single side if the wreath is to be hung on a wall or on both sides if it is to be hung from a bracket. Wreaths are watered by a gentle spray from a hose nozzle or watering can.

A slight twist to this technique is the living picture, in which a thick wooden frame, preferably pressure treated, is covered on one side with galvanized chicken wire. When the frame is flipped over, it becomes an empty box, and the wire bottom is layered first with sphagnum moss, then soilless mix, and then another layer of sphagnum. Chicken wire is stapled to the open side of the frame to hold everything in place. Plants are pressed through the openings of the chicken wire (which may be enlarged with tin snips if necessary), the sphagnum, and into the soil. The many varieties of *Sempervivum*, or hens and chickens, are especially good for this, but plants such as those suggested above for wreaths may also be used.

Troughs originated in England as carved stone containers used as sinks, animal watering vessels, grinding mills (querns), and even coffins. As these items were replaced by porcelain and steel in the early part of this century, the discarded stone basins were used to grow many varieties of alpine and rock garden plants. Nowadays, because of their increased rarity in England (and complete absence in this country), such hand-carved containers are being replaced by replicas. These replicas are traditionally made from variations on a mixture of one part sharp sand, one part portland cement, and two parts wet peat moss. (This mixture gives a somewhat sandstonelike finish. I use one part perlite, one part peat moss, and one part portland cement, which gives a granitelike effect.) Water is added to the mixture until it reaches the consistency of cottage cheese. The amount of water depends on how wet the peat moss is. This mixture, called hypertufa, is molded in any way that serves the purpose. The simplest is to use a bowl or box turned upside down. The form should be covered with several layers of wet newspaper to help remove the casting when it is finished. (Plastic is often recommended, but I find it is easier to get the hypertufa to stick to wet paper than to plastic.) A mound of sand also works. The wet hypertufa is molded onto the form to a thickness of one to two inches. Generally, for a small trough, no reinforcing is needed. For large troughs, two forms (a larger and a smaller) are built from wood and the trough is filled like a concrete foundation. Usually these are reinforced with wire, but you can also use a fibermesh material that is sold commercially to reinforce concrete structures. It is just as effective as wire reinforcement, and I have been adding it even to my small troughs as insurance. After the troughs dry for several days (depending upon size) but before they are completely dry, they are roughed-up or chiseled to give a hand-hewn, carved appearance. Drainage holes should be made either at the time of casting or drilled at this stage. These rough, rather unrefined planters are perfect for dwarf plants of all kinds but especially for rock and alpine plants and conifers.

Many people have not heard of troughs and even more want one when they've seen one. Troughs are rarely available commercially, and so we are left to create our own. I have spent many a wintry day making troughs for myself and others.

To return to the garden, one must walk through the greenhouse. Inside is a demonstration on how to root cuttings, on making living wreaths, and on how to use parasites to control the greenhouse whitefly. Immediately upon exiting the greenhouse to the right is a demonstration on composting. This is well screened from almost every aspect of the garden so as to be as unobtrusive as possible. Part of the camouflage is created by incorporating a potting bench and pot storage area built from the same material as the three-bin composting structure.

Moving onward one now sees the mountain in all its finery and can hear the double waterfalls. Interestingly, birds have found the water and are using it for their private rituals. The garden show is in a large building called the Cow Palace, and sparrows have been our constant companions since we started building the garden. They were quite interested in our straw bales, and one of the workers here, Gaye Williams, decided to place birdseed in the finished garden to attract them. Obviously, it worked. At the waterfalls one can either exit the garden to the concessions area or turn left and go back through the other half of the garden through the orchard, the house, and the vegetable garden.

The orchard is composed of three of the five large apple trees that were taken directly from an orchard that was being cleared for replanting. As such they are substantial trees. Also in the orchard is a beehive and the equipment to work it; this emphasizes the role of the bee in making fruit by pollinating the blossoms. No bees, no fruit. The orchard is underlain with sod and looks much as if all the weeds and grass had just been mown. Around the edges are clumps of daffodils. (In some geographic areas, bulbs are naturalized within the orchard, but not so much in this country. It might not be a bad idea for a little extra beauty in the spring.)

Walking up the steps and crossing the deck, one arrives at the "house" (represented by half a room) and can sit down and enjoy the view of the mountain from the eight-sided sunroom or peer out the living room window and see the rock garden, ornamental grass garden, and vegetable garden. Walking out the side of the house, one sees a small grouping of herbs, and a little beyond is a triple set of raised beds. Here one finds various lettuces, radishes, beets, cabbages, beans, broccoli, and even tomatoes. Here, too, is a large bed of annuals, including zinnias, alyssum, marigolds, gomphrenas, salvias, and rudbeckia. The most soothing combination of colors is a patch of great borages with their forget-me-not blue flowers and in front of them a patch of the zinnia 'Rose Pinwheel'. It is not often that a color match is so harmoniously made. The simple beauty of the combination dwarfs the remainder of the garden in my mind and certainly is the gardening lesson I will remember most about this show.

This may be the last garden that the group of us will make. Perhaps the third time really is the charm. An enormous amount of work went into it: at least thirty-five people volunteered their time over the course of many months, and almost forty firms loaned or donated plants and materials to the effort. I think all of us worked well together to produce this gardening extravaganza. I cannot say I would care to work this hard again—even in my own garden. But it is invigorating to challenge oneself beyond all expectations and to create in a week's time a garden that might ordinarily take a lifetime of work on the part of one person. It is an inspiration, calling us to do better in our own gardens and perhaps to encourage others to accept the challenge of gardening.

For gardening is a challenge, and don't ever let anyone tell you otherwise.

Week Two

And so the show comes to an end. This week we dismantled the garden that took months of thought, weeks of work, and a few years off our lives. It seems a shame to utterly devastate an entire garden, but it must be done. We had two and a half days to do the unpleasant job.

I went up Sunday night to help begin the task and arrived an hour before closing. The place was still awash in visitors after five days of show and about 150,000 paid tickets. Parking, even an hour before closing, was nearly impossible to find. At the peak of visitation, on Saturday, cars were backed up for three miles to get into the state fairgrounds. This surpassed all expectations and in a way, I suppose, justified our intensity not only in terms of labor but also in terms of the garden's short life span—few gardens receive a fraction of this many visitors in a lifetime.

All the local Baltimore newscasts took footage of the garden, including overhead-boom shots. One ran shots of the waterfalls behind the credits at the end of their program all week. As a result, visitors came to the show with some expectations, especially with respect to our garden. It was supposed to be worth the arduous trek. Since the display garden was unjudged, I cannot, for example, say that it was a "prize-winning" garden or "best in show." We were left to our own devices to discover if we had done a good job or not. We all felt we had, but it is nice (perhaps even essential) to receive some feedback now and again.

Judging by the sources who commented on the garden (including two past judges of the Philadelphia Flower Show), the amount of positive media publicity it received, and the density of the crowd, it was a complete success. We could not have been more soundly rewarded if we'd won best in show. The immediate feeling was exactly as if someone had visited my garden (or yours, I'm certain) and made an extremely kind or even exuberant remark about a small planting that was especially wonderful (even in our own minds).

There is something to be said for creating a work of art, no matter how small, and recognizing that we have accomplished something worthwhile. It feeds the soul, I think, and encourages us onward in our work. If someone else recognizes that we have accomplished something, then it nourishes not only our soul but our creative ego as well. And that is not entirely bad. There is little enough reward in life so that some unsolicited praise will always fall upon receptive ears and propel us forward with unsuspected vigor.

So now the show is over. The tent is folded and the circus moves on. What was once a big, flat, cold expanse of concrete pulled itself to great heights (well, at least ten or twelve feet) and unexpected beauty. A sow's ear really can be made into a silk purse—at least for a while, and with the magic of plants. Now the magic is over, the concrete has returned, and it is on, one hopes, to bigger and better things.

In talking with the various volunteers, I sense that although our collective feelings are of almost complete exhaustion and the certain emptiness that comes when a preoccupying, fanatically compulsive project is completed, we are still a little too close to the work phase of the garden to appreciate its true impact. I find myself thankful that the entire affair is over, but in a few weeks or months I will look back on the project with great satisfaction. In a few years I might even talk myself into doing it again if asked. But not next year. Never next year! I know too much work when I see it.

Would that I could work as diligently in my own garden with the same results. But my garden lies in the realm of reality, not illusion. What took weeks to build as fantasy takes years to achieve left to our own brawn and brains (and weeds). Certainly for a few moments, in the lives of thousands of visitors (and not a few of the dozens of us who put the show together), illusion had given way to possibility. If the public learned anything from our efforts it was that unimaginable results may arise from unimaginative spaces. If we could turn 5000 square feet of flat, lifeless concrete into a living garden, just imagine what can be accomplished within the nurturing space of our own earth-bound gardens.

After five months of seemingly total inactivity in the garden, I am ecstatic to announce that THE GARDENING SEASON IS OPEN—at least *my* official gardening season. I am what you might call a fair-weather gardener. I don't like to dress up in a down jacket, wool hat, and gloves just for the dubious privilege of working in the garden. If it is not entirely warm, as it is today (in the midfifties), at least the wind can't be blowing. I can handle midfifties to high nineties, but I don't like to work in the wind. Sorry, but that's the way I am.

Today is the first warm, windless day in months. And about time, I might add. The front garden is just starting to take off, but it looks a little tattered after the winter. I always strive to have an area of potential interest spruced up in readiness for its performance. That is one of the self-imposed rules that I try to follow. Often it doesn't much matter if parts of the garden look a bit dowdy as long as there is nothing to contrast with the dowdiness. But quite the opposite is true if something even slightly interesting is going on. Then the dowdiness is intensified at the expense of the show.

I have worked half a day to ready the front garden for its opening spring show of bulbs. Not that the show is spectacular, mind you, but it will be, some year in the near future, and it doesn't hurt to keep up appearances in anticipation. Up to this point the front (and the back, too) has been covered by the vagaries of winter, including broken twigs and branches from nearby trees, some leaves left over from last fall's raking, shattered ornamental grass sheaths, and dead herbaceous vegetation.

Now that the front is cleaned and the miraculously few weeds pulled, it doesn't look half bad—even with scarcely anything blooming. There are a few species crocus still hanging on from years gone by, but they are declining a bit every year. Some giant Dutch crocuses are putting on an overly extravagant show, except that they have been totally overgrown by *Rhododendron* 'English Roseum' in the course of five years. In the beginning, these crocuses perched at the drip-line of the rhododendrons, but now the drip-line has expanded enough to cover them. I should move the crocuses, I suppose, but it is just as easy to buy a new batch this fall (actually this spring for next fall would be more technically correct). The next actors awaiting in the wings are the large-flowered daffodils that are just now showing a little color at the tips of the buds. 'February Gold' has been blooming for a few days, but it and its cousins were set back a little by some sleet and snow that fell last week.

I cleaned down the side of the drive, too, and found some major damage done to *Rhus typhina* 'Laciniata', the staghorn sumac. A large branch (about four inches in diameter and twelve feet long) broke off the tulip poplar overhead and smashed the sumac in half. This cleanup consisted of removing the branch and sawing off the tattered remnants of the sumac, which will resprout from almost any cut any place on the plant.

I am fond of *Rhus* for it is beautiful year-round. In spring the branches are covered with fine red fur; in later spring and summer with gorgeous fernlike leaves and eventually red berries; in fall with brilliant orange, fiery leaves; and in winter the branches are strikingly architectural. This sumac is not without its problems though. It is a "thicket plant," creating a forest around itself by way of wandering underground shoots that may come up at some distance from the parent.

I'd had my plant in a different place for several years when I noticed shoots erupting from the ground a yard or so distant from the parent. This did not disturb me until I read a short piece on the sumac in Allen Lacy's book *Farther Afield* (New York: Farrar, Straus, and Giroux, 1986). His fear of the invasive habit of this sumac infected me, and I dug up my plant with the intention of tossing it out. But I couldn't. It is such a complete plant in itself, and this is such a rare commodity in plants, that I decided I would give it another chance. I put it on top of a hill in a tough spot in some rough ground where it has really had to struggle to survive. It has been there for five years and although it puts out a few weak runners from time to time, I simply pull them up and that seems to do the job. The site on which I had first planted the sumac had light, sandy soil, improved with yearly doses of horse manure. The new site was three feet of excavated clay subsoil mounded on top of three more miles of clay. The difference in sites now makes the sumac an acceptable plant in my garden. It is, however, a plant to be wary of. I still keep one eye cocked on that old, beat up beast, just in case it suddenly springs to life like the hydra it is supposed to be.

Another even more splendid day has gone by and I've gotten 'round to the back side of the garden. Here the major task has been to clean up the grass hedge that I put in several years ago. At the time it seemed like a novel idea. Now it just seems like a pain in the hands, mostly.

There was a long, narrow expanse of ground that I wanted to use as a screen to separate the soon-to-be-built large rock garden from the lawn and perennial borders. I had started a mixed shrub hedge that included, by the way, the above-mentioned sumac. When I decided to move it, I began to rethink the concept of hedges and opted for an experimental ornamental grass hedge. I can't say I'd seen it done before (or even since), but some grasses can grow quite tall. Too tall, in fact, for the modest garden. I decided to stick with grasses in the five-to-six-foot height range, and I was particularly anxious to include a grass I'd seen in England several years before called *Miscanthus sinensis* 'Variegatus'. The leaf margin of this variety is edged in white for its entire three- or four-foot length.

After consulting with Kurt Bluemel, one of the leading growers and proponents of ornamental grasses in the United States and who, co-incidentally, lives about sixty miles from here, I created a sixty-five-foot-long, four-foot-wide sinuous hedge from *Miscanthus sinensis* 'Variegatus' (variegated Japanese silver grass), *Panicum virgatum* 'Rehbraun' (red switch grass), *Panicum virgatum* 'Strictum' (tall switch grass), *Pennisetum caudata* (white-flowering fountain grass), and *Calamagrostis* × *acutiflora* 'Stricta' (feather reed grass). I used a total of three dozen plants, which in five years have more than filled in the original swath of ground.

Grasses, along with perennials, are often touted as maintenance-free plants. Well, anyone who thinks that perennials are maintenance-free has a large, gaping hole where his or her brain should be. Grasses are no different from perennials! Every year they must be cut back to the ground in the spring. For most grasses this is no problem. Making them stand up the rest of the year *is* a problem. *Miscanthus* and *Panicum* must be trussed up, in my garden at least, or else they splay apart when it rains. This is true of plants that are two or more years old (mine are five), but I've read recently that if you replant some species of *Miscanthus* every two or three years, they are not so prone to falling over. I am going to reset my plants this year, but it is, of course, labor intensive (and a far cry from maintenance-free).

An additional point of contention concerning *Miscanthus sinensis* 'Variegatus' (and some of the other varieties) is rather contradictory. On the one hand, the plants are darn hard to cut down in the spring. I've used a pruning saw, hedge clippers, grass knife, loppers, and hand-pruners in various attempts to make the job easier. No such luck. They are just plain hard going. But on the other hand, they shatter terribly in the late winter. Great hunks and pieces of the leaves blow all across the garden, making it a total mess. If you take the plant down in fall, you lose one of its more attractive features, which is that its winter silhouette, which is quite architectural, makes for good snow mounding. There-fore, I leave the foliage all winter and I pay the price now.

And finally, a problem peculiar to *Miscanthus sinensis* 'Variegatus' or to me: the edges of its leaves are abrasive, and working with them without a long-sleeved shirt and long pants is tantamount to death by 10,000 paper cuts. This is especially bad in the late summer when the damn things fall over no matter how many times you stake them. It is hot, the humidity is well over the point of steam, and it is no fun to be dressed from head to toe under these conditions. Unfortunately, the only way to stake up the plant is to wrap your whole body around it and then tie for dear life. Even when I am well wrapped (and I usually am not), all the cuts in my face and hands swell up and itch—and stay that way for several days. I know at least one other person who has an aller-gic reaction to this plant.

I guess you have to like a plant a lot to put up with this sort of nonsense five years in a row. I'm to the point now where I believe I will remove some of the troublesome *Miscanthus* plants—I have twelve huge clumps of it—and replace them with a tamer, more refined species such as *Calamagrostis* × *acutiflora* 'Stricta'. This is a stately, dignified grass with a crop of flowers that grows upward in a straight, columnar form for four to five feet. It also has the good feature of producing much softer fo-liage that is easy to cut back and causes no paper cuts. And in another contradiction, this soft, ramrod straight grass is scarcely bothered at all by the rain. I never stake it. It does lean over when it rains but then straightens up again when the sun comes out. It doesn't increase as rapidly as *Miscanthus* either, thus requiring fewer replantings.

Although I crab about the grass hedge (and almost everything else whenever I can), I enjoy its presence very much. Each spring it grows rapidly to its prescribed height and needs shearing (to the ground) only once a year. It gives a lush, savannahlike look to the garden from one side yet acts as a good foil for the rock garden on the other. It is as dependable as a rock, too. No plant has had a single trace of dieback; there are no bugs, no fungi. No cat or dog or rabbit has hurt it. Nothing will hurt it, I am convinced, except rain, and that doesn't hurt it very much—just musses its hair a bit. And finally, it is easily animated by the slightest breath of wind, and in summer and fall gentle, warm breezes make a comforting rustling noise as they travel through its tangled vegetation.

I would recommend a grass hedge to anyone who doesn't mind a little work, a little aggravation, and not a little pleasure.

Week Three _____

The first day of spring. Is it possible? Months have gone by—dark, cold, stuporous months—when spring seemed impossibly far away. Yet here we are at the brink of another gardening year, and today had better not portend the days to come for it is overwhelmingly dark and gloomy!

What do you suppose this gardening year will be like? Will everything go according to plan? Don't be ridiculous. A better question is "Will *anything* go according to plan?" Here, the answer is "certainly"—if you don't make too many plans. Let's be realistic, shall we, and say that some things will go as planned, some things won't—and that's no different from anything else in life. The garden is only a small slice of semi-reality, after all.

To be honest, I have not thought too far ahead for this year. Some seeds and plants have been ordered, to be certain—a garden can always use plants. But I haven't yet made any plans for major structural change because most of the garden is laid out about as good as it's going to get, for now, anyway. If anything, this is going to be the year of planting and replanting. In previous years I have turned the soil, moved the soil, removed the soil, put it back, laid the rocks, laid the flagstones, taken out the trees, put in the trees, and planted rather sparsely with small subjects that would eventually fill in. Well, some things have grown and some haven't, and a lot of space has not filled in as well as expected. This year is to be a year of stuffing things into every spare space I can find. If I have to take them out next year, so be it, but I am tired of so much bare ground. It's about time the garden's bones were fleshed out.

There are a few small moves that are necessary to bring the structure back into focus, and I plan to make these as soon as possible. This weekend should be the start. Two buddleias need to be moved, and I will use them to replace *Chamaecyparis lawsoniana* 'Oregon Blue', a tree that died this winter. I wasn't aware that these trees could be killed, but it may have dehydrated once too often in last August's dry period. I failed to water such things as trees on the presumption that they could take care of themselves. Apparently I was wrong. (It is not always possible to blame a winter's loss on winter. This tree looked pretty stressed out last fall, and I think it was a goner long before winter arrived.) I am also going to replant parts of the grass hedge, as I mentioned last week. And a waist-high pussy willow with black catkins, now in full, furry bud, needs to be moved from its present cramped quarters to a position where it can mature to its full height. Based on this list of plans, then, I ought to be finished with the year's projects by tomorrow afternoon.

As I said, my plans are not yet firmed up.

ARGHHH!! The first weekend of spring and all it's done is rain since day one of the season—one and a half inches in dribbles and dabs. If it's not raining, then, just as bad, overcast. I'd hoped to finish cleaning the garden today, but it is raining now and does not look to get better. The weather-guessers said it would be beautiful today, but their crystal balls must need recharging. (It certainly would be nice to have a job where you are paid for being wrong half the time.)

I'm a bit snippy today. I get that way when I plan (no, *dream* would be a better word) all week long to do something in the garden and then can't because of the weather. I've never come to grips with myself on this one. It's wrong of me, I know, but still I chafe at the unfairness of the foul-weather weekend. (I remember the second or third spring after I arrived here it rained every other weekend for months. My plans were continually being rained out. Even now I recall the agony and frustration of so many plans and so little progress—it's a wonder I didn't have a coronary.)

The secret to survival, I suppose, is to realize how insignificant these problems are in terms of the real world and then to be happy that everyone else is suffering, too! In the West, for example, they don't have enough water and they get cranky because the sky is so clear and beautiful. What they wouldn't give for an inch of rain every week. I would be just as happy to send California our excess rain and thus solve both our problems at once, but life doesn't work that way. If it works at all (a hypothesis I seriously doubt), life is designed merely to place as much stress on an innocent victim as is absolutely necessary to produce nearly total collapse—but no more. It is simply a test of our ability to survive. Anyone who understands the purpose of life can outwit it at almost any time by realizing that it is a test, merely a test, and can largely be ignored. We will survive almost automatically, in spite of nearly any stress. We are programmed for survival, and a nice solid D is enough to pass the test of life, so why take it too seriously if you can avoid it?

Unfortunately, each of us has one window of vulnerability that can override the code of minimalization. George Orwell aptly demonstrated that window in *1984* when he had his protagonist, Winston Smith, face his own worst mortal fear—rats. (Why anyone fears rats is beyond me, but then I suppose there are those who wouldn't understand my fear of rainy days—especially rainy weekend days.) Big Brother knew that each of us has a secret fear that goes beyond all reason, and Big Brother knew how to manipulate this fear toward its own needs. Big Brother knows that I detest rainy weekends and so would use it to its advantage if it ever came to that. Fortunately for me, Big Brother can know, or do, no more about the weather than your average weatherman, so I am as good as free from any form of unnecessary persecution (except that which I impose upon myself).

It is the evening of the same day. I'd thought the day couldn't get any worse than a simply wasted, rainy Saturday. I was wrong and I admit it. Being wrong is one of the things I do best, and I'm getting better at it. Shortly after ten o'clock this morning it became black out and thunder and lightning began. Then it hailed. Not for long, but who's keeping records. It was good-sized hail, too, for those who collect such things. I reached out the back door, picked up a big piece, and measured it at three-quarters of an inch. This was the biggest hail I've seen here. But as I say, the hail didn't last long.

After the hail came the deluge. It didn't last long either. About ten minutes and an inch of rain. As I watched out the window, a river of water came down the driveway (washing over the cement berm I'd built to keep it from doing exactly what it was doing) and washed out the gravel pathway on the western flank of the garden. Meanwhile, on the east, a raging river washed across my neighbor's property (leaping the earth berm I'd built to keep it from doing exactly what it was doing) and washed out the mulch path on the eastern flank. Not to be outdone, the central garden area was being washed away by the combined discharge of the two house gutters.

As a final insult, all this water combined to form a single four-inch-deep creek down at the northwest end of the garden, which then charged off down the swale, eroding its way to my back neighbor's property.

"How," you might ask, "did you know the creek was four inches deep?"

"Well," I would answer calmly, "because my duck shoes are four inches tall, and the creek filled them up when I stepped in it."

"Hmmm!" you might say, "Why would anyone be out wading in a creek on a day like that?"

"Well!" I would say, "Because I really didn't have anything better to do, and hydrology is another of my many hobbies. I practice every chance I get."

This is true. I do study the movement of water on my garden in an attempt to control its flow. The only way to study water flow is when it is flowing, and that means: (1) it has to be raining hard, and (2) I have to be near (or in) the flow to study it properly. I've been doing these studies since I've lived here, and over the years I've built an intricate series of underground drains, gravel seeps, and concrete and earth berms. My study today was an attempt to understand their failures: Why didn't the berms do their jobs?

Now, after patient, wet, cold, detached examination, I know why the berms failed to hold the water back—they weren't high enough! Half an inch more and the driveway berm would have stemmed that tide. If it ever stops raining, I will slap another layer of concrete on that ridge. The eastern flank, it turns out, has a low spot—a breech in the dike, so to speak. There, too, I will haul in some soil (or dig a deeper trench) and bolster it up a bit.

This was an unusually heavy storm based upon previous observations. I haven't had any problems in several years (except for some minor basement flooding, quite a different story, indeed), so I figured I'd built my levees high enough to do the job. Apparently not so. This time, however, I hope I've hit the high-water mark; any more water and I'll be building an ark.

As it turned out there were 1.6 inches of rain today, mostly falling in the aforesaid ten-minute period. As days go, it was not a total loss. At least I was able to understand, through the destruction, how to better direct water around and off the garden. If I'd had my options, I'd have rather been gardening. But still, finding out how to save the garden through the proper application of hydrological principles (of which the Army Corps of Engineers and I know only one: "If in doubt, dam the thing") is not a totally wasted day. It just seems like it.

I would like to point out that the magnolias (*M.* × *soulangiana* and *M. stellata*) are putting on a magnificent display this year in the capital. Despite the frost damage that occurred on several trees out here in the suburbs, the downtown trees don't seem to have been clobbered as they usually are. They may have been spared the cold, though with a gale-force wind blowing this evening, there is no telling what the sight will be tomorrow when I go to work.

The Bradford pears are also making a big splash downtown, but out here where I live the buds are only just now showing a little white. It is routinely about five degrees cooler and about ten days earlier here. Thus plants bloom later out this way. Downtown the Dutch crocuses and later varieties of daffodils are making a great display.

The main attraction, however, for visitors and locals alike, is about five days away from bloom. These are, naturally, the infamous cherry blossoms, which are scheduled to be at their peak next Friday at 9:42 a.m. After thirty minutes or a gentle breeze, whichever comes first, the cherries will be finished and spring will be officially over in the nation's capital.

Week Four

I knew it was going to be another one of those Saturdays as soon as I awoke. The wind was howling mightily. As I stumbled about without my glasses in the early morning light, I could sense a brightness not of the normal kind. It didn't occur to me what the problem was until I put on my glasses and looked out the window.

"Good Lord!" I screamed inwardly. "Snow." (Actually, I said a bit more than that, but it doesn't bear repeating.) I rushed to the in-door-outdoor thermometer and looked at the temperature.

"Good Lord!" I fumed. "Freezing! Why don't you just take me now and get this misery over with?" (Mornings bring out the melodramatic in me, especially before coffee.)

I rushed downstairs, slipped on my work shoes, and went out back to save the plants I'd put out just last week to begin the hardening-off process (sometimes referred to as the killing-off process by gardeners of experience).

"The damn weatherman didn't say anything about snow or freezing weather," I explained to the plants as I brought them in. "It's his fault, not mine. It was supposed to rain, not snow."

Three flats of overforced rock garden plants, lately from the flower show, listened with no sympathy whatsoever as I tried to explain my way out of this one. They were covered with a half inch of wet snow, and while they didn't look damaged, it's difficult to tell just when the moment of death arrives for a plant. It might be tomorrow before I knew.

What I should have known was that all was not well last Wednesday when the temperature hit almost 80 degrees. These days are made just to throw the innocent gardener, and long-suffering winterite, off balance. A cruel hoax it is, and it should have been obvious that someone was out to get me. Now that I know it for certain, I will be prepared the next time (which is not far off, I'm sure). I don't know which is the worse offense, being tricked into a false sense of spring by the gods of frost or having long-pampered plants die just weeks before the day of last frost. Either way, it is not what this poor soul, who has waited through six months of winter, wants to see.

I'm all right now. I've had my coffee and I'm used to the idea that this Saturday is a nongardening one—so I have nothing to do but indoor work or writing. After protracted thought, I've decided to work first, then write.

A number of seeds have sprouted (planted five weeks ago), and they demand transplanting. Already some are markedly overgrown for their containers. The most overplanted seed is *Myosotis sylvestris* (the 'Tetra Azur' forget-me-not). There are not a lot of solidly blue flowers for the garden, but this is supposed to be one of them. The seed came from Thompson & Morgan with the hype that it was the "world's finest" forget-me-not and theirs exclusively. There was also the admonition that they were genuinely "unable to say if [they] will be able to offer it again."

A statement like that is designed to appeal to weak-willed, susceptible gardeners like me. As soon as I read the script, I knew I had to have the damn thing. Why? I don't exactly know. Don't get me wrong, I like forget-me-nots. As I say, they are a color of blue rarely duplicated by any other flower—especially an easy-to-grow one. We can't all have massive beds of gentians can we? Forget-me-nots make a more than acceptable substitute, and we *can* have massive beds of them.

As a kid, I always thought forget-me-nots were weeds. They seeded around like weeds, anyway, and the job was not to plant them into the garden but to take them out of places they weren't wanted. Thus, they were a "work-plant" to me, meaning I had to work to get rid of them. As a novice gardener (and weeder), I never much liked this in a plant. Now, however, I find that plants that reseed themselves (but not too thickly) have a virtue all their own. They save a lot of time (and money) in the spring when time is at a premium. There is no involved process of sowing and no transplanting. They save space in the greenhouse and basement for so-called choicer plants (though what this really means is that self-sowers are simply scorned for their commonness). And in many cases, the self-sowers are as beautiful as any pampered plant. I try to appreciate this virtue whenever I can, and it is not too difficult with forget-me-nots.

I decided late last year to incorporate some taller forget-me-nots into the shadier parts of the garden. I already grow some of the more compact forms of *M. alpestris* in the rock garden where they reseed with great reluctance. Like many old-time gardeners (that doesn't seem like the right choice of words, but I don't think "gardening snobs" is quite right either), I was a little hesitant to introduce the common weedy form I knew as a kid. Also, since I didn't know what name to call the weedy form, I wasn't sure what to order from the catalogs. So I studied the problem a bit, and the more I studied the more confused I got.

By the time I'd read through the catalogs and books I was awfully confused as to what sort of forget-me-not I'd grown up with. I thought there was only one common sort, and I think I am basically correct in this. However, there are some problems with names and evidently a lot of problems with behavior. There seems to be basically the common variety, *M. sylvatica*, which occasionally gets confused with *M. alpestris*, but is so mixed up biologically as to be nearly a basket case. Several books state that *M. sylvatica* is a biennial in cultivation but a perennial in the wild. Well, OK, I guess things like this happen. Burpee sells *M. oblongata* as an annual, but according to the *The Royal Horticultural Society Dictionary of Gardening*, Second Edition (Oxford: The Oxford University Press, 1956), this species is really *M. sylvatica*, which, as we already know, may act as a biennial or perennial. Oy! Park Seed states that *Myosotis* is a biennial but then says of *M.* 'Victoria Blue' (which so far as I can tell is a form of *M. alpestris*) that it blooms in six weeks from seed. Double oy! Sometimes it doesn't pay to know so much.

That is why, today, I transplanted seedlings of *Myosotis sylvestris*: because I couldn't figure out which variety to buy so I went straight for the catalog hype. Accordingly, this species is supposed to have flowers double the size of other forget-me-nots with strong stems and longer-lasting flowers. According to the RHS dictionary, the species is a perennial with the proviso, alas, that it may be short-lived. I will plant this, then, the world's finest forget-me-not, with the belief that it will bloom next year and may or may not live beyond that. As an added piece of insurance, I have also planted Burpee's annual forget-me-not with the hope that it will bloom this year but with the expectation that it will probably bloom next year and promptly die as a biennial.

I would never have imagined that this, the simplest, most common, and most beautiful of garden plants could have so much confusion built into its simple little weedy soul. Possibly the best thing that one can say of forget-me-nots is that they should be called forget-me-knots. It would seem more appropriate.

Well, I must admit that I had no little trouble transplanting the seedlings of the world's finest forget-me-not. The small pot that I'd planted them in was completely overgrown, yet scarcely any of the plants had developed their first set of true leaves. This is the standard by which transplanting is gauged. I decided I'd better transplant them, leaves or no leaves.

The bunch of seedlings came out of the pot easily enough and for good reason—they were as rootbound as a ten-foot tree in a ten-inch pot. It is not good to let this happen. I had obviously overplanted the seedpan. What to do? It is not terribly effective to try to pull the seedlings apart because you generally end up pulling the tops off the bottoms. Seedlings resent this as a rule. It is not even possible to try to reroot them in the cutting bed. Two easy measures struck me. The first was to toss out the seedlings and start over with new seed, only planting them a little more thinly this time. This would not work, I decided, because I had used up all the seed the first time. The second idea was to plant the entire plug in a six-inch pot and grow one big plant. I've never tried it, but my guess is that you'd get a hundred little tiny eenie weenie worthless plants, all of them half-dead.

Then I remembered a technique suggested by Don Humphries, the chairman of our rock garden chapter. This was a technique he used for alpine plant seedlings that were too thickly sown. You take the entire wad of seedlings, hold them underwater in a container, and gently pull and shake them apart in little bunches. Then you take the little bunches and repeat the process. The water acts as a lubricant, and if you are quite gentle about it, the roots just sort of float apart. I tried it and it works. There is nothing very pretty about the method, though. It is messy, with a capital MESS.

To begin with, the water in which you hold the plants turns into an instant mudpie (unless you use a great big bucket), and if there is any perlite in the planting soil, it floats to the surface along with any peaty bits. Therefore, the surface is entirely dirty, and when you bring the seedlings out they become caked with flotsam and jetsam. It would be well at this point to have a rinse stage, but I didn't.

Next, when you take the wet, dirty little seedling and stick it in the prepared six-pack, several things happen. The seedling picks up more dirt as you lower it into its little hole, and your fingers pick up more dirt as you try to keep the seedling from becoming a big dirt ball. Soon you can scarcely pick up anything because your fingers are so heavily coated with soil particles.

In hindsight, this could all have been taken care of with a little forethought. A large first rinse would have been useful—a bathtub would work fine. I used a cup of water, and it didn't have the dilution factor needed. Next, have another bucket (or bathtub) of water ready for a quick rinse. (It helps if you take your clothes off first.) Then lay the laundered seedlings out carefully, pat them dry and dry your hands. Now you are ready to transplant.

It's no wonder I never get anything done around here!

This week ended with distressing news. As you may recall, I wrote to Henry Evans, the noted printmaker, to see if he might be interested in illustrating this book and to obtain a listing of his available prints. It had been about six weeks, and I was of the opinion that my letter to him had gone astray. In fact, I had drafted a new letter and was awaiting the eight-week mark, when I received a small package by parcel service. Along with the information I had requested on the prints was a letter from his wife, Marsha, informing me that Mr. Evans had passed away about a year ago. The thought had never even entered my mind.

I would have liked to meet Mr. Evans, the more so because his wife graciously said that we "would have found pleasure in each other's company." Now, however, I will simply have to take pleasure in his art. I will purchase his print called *Sunflowers* because I collect, in a small way, things that depict these glorious paeans to summer.

It is still possible that his art will be used to illustrate this book, but it will not be quite the same working without its creator.

6

APRIL

——————————————————————————

This was a plant week, pure and simple. All energy went to the increase of plants, but it was still a bit too miffy outside to move much out (as I learned last week). Also, since there's little daylight available between the time I arrive home and the time the sun goes down, there hasn't been much opportunity to practice the art of physical labor in my attempt to catch up with last winter's cleanup. As I've already noted, weekends have not been much use for this so far.

Most work is confined to looking at the newly emerging plants, potting up a few odd seedlings in the potting room after dark, and rearranging this room to put some seedlings under lights. There is no space left in the greenhouse, and I am in need of places to put seedlings until it is warm enough to move them outside. Logically, it should be the potting room, since I did, after all, build racks and shelves for this very purpose. The only problem is that there has been no way to get at them up to this time.

All winter long I've stacked firewood in front of the shelves and have also piled up boxes, bags, bulbs, dirty pots, potting soil, and used soil (for the compost heap). Now I must remove all of this clutter so that I can use the shelves. Fortunately, I solved the firewood problem last weekend—I burned it all.

After some little effort I cleaned up the entire area, found four old shop lights that haven't been used in years, cleaned them off, bought eight new fluorescent bulbs, set up the timers, plugged the whole mess in, and amazingly, it worked. There was no excuse now not to pot up more seedlings. This week it was several forms of pinks (*Dianthus* spp.), *Verbascum* 'Arctic Summer', and more forget-me-nots (*Myosotis* whatever). Speaking of which, I'm reminded of some more forget-me-not-looking plants.

As beautifully blue as forget-me-nots may be, there are several other perennial plants that are remarkably like their namesake in flower. These are creeping forget-me-not and Siberian bugloss. Siberian bugloss (*Brunnera macrophylla*) is also called heartleaf brunnera and, to make matters more interesting, may be found under the scientific name *Anchusa myosotidiflora* (the species name means with flowers like myosotis). This is a large-leaved, clumping plant that blooms in early spring. My four-year-old specimen will probably start blooming in a week or two.

Creeping forget-me-not, *Omphalodes verna*, also sometimes called blue-eyed Mary, is a marvelous plant and one that I obtained entirely by accident. Such accidents rarely happen to me. I was visiting Andre Viette's fine nursery in Fishersville, Virginia, with my friend Dee. It is the sort of place you can spend an entire day. So we did. There are expansive display gardens featuring most of the huge selection of perennials that the Viette family sells.

In these gardens you can walk and talk about plants and take notes on named ones that you might like to buy if they have them in stock at the retail nursery. Generally, most retail business is done by mail order, so the nursery does not have all the plants on display (or listed in the catalog, for that matter). (For those who might like to see a catalog, the address is Andre Viette Farm and Nursery, Route 1, Box 16, Fishersville, VA 22939.) By the end of the day I have a fair list of plants that I want, but since they seldom have everything I write down, I generally get off for under a hundred dollars when I visit. (I try not to visit too often!)

One day several years ago after purchasing my two dozen odd plants, the cashier told me that I could take a free plant from among a large selection of labelless pots. One plant appealed to me in particular, but no one in the growing area knew what it was. It was about six inches in height with elongate yellowish green leaves with nearly entirely yellow veins. The effect was of variegated leaves, but there was also a slight sense of malnutrition in the air. That is, the variegation could have been a form of chlorosis. As there was no other plant I liked, and I liked this one, I decided to take it and see what happened.

The next year, in very early spring, the plant put out a flush of the most intensely blue flowers imaginable. The foliar yellowing, which had been nutritional after all, disappeared after planting in the ground. Not to worry, I still liked the plant in spite of its healthy appearance.

It was some time before I found an identified plant of this blue-eyed Mary, and I can't recall exactly where it was. Most likely it was Brookside Gardens, where I spend a lot of time reading plants (a botanic garden is, after all, a library, isn't it?). One of the distinguishing characteristics of this plant, as its other common name, creeping forget-me-not, implies, is that it looks like a creeping forget-me-not. Common names sometimes are just as useful as scientific ones. It has stoloniferous stems that run along (or under) the ground and root from time to time. It is relatively tentative about this rooting and is not the least bit invasive in my garden. At least yet (one must always reserve judgment on creepers— Grissell's rule number 437).

I mention the plant at some length because I have just seen it blooming here in the first week of April, and it is so sensuously blue that I want to run around shouting for everyone to come and see it. It may come to pass that I will do a lot of yelling on these pages now that spring is almost really here.

Well, I finally did something about the grass hedge. It was not particularly warm out today, so hacking and digging had to replace sun-induced warmth. I decided to finish cleaning up the hedge area begun several weeks ago. First, I cut down the old, weather-beaten foliage of two clumps of variegated Japanese silver grass. This, as I've said before, has to be done every year. As I cut and hacked, my mind wandered back to last year when I staked and restaked these plants every couple of hours or every raindrop—whichever came first. As each dozen stalks fell at the crunch of my pruners and as my hands became increasingly pierced and gouged by the pencillike, upright basal stalks, I stopped thinking altogether, walked to the tool room, picked up the spade, spading fork, and axe, and returned to the patch I was working over. Something came over me and I went for their throats (wherever those might be). Before even I realized what I'd done, those two clumps of variegated Japanese silver grass were out of the ground and in the compost heap.

Next I went to the spot where last year I'd planted two clumps of feather reed grass. I dug them and divided each into three smaller plants. Then I replaced the Japanese silver grass with them. That is one area I will not be staking again!

I must have been in a hatchety mood this day, because upon completion of the grass removal, I stalked right over to another area that had been giving me some planning problems and started tearing it apart willy-nilly. This time it was the old wisteria area.

When I moved here some thirteen years ago, one of the few plants on the property was an old wisteria that had been trained into a sprawling tree some eight feet tall and ten feet in spread. Creating and training such a tree is not an easy undertaking, nor a common one, and judging by the remainder of the yard, I have no idea what possessed the owners to engage in such a time-consuming endeavor. I am just glad they did, for the tree is spectacular when it blooms. (Which, by the way, is not a yearly occurrence. If it does really well one year, it often skips a year or so before repeating its performance.)

The tree was in some need of repair and rejuvenation and also was at the site I had pinpointed two weeks ago as the place where the majority of rain was running off my neighbor's property. I decided, in my hatcheting pique, to clear out the eastern front (as I call it because it is the eastern flank of my war zone—excuse me—I mean garden). The biggest obstacle to progress was a large branch at the back of the wisteria that was not in good condition to begin with. Uncharacteristically—that is, without a week's worth of agonized planning—I simply took out my pruning saw and cut it off. For years I have recognized that this branch was not as vigorous as it ought to be, but I had never been able to convince myself to remove it. At four inches in diameter and supporting roughly one-fourth the growth of the tree, the branch had always made me feel a reluctance to do what was necessary, and if I'd been thinking today, instead of reacting, I probably wouldn't have removed it. Subconsciously, I knew the branch needed to go, both for its own good and the good of the garden.

Some years ago I created a pathway called the Maginot Line on the west side of my garden. It is the first line of defense against all sorts of plants that spread out from the communal fencerow I share with my neighbor. Such plants as smilax, seedling wisterias, Virginia creeper, Japanese honeysuckle, ivy, poison ivy, and multiflora rose become too rambunctious for the good of any garden. But once something crosses into the Maginot Line, I am fully at liberty to attack it. I have been building up a similar defense in the old wisteria area because the same plants grow along my eastern flank. On this side, however, I have the added problem of the water runoff from my neighbor's property.

First, I pulled up all the creepers that annually sneak over and under the fencerow. Then I raked off all the debris that had accumulated, including the ivy and honeysuckle, and piled it up for its designated purpose (which I shall come to in a moment). Taking the shovel, I excavated the top two inches off the pathway and used it to fill in the low spot in the berm. I hope this will solve the drainage problem, but water has a mind of its own, and there's no telling where it will break through next. Some new low spot will undoubtedly pop up (in my basement, for example), but for now I am content that no water will spill across from the east.

Having satisfied my innate hydrological tendencies, I chopped up the pile of debris with spade and pruners and redistributed it back on the path. This is a method I use on the service paths at the back of some beds to recycle organic matter. It is a method of sheet composting that also keeps the paths from becoming muddy and disposes of great quantities of organic matter that otherwise would fill up my compost area—itself stuffed beyond capacity with excess garden material.

The wisteria reminds me of a pleasant memory I have of an unintentional combination of plants I once saw. It was a gardener's dream. At least this gardener's. It is a combination I would plant myself if I had the space. It would take a few years to duplicate, but I would spare the time, if only I had the space.

Not far north of where I live there used to be a small crossroads and a quiet rural town. This was less than a decade ago, but all is now irrevocably changed. For some years, during the changeover from rural sleepiness to suburban sprawl, there was an abandoned farmhouse just before the crossroads. Growing outside the old, dilapidated building was an even older, more dilapidated pink dogwood. The tree was nothing to look at, but it was big—I would guess twenty feet across and fifteen feet high—and since it was leaning every which way, it was hard to say just how big it really was. It was big enough to see from a long way off, though, I can tell you that.

I had never noticed the tree until one spring day when it was in full pink bloom and would, itself, have been a glorious sight. But it was not alone. Apparently some years before, a wisteria had wound itself up the trunk of the tree and invaded all its limbs. Now, hanging from the limbs were hundreds of bunches of lilac-colored flowers. So closely was the wisteria appressed to the dogwood that the flowers looked like the dogwood's own. The combination of colors was such a sight that gladly would I make it my last on earth.

After I saw the spectacle the first time, I swore I would go back every year thereafter to witness its beauty. Fool that I am, I imagined that such beauty could last. In less than a year's time the entire area was bulldozed and apartments built.

I would have made it a national monument.

Week Two

Two weeks into spring and summer has arrived. Forget all that whining about foul weekend weather. We've just had two glorious days in the upper eighties and lower nineties, and I'm already worked-out for the season—whichever season it might be. The body is not yet used to honest-to-goodness working weather. That's what spring is for, after all, a chance to slowly work the body back into condition after the sit-and-stuff-your-face fest of winter. It prepares the body for summer and fall and the chores those seasons engender.

To make matters even better (or worse, depending upon your work-ethic outlook), daylight saving time has arrived, and now we can damage our bodies late into the evening for the next six months. That's what winter is for, after all, a chance to repair the damage done to the body during the work-your-butt-off fest of summer and fall. The life of a gardener is not necessarily an easy one, but it is a predictable one, that's for certain. At any given season you can fairly accurately predict what your body will be doing—except for spring. At this time of year nearly anything can happen.

I rarely offer concrete advice to anyone on two general principles: (1) Who am I to give advice? and (2) No one listens anyway. But today I am going to give you some very stern advice, and that is, do not ever plant a walnut tree on your property or even move next door to a person who has a walnut tree on the property line—they are just damnable nuisances (the trees, not necessarily the neighbors).

I have had no little experience with walnut trees, both as an insect researcher and a gardener. While they are acceptable in a walnut grove, where they can't hurt anything, in a garden they are a living monument to distress. The house where I grew up in San Anselmo, California, had an English walnut tree that hung over the patio and the service area. Here it was only a relatively minor problem. The leaves that fell all during the long, hot summers were relatively innocuous. You just had to sweep them up every few minutes or so—no problem really. The nuts and their spongy green husks, which were always attacked by the walnut-husk fly, rarely did much more than fall on the ground, unless you happened to step on a nut and break your collar bone or track one of the husks into the house where it made an indelible black impression on the carpet.

My neighbor on the east has a volunteer black walnut about ten feet from my wisteria and about two feet from our common property line. Note especially the word *volunteer* as it plays no small part later in this narrative. The really messy time of year for this tree is fall when all the nuts and leaves fall down over as long a period as is inhumanly possible. This is the normal state of affairs because here the trees are not bothered by husk flies and the nuts reach a full and synchronous maturity. They just don't fall with any synchrony. I don't mind picking up fallen nuts for weeks on end or raking up the leaves—I rather enjoy the job. I like indelibly blackened hands because it reminds me of my childhood, something from which I am becoming increasingly detached.

The full impact of my neighbor's tree is not felt until sometime in the spring, summer, or fall when I find a walnut tree coming up, for example, in a flower pot containing, say, geraniums. Or in amongst the primroses. Or maybe in the Shasta daisies. Occasionally I find a three-foot walnut tree emerging from under the skirts of a cypress, where it has no doubt been growing for several years (wisteria seedlings also do this).

It is the squirrels whom I have to thank for this generous planting scheme. There are lots of squirrels in this area, and they apparently like walnuts. They like to hide them deeply, securely in the ground or in a flower pot and promptly forget them. Once entombed, the nut goes to work putting down a sixty-five-foot taproot before any surface foliage shows. Thus, when I grab the tree to yank it out, it might break off cleanly at ground level. Or it might rip my hand apart as it slips through because I haven't the strength or the grasp to overcome its root. Or, if embedded in a soft, humusy bed of primroses, it comes forth from the ground uprooting half a dozen primroses in the process. In a pot it may even become necessary to disembowel everything and separate its roots from those of the rightful owner of the pot.

Finally, if I haven't already said too much about walnuts in the garden, let me add that the tree's roots are now known to produce a secretion that inhibits or interferes with the growth of certain plant genera within the tree's root zone. Azaleas are susceptible to this phenomenon, and I can attest that none of the half dozen azaleas I've planted near the tree has survived. I've always blamed myself for this failure, but I've read several accounts in gardening magazines about the walnut connection and absolve myself of all responsibility. Occasionally it is heartening to know that I am not responsible for every disaster that occurs around here.

Next to the wisteria is a wonderful old Japanese red maple, planted well before I arrived. I suspect the tree is in the vicinity of twenty-five to thirty years old. It is about fifteen feet tall and the same in spread with an intricately branched inner structure that no gardener could train as gracefully. This is the tree's natural form and results from a dense outer canopy that shades the inner branches until they gradually die. From an annual self-pruning these small, dead branches fall away revealing the tree's inner self more beautifully than any hand of humankind could.

At the present moment, the entire tree is a garnet red mop of new leaves that would stop the heart of even the most callous observer. In a few weeks the leaves will turn green for the summer, but in the fall, the red will be back in even more glorious brilliance. There is a companion tree, even bigger, about thirty feet away that embraces the eastern corner of the house. Although my predecessors were not much as gardeners, I cannot praise them too highly for doing three things correctly: planting the two maples and training the wisteria.

Beneath the smaller of the two trees, which, by the way, grows without undue influence from the root zone of the walnut, I am experimenting with an all-foliage garden. These foliages, at present, are in shades of yellows, chartreuses, light greens, blues, and whites as well as variegated combinations of these colors. So far I have avoided planting "flowers" there entirely, and I don't think it is any the worse for the experience. (All flowering plants flower, of course, or nearly all, but many have flowers that are not really worth looking at.)

I am of the firm belief that a garden should be a garden in spite of flowers. Flowers, certainly, are a great part of the garden, but there is room for color from other sources, including foliage, bark, berries, and seedpods. Additionally, much of the garden should reside in the architectural structure of the plants and in their texture. There is no need for blind, unquestioning subservience to flower, when, in many cases, flower is an end point as well as a high point. With many pet exceptions (a garden without hollyhocks, after all, is simply a desert), I am striving toward a garden that is attractive in or out of flower.

To keep a garden in a constant state of flower everywhere is, to me, akin to working a Chinese puzzle with your hands over your eyes. I suppose it can be done, but who really wants to? This is what botanical gardens, private estates, parks, and shopping malls are for. It takes incredible planning, an enormous work force, and lots of money—all things the average gardener is lacking in abundance. We gardeners shouldn't be tricked into thinking we must provide a nonstop exhibition of flowers for the occasional visitor any time one drops by. Should we? Well, I used to think so, but I don't anymore.

My goal now is to make the garden respectable most of the time, with something blooming and everything else interesting to look at. (Everything should be neat, too, but I have yet to master that piece of magic. That is why I try to have at least the blooming areas neat.) And that brings me back to the foliage garden under the Japanese red maple.

The backbone of this garden is supposed to be hostas, but they are taking so darn long to grow that I am about to lose patience with them. Six big-leaved, powdery-blue-foliaged *Hosta sieboldiana* 'Elegans' are the anchor plants of the area, but so far they have yet to reach a foot in height. I know that these big sorts take time to mature, so I'm still counting on them, but for three years now they have not shown much inclination to grow. I am concerned that they may not compete well with the maple roots. To fill in during their reluctant period, I have interplanted the white-leaved *Caladium* 'White Christmas', which is not hardy here and has to be replanted like an annual. It makes a nice display in the shade of the maple. There is also *Hosta* 'August Moon' with yellow leaves, *H. undulata* 'Variegata' with white and yellow-green leaves, and *H. tokudama* with white and blue-green leaves. This last-named hosta is a large-leaved variety like 'Elegans' and also appears to have some trouble growing under the tree. The two smaller-leaved sorts fare much better.

Other yellow-leaved plants include the grass *Milium effusum* 'Aureum' with its upright, pointy foliage that grows best in shade; *Filipendula ulmaria* 'Aurea' with its ferny, dissected foliage and unnecessary flowers; *Spiraea* × *bumalda* 'Limemound' with its pink flowers that clash mortally with its foliage (and are thus removed as quickly as possible); *Melissa officinalis* 'Aurea' with leaves the fragrance of lemon when crushed; and last, *Lysimachia nummularia* 'Aurea' with yellow flowers that are invisible next to the foliage. This last-named plant is a rapidly spreading ground-cover, and I am now debating whether or not to take it out—provided it is not too late. Based upon its ground-clinging nature and thin, fragile stems, it appears to be less wantonly aggressive than its sister species *L. clethroides*, but one never knows quite what the garden is in for with these spreading sorts of plants.

Lime green or chartreuse colors are provided by the New York fern, *Thelypteris noveboracensis* (which I purchased many years ago as the lady-fern, *Athyrium filix-femina*, and which it so much resembles that it really doesn't matter which one I ended up with); *Tanacetum parthenium* 'Aureum', whose seedlings were discussed way back in November; and *Hakonechloa macra*, another shade-loving grass. This last-named plant is slow to spread but is worth the wait. The slightest breeze makes the one-foot-tall wiry leaves dance and cavort; they undulate and crest like waves in the ocean. The variegated forms are exquisitely beautiful and exquisitely priced, costing many arms and legs and other body parts dear to oneself. I have a plant of *Hakonechloa macra* 'Albo-variegata', which is composed of two leaves and cost about two dollars and fifty cents a leaf. When I die it will be worth a fortune.

A few other varieties of plants round out the area and are grown as foils, or contrasts, to the main planting. *Lamium maculatum* 'Beacon Silver' is a green-and-white ground cover that grows under the variegated hostas just to confuse the eye a bit. Where does one begin and the other stop? *Alchemilla mollis* is grown as a patch of light green color (heightened by grayish pubescence) simply to break up the other yellow-green foliage, but when it blooms it is right in the fracas with its own unique yellow-green flowers. *Polygonatum odoratum* 'Variegatum', the fragrant Solomon's seal, is grown for its uplifting, arching foliage and variegated leaves. In early spring, as the shoots emerge from the ground, there is a reddish stripe around each whitish bud, reminding me of candy canes stuck in the ground.

Overall, the effect of all this foliage is pleasing, and the planting is not even approaching maturity. Eventually, when the big powdery blue leaves of *Hosta sieboldiana* 'Elegans' come of age, I think the area will offer a good advertisement for the absence of flowers. It is not the least bit labor intensive, either. Just an annual cleanup that takes about an hour and it's off and running for three seasons at least. Come the winter and it disappears for a well-earned rest. Just like me.

The heat has taken its toll. Spring is over as far as the daffodils are concerned. The anemones, too. Even the tulips, which ordinarily would have a few weeks' worth of color left, look a little stewed. I knew the weather was too good to last, though. Now the weatherpersons are calling for a drop in temperature and a little rain toward the end of the week. I've had a number of perennial plants out hardening-off on the terrace, and they are now ready to go into the garden. A little frost or two won't bother them, and that's good because we've still got at least three weeks to worry about frost.

Now that daylight saving time is here, I have a few spare hours after work to devote to the garden before it gets dark, and planting things out is one of the more enjoyable aspects of this time of year. I sense that anything put in now will grow like gangbusters in the next few weeks and months. (Or, being a realist, I know it might just as easily die. Being an optimist helps a lot if you're a gardener, and that is why I sometimes have so much difficulty with the concept of gardening.)

I prefer to transplant just before a rainy period as it gives the plants an extra margin of care. I've been waiting for a projected period of rain to get the job done. The problem is, though, that depending upon the weather-guessers to make a correct foreguess is about like depending upon a lottery to pay your monthly bills. So I made my own guess this evening and decided to plant out as many things as I could—about two dozen in all. This is Wednesday, and they are predicting rain by Friday. It might happen.

(From the late news Thursday evening, after I've transplanted another two dozen plants, I learn that the rain will not come until Sunday. It is a good thing I watered the transplants in. We could be in for a drought.)

Week Three

As usual, I spoke too soon about summer. My penalty: a Saturday and Sunday of unremitting solid, overcasty drizzle. Everything has been constantly wet since predawn Saturday. At least I was justified in planting out as many plants as I did last week. Based upon the weather-guessers, I had anticipated the cooler, slightly damp conditions that are just right for newly transplanted subjects. I'm not so certain that swampy weather is equally as good.

When you can't work outside, you just have to make do. That usually means cleaning up, reorganizing, or performing some other more onerous task, so that's what I did today: both an onerous task and cleaning. The onerous task was my taxes, but I won't bore you with those details. This is not a horror novel, after all. The cleaning task was a general cleaning and puttering party in the potting room.

The potting room went largely unfinished for three years until last year when I almost finished it. At that time I spent an entire month of labor upgrading the room from a simple studded shell to a nearly completed masterpiece: double-stud walls, insulation, electrical outlets, new lighting fixtures, drop ceiling, sheet-metal heat ducting, new shelving, priming, and painting. But—and here is the important point—I did not finish painting four small switch plates at the time. They were primed and placed on a block of wood to await the last coat of paint. After a year, however, they have a very nice coat of dust. Sometimes I have enough steam to get a job almost finished, then something better comes up—such as anything else—or good gardening weather.

Today I finally painted the plates and screwed them to the walls where they belonged. Fifteen minutes and I essentially finished the necessary work on the basement. It is amazing even to me how a person can work up an entire job yet postpone the final fifteen minutes of work for a year. Sometimes I think there's a great deal of truth to the old saying that anticipating is better than finishing!

As part of my basement cleanup and reorganization, I'd bought a tool rack upon which to hang my tools. Perhaps reorganize is not a good choice of terms because for years my tools have lain higgledy-piggledy against the potting-room walls—or, to be technically more correct, the studs of the walls. I was not reorganizing them, then, so much as organizing them for the first time. I have never been one for overly strict organization. In my life there have never been Peg-Board walls with hooks and the painted outline of a spade to show me where to put the spade when I'm finished with it. This is entirely too much work simply to know where to hang your spade. My system is much simpler. I just plop the spade next to the door so that it's handy as I rush headlong into the garden. The fact that I also plop the shovel, spading fork, rake, bamboo rakes, lopper, hedge shears, axe, grass shears, swan-neck hoe, screwdriver, hammer, nails, level, and so on next to the door doesn't slow me down a bit: I know exactly where everything is even if it takes me ten minutes to find it.

And while I'm at it I might as well tell you one other thing about me. I don't clean my tools. I know this must make me some sort of degenerate. All the gardening books tell you to scrape your spade when you're finished or to keep a bucket of sand soaked with oil to stick your spade in or to wash off the spade and pat it dry and rub it down with baby oil and talcum powder. Phooey! Garden tools are meant to get dirty and be dirty and stay that way. As far as I'm concerned, the only clean tool is one that's still for sale.

I firmly do believe in buying the best tool that fits the job at hand, but this does not mean the most expensive tool. I have paid high prices for a high-quality spading fork, spade, and shovel because these are the three tools that see the most duty in my garden. I have heavy soil, lots of sod to remove, and lots of beds to dig (and redig). Well-built tools are not only a necessity, they make the work much easier—I don't have to worry a whit about breaking, bending, or banging them up. If I only had to use a spading fork ten minutes every sixth year, I would buy a cheap one, or even more wisely, borrow it from a gardening friend. (And, no, you may not borrow my tools—never. Ever. That is the best way to lose a gardening friend. Better I should have written "borrow it from a gardening enemy"-—who cares if you lose one of those?)

I don't have many power tools because I don't like them. When I garden I want to contemplate the outdoors, not smell exhaust fumes or have my ears ripped off by sonic waves. I have a power mower and I hate it. But since I hate mowing even more, I decided the best strategy was to get it over with as swiftly as possible. On the other hand, I've decreased the size of my lawn by two-thirds, so I have much less to mow than I used to. I have seen city dwellers using power mowers on lawns so tiny they could scarcely turn the mower around—three passes and they are finished. A power mower in that case is just plain silly. Then, too, I once saw a city lady sitting on her lawn (which was scarcely larger than she was) using a pair of household scissors to cut the grass. I greatly admire her attitude.

I do not have a huge expanse of open ground to prepare every season as do many food gardeners, so I do not begrudge them their gasoline rototiller. Turning the soil is a hard job. I would prefer to do it by spading fork, but I understand the need for a rototiller. If I were making a great, huge perennial bed (several acres) I'd probably use one myself. Still, I would resent the smell and the noise.

If you have endless hedges, topiary, or arthritis, I suppose you can have your electric hedge clipper if you must. Or your electric lawn edger. I've tried both and do not like either. It takes longer to get the eight hundred feet of electric cord unwound than it does to cut a small hedge by hand (and I would be cutting the cord or my hand more than likely anyway, so what's the use?). Electric lawn edgers of the hand-held variety can only cut one or two blades at a time without binding up, and I prefer to edge and weed simultaneously. This is more easily done by hand than by machine so far as I have found.

I would personally disavow any knowledge of (or relationship to) a person who used an electric sprayer for insecticides or herbicides. Using chemicals is an important and hazardous undertaking. Spraying should be made physically demanding and excruciatingly difficult. The easier it is to do, the more chemicals will be sprayed. There should be a vast amount of thought put into spraying beforehand, and the harder the equipment is to use and the more time it takes to set up, the better it is for the rest of humanity. Most people do not know anything about the chemicals they use; they shouldn't be using them in the first place—except on themselves. They should not be encouraged to spray faster.

Well, I do seem to be getting peevish. And off the main point, which had something to do with a tool rack. Which had, as I recall, something to do with the damn weather. (Ah, yes. Now I know why I'm peevish.)

The tool rack is a forty-eight-inch maple bar with holes and pegs in it that allows me to arrange the tools any way that I think is most expedient. I decided to put the bar to the left of the door, opposite the normal leaning place, so that the tools would then be totally out of the way. (I neglected to mention that leaning the tools to the right of the door partially obstructs the narrow passage leading to it.) Removing the tools opened the passageway but made an extra five- or six-foot trip necessary to get to the rack, pick up the tool, and return to the door. Sometimes efficiency is a trade-off between clutter and organization. A well-cluttered mess can be more efficient than well-ordered organization, if you have a good memory for detail.

Foul, cold, rainy spring weather is good for only three reasons: it does most plants a great service, the gardener doesn't have to spend valuable time watering, and weeds pull easily when the ground is wet. I prefer to pull weeds the day after a rainstorm when the sun is shining and it's too wet to do anything else. I was so anxious to do something outside this week, however, that I went to work weeding the gravel paths when it was still misty out Monday afternoon when I got home from work. If one has to work in the mist, weeding gravel is not a bad job. A gravel path is not muddy, and the seedling weeds pull easily from the chunky bits of stone.

Along with the paths I once built a large, flat expanse of graveled space (about ten by fifteen feet) that I christened the "container garden."

It stands between the holly hedge to its south and the rank border (which I will undoubtedly discuss at an appropriate time) to its north and was the solution to the root zone of the gigantic silver maple that once stood at its corner. Before I had the tree removed, I built a knot garden at the site, but it was a failure. Then I built the container garden with the rationalization that if I couldn't grow plants in the soil under the tree, at least I could grow plants in containers under the tree. I was going to place various pots and troughs as containers on the flat gravel area, and behind them, bordering the north side of the holly hedge, I built a heavy-duty, industrial-strength wooden container.

Then, as it turned out, I had the tree cut down. Now the container garden seems a waste of time and space because I can have a real garden there: one that grows in the ground. I am going to slim down the gravel part by half, leaving a narrow strip of gravel as a path. I will keep the wooden container, although I admit it probably should come out, and do my best to adapt it into the design. Then I'm going to capitalize on a phenomenon that has occurred naturally in the gravel bed and see where that takes me.

A garden can be a constant battle, especially with weeds. Occasionally, however, the gardener should evaluate the situation objectively and attempt to put some weedy plants to his/her own good use. That is, "If you can't pull them, enjoy them," which is what I am planning to do with certain weeds that have self-sown in the gravel bed.

Several years back I planted two rather nice but exuberantly self-seeding perennials that ought to be more widely grown than they are (as all garden writers must say). One is *Linaria purpurea*, the wonderfully named toadflax. The other is *Agastache foeniculum*, or anise hyssop. Toadflax is an upright, gray-leaved pillar of small lilac- or pink-colored flowers. The leaves are tiny but profuse, and the effect is of an airy column—two to four feet of almost constant summer bloom. Anise hyssop is a squat, widespread plant, two to four feet in every direction. It has large, poplarlike leaves that smell of anise when crushed and sends up one-to-two-foot flower stalks with small purplish or lavender flowers. It, too, blooms for an extended period of time.

Both plants are absolutely wonderful because they never, ever (and

I do mean *never, ever*) need staking, bloom for a long time, reseed generously, and are beautiful in their own right. But that is not all! The thing I particularly like about them is that they attract insects, especially bees and wasps. I suppose this will put off most people, but any preconceived notion about such matters is strictly poor press, I can assure you.

The flowers of each type of plant are small, so they attract the smaller sorts of bees and wasps, including mostly solitary or nonsocial species. Colonial honeybees, for example, or yellow jackets are not particularly attracted, but many sorts of tiny, lone-dwelling, essentially nonstinging bees and wasps will come calling. As will butterflies. The insects become so frantic in feeding and so engorged with food that the passing by of a mere mortal holds no interest for them whatsoever. They will not harm you in any way, even if you stick your face right up to them. I do not recommend this, necessarily, because there is always the chance you will breathe in. This could complicate matters a bit. I do not know what happens when you get a bee up your nose, but even I would hesitate to find out. The thing is to just accept the plants and their fauna and all will be well.

Many people are surprised to learn that there are nearly 17,000 described species of bees and wasps in the United States and Canada. This figure doesn't include ants (another member of the insect order Hymenoptera to which all belong), of which there are nearly 600 species. All told, the total figure for the entire group would probably double or triple if we knew all the species, which we don't. (A very small part of my job is to determine if species of parasitic wasps have been described or not and to describe them if necessary.) The most familiar bees and wasps are the big sorts that live in colonies: honey bees, hornets, yellow jackets, paper wasps, and bumble bees. The females (and only the females) of these wasps and bees sting, and all are aggressive to varying degrees. Bumble bees, for example, rarely ever sting. You darn near have to squeeze the life out of them to get stung. Paper wasps are not too bad either. But hornets and yellow jackets don't take kindly to being disturbed, especially at their nests. They will defend their colony to the death . . . either theirs or yours. In general, working bees or wasps do their best to ignore humans and take care of their business, which varies with the group.

Honey bees gather nectar and pollen to provision their nests and water to cool them. All social wasps gather other insects (or meat products, such as hamburger) to feed their young. The adults visit flowers to feed on nectar. For the most part, these larger bees and wasps are beneficial for the garden, but not all gardeners accept this as good news. If you are allergic to honey bees, for example, then one bee is too many.

Aside from the social sorts of bees and wasps, which are relatively few in species but well-known to humans, there are thousands of solitary bees and wasps, which are virtually unknown and often invisible. Some of us have seen the more common of these, for example, the mud-dauber and potter wasps that build mud nests. But few see the parasitic wasps that are both abundant and everywhere about us, sometimes even in the house. Of these wasps we should be both ecstatic and worshipful, for without them we would be knee-deep in aphids, scales, whiteflies, leaf-feeding beetles, and all other manner of plant-feeding beasties. Parasitic wasps account for unknown amounts of natural control (i.e., population suppression of naturally occurring insects), and when put to use by humankind, result in what is termed biological control (i.e., suppression of target species objectionable to humans).

Having devoted my life's work to wasps as I have for nearly thirty years, I would be the first to admit that these creatures are scary to most people. Sometimes even to me—I've been nailed by the best of them. But in the garden all bees and wasps provide two services that are free to the gardener: they pollinate (for seed and fruit set), and they control other insects either through predation or parasitism. They contribute to a natural balance that is otherwise missing in a garden. An unbalanced garden is one that must be sprayed to tip the balance in favor of the gardener. For my part, I'd rather have the hum and buzz of a myriad of wasps and bees than the silence of a sterile garden.

Week Four_____

And so we reach the half-way point in our journey through the gardening year. Is it possible that half a year has gone by so rapidly? If there is anything that gardening (and perhaps life) teaches us, it is that time passes much more quickly than we give it credit for. Why should we plant an expensive ten-foot nursery tree when a ten-inch sapling will do? What's the hurry? Should we hesitate to plant an acorn simply because it takes years to grow into a tree? I think not. The joy of gardening lies in the planning and growing, not exclusively in the maturing. The former represents creation, hope, dreams, aspirations, new life; the latter, simply old age.

I'll give you one guess as to what the weekend was like. Give up? Well, no surprise really: forty-eight hours of solid overcast and drizzle. A stunning repeat of last weekend. If I didn't know better, I'd swear I was living in Oregon or maybe at the bottom of a well.

My friend Dee came to visit today. After a cup of coffee or two and a brief summary of our respective gardening activities for the past few months, we headed off to the garden. In spite of my usual rain-reluctance, I was coerced into leading the tour. It's not all that often I have truly interested visitors, and so what if it was raining? That's what the umbrella was invented for, wasn't it? All one needs to think of is England, the mecca of all gardening, and one immediately recalls the two things it's most noted for: gardens and umbrellas. And tea. Better make that three things. After examining the garden in the rain under your umbrella, you must go in the house and have a cup of tea—it is the proper sort of gardening etiquette. It was easy to emulate today.

The garden was not looking too shabby, even in the rain. In the front the mass planting of *Iberis sempervirens* 'Snowflake' was in full bloom. I first grew a half dozen of these from seed over ten years ago, and then five years ago made almost a hundred cuttings. The new plants were set out in a five-by-fifteen-foot-long bed as underplantings for four 'English Roseum' rhododendrons. The white candytufts were supposed to bloom at the same time as the pink rhododendrons, but they didn't know this. Generally, the white always comes first, then, just as they are thinning out a bit, the pink blooms. *Iberis* is one of the few perennials here that remains evergreen all winter. They are well worth growing in their various-sized cultivars. The annual sorts are equally nice but tend to bloom in this area in one splendid, rushed burst that immediately dies out. It's a real pity, too, for they are immensely cheery in their assortment of bright pinks and pure white.

Also blooming in front was a mass planting set out last year of seed-grown *Aubrieta.* This is its first year of bloom and it is showy in its mounds of multihued rose and purply red flowers. Although I set out six dozen plants last year, only about half that number survived the winter. This year I will take cuttings to fill in a few of the blank spaces, and I'll also add several dozen plants of *Dianthus plumarius* 'Highland Hybrids' that I am currently growing from seed. This will add the contrast of gray foliage as well as extend the bloom period in the low border for another two to three weeks.

After touring the front garden, we went out back and spent some time looking at the new foliage unfurling into spring. The rear yard was not particularly noteworthy today in terms of flowers (there was more *Aubrieta* in bloom in the large rock garden, but this was only a repeat of the front). A few odd anemones were still in bloom, the polyanthus and vulgaris primroses were acceptable, and the wisteria was a killer cloud of purple, not to mention the hoards of fuzzy black carpenter bees buzzing excitedly about as they attacked the plant with vigor. In their frantic, nearly drunken endeavors to collect nectar, those huge bees would not sting, but I have no doubt they could knock you down if you got in the way. In spite of my own attack on this plant a few weeks back, it appears to be about as robust as a plant ought to be. This was a good year for wisteria throughout the region, and now we'll have to wait another two or three years to see its like again.

Other than the few flowers just mentioned, the only admirable quality of the back garden lay in the foliage color of its newly unfolding plants. Although these colors may be slightly lurid at times, leaf color does not seem to be as visually belligerent as flower color. My current favorite foliages are purple or red combined with either yellow and chartreuse or white and gray. I repeat these combinations wherever I can in the garden. Today, for example, there is an eight-foot purple wall of *Cotinus coggygria* 'Royal Purple' backing a six-foot ball of the lacy yellow *Sambucus racemosa* 'Plumosa Aurea'. In another spot, the four-foot intertwined combination of purple *Berberis thunbergii* 'Atropurpurea' and

'Aurea'. In yet another, a year-old planting of the yellow *Philadelphus* ×
virginalis 'Aurea' and the purple *Prunus* × *cistena*. Even though all of
these flower, it is only for the foliage that I grow them. And fine it is, too,
especially in the spring, when it is all new and softly unfolded. At this
time of year it has a quality unlike any flower—a saturation——at once
more luminous than mere color alone and more sensuous to the eye.
When back-lit by early morning sun the leaves radiate an incandescent
spark that sets the plant aglow. Alas, like many of gardening's miracles,
the foliage of these plants becomes worn out by midsummer. It hardens
both in texture and color, often tearing and browning. Although it becomes slightly less wondrous as summer sears its way through the garden,
even then the colors are not completely gone, and it has served its purpose far longer and better, I would say, than peonies or irises.

By the time we'd taken a quick tour around the front and back
gardens, it was well on in the morning, and as we had plans to visit a
nursery some distance from the house, we cut short the remainder of
the tour and took off for greater glories. Our destination was a nursery
near Annapolis I'd visited once before called Bittersweet Hill Nursery.

The overall setting of the nursery is more scenic than average because it sits on the edge of a woodland knoll overlooking a broad valley.
(It would be perfectly situated except that the valley view is tainted by
several acres of wholesale greenhouses belonging to another, larger nursery. These should, of course, be removed, but I doubt anyone will listen
to reason.)

After examining the sales benches up front, we walked down the
hill to investigate several plastic tunnel-houses in various states of disrepair. As anyone who visits nurseries knows, it is these out-of-the-way
places that harbor all the good gardening stuff—plants often without
labels or prices but tempting nonetheless. It was here that I stumbled
upon today's find (or possibly the weed of the year)—*Kalimeris yomena*
'Aurea'. Nestled in a distant back corner of one greenhouse in a half-
gallon black pot, this low-growing plant looked much like *Solidago* with
variegated foliage. Although small in stature, the plant stood out because
of the intensity of its yellowish white variegation.

I knew nothing of the plant this morning, and finding anything about it in my references this evening has proven difficult. From my large array of books and catalogs I can determine only that We-Du Nurseries (Marion, North Carolina) sells it and that it is a blue-flowered composite from Japan. From the plant itself I have deduced that it might be a terrible weed because there are stoloniferous roots curling all about the rim of the pot (an almost certain prelude to disaster). I shall give it a chance to overwinter in the garden, and even take a piece or two into the greenhouse next fall for insurance. It may not be hardy, or winter may knock it severely back each year. There is no telling until I try it. Then, hopefully, if it is noxious, I can still get rid of it in time. Usually removal after a growing season *and* eternal vigilance rids the garden of weedy plants. But it's the eternal vigilance that really pays off!

Another find today of unknown stature was a purple-leaved clover, *Trifolium repens* 'Purpurascens'. Normally, clover does not seem like a plant to invite into the garden, but this small-leaved variety has chocolate brown central regions trimmed with lime green. It is a pretty little thing of flowerless interest (and thus, again, of almost continual interest) that the guru of rock gardening, Reginald Farrer, described in his book *The English Rock-Garden* as a plant for "hot and valueless places." (He must have had my garden in mind.) I will plant my little plant in just such a place in the large rock garden.

After poking about in several more greenhouses, all about equally interesting, we went back to the three main sales greenhouses and joined a growing crowd of shoppers. One of the houses was full of seedling annuals and tender perennials grown like annuals (such as geraniums and Transvaal daisies). Another was full of houseplants, including orchids, various foliage plants, and ficus, and most notably, topiaries created from rosemary or small-leaved ivies trained on wire-work frames. This is one of the specialities of the nursery. Its other, herbs, occupied the third greenhouse. Here, I am certain, can be found many more herbs than anyone has the time to grow. Hanging over each grouping was an inverted wooden flat with neatly painted scrollwork of ivy and the name of the category of herb.

I bought several artemisias, or wormwoods, for which I have a great fondness dating back to my insect-collecting trips to the Great Basin region. These silver-leaved plants have aromatic foliage that one either understands or not. It is a fragrance of intense heat, of concentrated sunlight, of distilled dryness that has built up over the millennia. It bursts forth with blessed relief whenever crushed. It is the essence of desert, and for this I love it. My own selections today, 'Huntington' and 'Powis Castle', may not be reliably hardy here (being, I suppose, sissified selections), but they grow quickly and can be overwintered as cuttings. I've grown 'Powis Castle' before but did not know of its questionable winter hardiness until it died. Now a few fall cuttings solve this problem. Whether it overwinters outdoors or not I will still have it come next spring. One word of caution: some artemisias, the commonly grown 'Silver Queen' being an example, are underground spreaders and easily take over an area they like. I've spent more time taking out 'Silver Queen' than seems reasonable, but it does withstand my winter-soggy clay soil better than other varieties have, and for that reason, it remains in the garden.

Now, to round out the day's collection of valuable-leaved plants, I found another curious little thing called *Hieracium marmorum*, or hawkweed. There are many native species of this genus, all of which have flowers (and apparently progeny) exactly like dandelions (which are pretty flowers, all other prejudices aside). Farrer has little nice to say about hawkweeds, and in fact, he states that its name alone "upon the gardener's heart . . . blows a chill." We shall see. The plant I purchased has small oval leaves, somewhat hairy, with an olive green background and miscellaneous purple swirls overall. It almost looks like army camouflage. I am going to plant it next to a specimen of *Hieracium lanatum* I received last year at the rock garden exchange. This is grown for its woolly, felted leaves which out-lamb lamb's ears for softness. Although the flowers of both plants are acceptable (*H. marmorum* was blooming when I bought it), their foot-tall stems are totally out of proportion for the small size of the foliage and probably should be cut off. I doubt I will have the heart to do this.

The day was one of those learning experiences that can happen when one goes to a nursery of character. Often the gardener can learn a lot from the proprietor of a nursery, or as was the case today, when all hands were at full customer service, the gardener, once home, can rely on books to help round out his or her knowledge. A little reading never hurt anyone. Nor, apparently, a little rain. And certainly not a nursery visit.

7

MAY

_____

Sometimes a person has to be sociable, like it or not. This was my week for sociability, and thus I was left with sparse opportunities for gardening. In normal times I don't begrudge the loss now and again: any excuse to ignore work is not without some merit. After a few rainy weekends, however, I become fidgety if I have to spend a perfectly good one being sociable. Sometimes the work of being pleasant is more effort than any physical work might be, and to put it bluntly, I'd much rather garden than cook and clean house. But then, what right-thinking person wouldn't?

Most of the week was taken up entertaining visiting colleagues who independently descended upon the area for professional meetings. Washington, D.C., is a good place for that sort of thing. Generally, when you haven't seen close colleagues and friends for some time, you are expected to act in certain ways. You know, be glad to see them, entertain them, actually listen to what they have to say. This is not always easy when the garden calls. I'm afraid I spent much of the week in a state of transfixion, mentally tuning in and out the various topics being discussed as I pondered some area of the garden that needed my attention more than did the conversation. It made for an interesting week.

In a way the distractions were not entirely negative. In the odd moments allotted to me—between dishes, cooking, taxiing, introducing, discussing—I sorted through some of the literature that has been piling up on the living-room floor. I have a convenient filing system wherein all the new gardening magazines, catalogs, and nonessential sorts of mail (like bills) are stacked chronologically on the floor until I can get to them. It's a simple system, really, and one that more people should make use of.

With my houseguests here this week I've used the television as a postdinner opiate on at least one occasion. This is not proper etiquette, I assure you, but sometimes a cook's got to do what a cook's got to do— namely the dishes. To have absolute privacy, I find doing the dishes provides about as good an opportunity as any. And I can even think while doing them.

I am not what you would call a television snob: I watch as much as the next guy, maybe even more. I try to limit myself to either educational TV (for example, PBS) or escapist TV (for example, sitcoms). Put simply, I use the television either to learn things or as a narcotic, whichever is necessary at the moment.

I wish television, in its endless search for mind-drivel, would make room for more gardening shows. They wouldn't have to be terribly sophisticated. Perhaps something along the lines of "Murder, She Weeded," starring a gardening detective who solves all her crimes while weeding. Or maybe "Hilarious Gardening Videos"—people stepping on rakes or falling in roses or anything even remotely funny about gardening. Would this be so difficult?

In my region there is only one show about gardening, namely, "The Victory Garden." Is the rest of the country as deprived as I am? It is hard to believe that this single program might service nearly the entire known world. And even it, of late, has turned into something of a cross between a travelogue, an endorsement for hotels, and a cooking show. In truth, we are left with two-thirds of a gardening show to elucidate the world of gardening. This is certainly not enough. Especially when we were recently told by a Gallup Poll that gardening is the nation's number one "outdoor leisure activity."

This revelation came as an utter and complete shock to me. Number one, indeed! How can the nation's number one outdoor leisure activity have two-thirds of a television show dedicated to it when the nation's number one indoor leisure activity, football-watching (I think it's still first, isn't it?), has roughly 4.3 billion hours of coverage per season? Can anyone answer that? Then, too, how can anyone label the practice of gardening as "leisure"? *Leisure* is defined by Webster as an adjective meaning "free and unoccupied." Anyone who gardens knows that the concept of free or unoccupied time is incompatible with the tenets of gardening.

Considering that free time is the occupational hazard upon which television is built, how do you explain its total indifference to teaching our number one outdoor activity—gardening? Of all networks only one—PBS—offers the remote possibility of such shows, and even it falls far short of its potential. It presents endless educational tracts on the joys of painting and the magic of watercolors; it admonishes us to cook cajun or cheap; and it advises us to tear down our old house and build a new one. Why, then, are there so darn few shows that teach us how, or more importantly, why to garden?

This lack of instruction may arise simply because the leisurely indoor arts are teachable and gardening isn't. After all, anyone can learn the art of cooking. You buy the specified ingredients, put them together in a cookbook sort of way, and out comes a culinary masterpiece. Nothing tough there. And what's so difficult about fixing up a house? Anyone can tear one down and rebuild it—all it takes is money. And it's exactly the same, except cheaper, with painting. Children do it with no effort at all. Even slugs can be taught to paint. Just dip one in blue, say, and let it slime away on canvas. One sees this sort of thing in all the best galleries.

I guess it's not so simple with gardening. You don't just plant a package of seeds and life springs forth. Oh, it might. Just as likely it won't. Seeds are like that. Independent. If they sprout they might grow, or they might not. Slugs might graze them to the ground. (Artists have it so much easier. Have you ever seen a slug eat a van Gogh?) What's more, if the seeds do grow into big, husky, slugless plants, the neighborhood dogs might come by and take umbrage. (Have you ever seen a dog take umbrage at a Picasso? I imagine it's not a pretty sight.) And even if the seeds sprout and grow and eventually flower, someone with scissors could come along and cut them all for some decorative purpose or other. (Have you ever seen a person take scissors to a Pollock? Well, then, you're a damn sight luckier than I am.)

Perhaps the reason there aren't more television shows about gardening is that it is not really a manipulative art as is painting or cooking or even house demolition. Gardening is a state of mind, and more than any other art form it requires patience. But patience, after all, is not yet one of America's defining characteristics, and television is well attuned to this fact. As anyone who watches television knows, major problems are solved in one hour, minor ones in half that time.

The American public would never watch a miniseries, for example, in which a seedbed is viewed for ten days while the seeds slowly break dormancy and germinate. This is asking too much. But by viewing cricket matches for days on end, which is not much different, really, from watching grass grow, the British have developed a sense of patience monumentally adapted to gardening. And this is exactly what has made Britain the greatest gardening nation on earth. It is, in fact, what separates the gardeners from the colonists.

As a result of the week's commitments, any hint of organization became totally submerged by reality. Usually I try to set out at least one or two goals to strive toward. When I wake up on Saturday or Sunday morning, I know pretty much what needs doing and I do it. But sometimes when I wake up on a weekend morning, I say to myself: "Self, of all the endless tasks that await you, which one will you do today?" And then I wait for an answer. Occasionally it isn't until Monday morning and I'm at work that I receive one. Other times I get up, have several cups of coffee, and survey the garden for tasks that need immediate attention. This is dangerous because every task needs to be done and re-done constantly and immediately in the garden.

The most obvious solution to any garden-based dilemma is the old maxim: "When in doubt, weed." So that is what I did for the largest part of this Saturday. Weeded the gravel paths, weeded the terrace, weeded the woodland garden, weeded the rock garden, weeded the front garden, weeded the lawn (with the lawn mower), and weeded the bamboo garden. Which is interesting, when you think about it, because I don't have a bamboo garden. I should have said that I weeded my neighbor's bamboo garden.

The northern border of my garden is demarcated by a hundred-foot row of bamboo planted by my neighbor at the fence line. There is much that could be said about such neighbors, but very little is suitable for print. I will write, instead, of practical ways to eliminate such problems—the bamboo, that is—but we both know where my true thoughts lie.

In anticipation of battles to come, I dug a trench along the fence line, then cleared a two-foot-wide Zone of Death, or ZOD, as I affectionately call it. (Bamboo is a much more serious enemy than the vines that cross the western front along my Maginot Line, and its defense calls for a much more serious title, too.) I do my best to keep the ZOD as clear of plant life as I can. This is the debamboozlized area. No bamboo is allowed to cross (at least above ground). I find it helps to have a clear view of the enemy lines so that I can spot potential invaders. This doesn't always work, though, because the stolons mostly sneak underground. The ZOD does, however, allow me room to work to make surgically clean strikes with axe, spade, and backhoe.

This week I spotted several bamboo shoots coming up on my side of the fence—some in the ZOD and one already five feet into my garden. Generally, the stolons run underground, throwing up a vertical shoot every foot or so, as straight as the obstacles in the ground will allow. Only the one stolon had made a headlong dash for my inner sanctum, hoping that I would overlook it. But I didn't. It is tough to miss a one-inch-diameter spear sticking four feet straight up out of the ground.

Once a shoot erupts on my side, I let it get about a foot high (except in the case of those sneaky ones that surprise me). Then I cut off the top couple of inches below a joint, leaving a perfect hollow stem sticking out of the ground. This I fill to the brim with undiluted weed-killer. The bamboo gets a nice drink through its own built-in straw, and a few days later the runner dies. Amazingly, only the poisoned stolon dies; the remainder of the plant doesn't feel a thing.

I've been treating the bamboo in this manner for about five years, and the plants are ten to fifteen feet high on my neighbor's side of the fence and relatively nonexistent on my side. This treatment is rendered as often as necessary, but generally twice a year is enough. Only a dozen or so stolons cross the line, and, so far, if they are dealt with promptly, they create no real problems.

In the fall I dig up all the thoroughly dead but still immensely wooden stolons that have succumbed during the summer. It is as if the things were cast in concrete. They last for years in the compost pile, so I've stopped putting them there and instead cut them up and throw them on the service pathways.

One man's garden is often another man's compost, but in this case, my neighbor's garden becomes my pathways.

Week Two _____

Last week's weeding continued into this week's work as I moved from my neighbor's bamboo garden back to my own rank border. By rank I do not mean malodorous, putrid, tainted, fetid, or even slightly musty. I mean coarse—as in rough. A garden composed of big and small, rough and tough plants that can take care of themselves. You wouldn't think that a rank garden would need much weeding; generally speaking, the plants themselves are weedy enough to discourage any transgressors. And a good job they do, too. It's not so much that there are weeds to pull from among them but rather that their various proportions need to be adjusted so that one of them does not take over the entire garden.

The rank garden is backed by the Zone of Death. It would do little good (as I have found) to plant subjects of an endearingly petite nature in proximity to the ZOD. Whatever grows near there must endure the wrath of the bamboo removal squad (i.e., me). The plants must put up with root disturbances, spades, shovels, axes, weed-killer, flamethrowers, mortar rounds, and the odd stick of dynamite now and again.

When I first planned the garden (before bamboo), an immense silver maple strictly limited the use of the area. After some gardening failures and soul-searching on the subject of trees in the garden, I had the maple removed in the belief that I could make a much more complex and interesting life zone of mixed plantings. Anything would be better than the single-species, all-wrecking silver maple that took up a fifth of the sunlight that fell in the back garden. I did not count on a solid fence-row of bamboo taking its place.

Long before thoughts of removing the maple arose, I had designed and planted a narrow area of shade-adapted shrubs to act as a screen between my neighbor's yard and my garden. The only obstacle between us was a four-foot-tall wire fence that functioned only as a boundary marker. Little did I know that my neighbor had planted his side of the fence with small, evenly spaced bamboos. It takes these plants a fairly long while to become established, so at first I did not think much about them (except to put a simple, eternal curse on my neighbor—that the bamboo should grow only in his direction).

When the tree was finally removed, I knew the screen I'd planted was a total waste of effort. There were several forms of holly and a few rhododendrons and azaleas that would not grow in the blast furnace the space quickly became. So out they came, even though some had been in only a few years. I did some recalculating and decided that there were a number of gross types of herbaceous plants that I liked and that I'd never had a place to grow. Also, as you know by now, I am partial to bee- and wasp- and butterfly-attracting plants, and a number of these tend to be rank in nature. The new area would be the perfect spot to build such a garden: open (ignoring the bamboo for a moment), sunny, and a place where coarse, unrefined, tall, broad, and floppy plants would fit well together to make a living screen.

The rank area is now several years old, and at least one plant has proven far too rank even for its own environs. This is *Lysimachia cleth-*

roides, about which I wrote last fall. This plant is invasive to the point of noxious, so I've banished it from the garden (well, I'm trying anyway). The successful plants, some of which are exceedingly abundant, are now doing well. They are not for everyone, but then what is. They are simply great plants for a rank, bug-infested garden.

The two biggest-leaved plants are *Inula magnifica* and *Crambe cordifolia*, both of which are about six feet tall in flower. This growth comes up from the ground entirely in one season—in the case of *Crambe*, in about six weeks! Wimpy gardens need not apply for this fellow. *Inula* is a bit more sedate, but not much. Both species (in fact everything in the rank garden) are cut down entirely in late fall or early spring. *Crambe* is a member of the mustard family and looks in foliage somewhat like a giant mustard plant with one-foot leaves arranged in a pyramid three feet across at the base. Great, tall stalks of bloom erupt in May with hundreds of tiny white flowers much like baby's breath (*Gypsophila*).

Inula is a composite with typical yellow daisylike flowers about three inches in diameter. The plant grows essentially upright with three-foot-long narrow, hairy leaves and another two to three feet of flower stalk. It blooms in midsummer. A plant similar to *Inula* is *Telekia speciosa*. I grow it in dark shade where it seems to do just as well as if it were grown in full sun. Either plant creates about the same presence in the garden, so if you can't find one, try the other.

No garden, rank or otherwise, is complete (garden writers always say this, don't they?) without *Helianthus*, or sunflowers, especially the perennial kinds. I have several species in various parts of the garden, but the rankest grows in the rank garden. It is rank not because of any physical lack of beauty but because it is apt to run a bit underground and insert itself here and there and just about everywhere. This sunflower is *H. maximilianii*, which reaches about eight feet in my garden, definitely a back-of-the-border plant. My plants are situated behind the stump of the old silver maple (about four feet in diameter) and are trapped between it and the ZOD. They can only go sideways, and I keep an eye on them (just like the bamboo). Once they grow past the edge of the stump, they are themselves stumped. The plants are covered up and down the stalks with hundreds of three-inch yellow flowers in very late summer. Similar sunflowers that would do the trick as well are *H. angustifolius* and *H. salicifolius,* which bloom one after the other (but I can't remember which comes first). They are about the same size as *H. maximilianii* but not so aggressive. Therefore, I plant them not in the rank garden but in spots of honor where all sunflowers belong. *Helianthus decapetalus,* another wonderful species in its many cultivated forms, only grows about five feet tall. It, too, is relegated to the nonrank parts of the sunny garden.

Looking exactly like *Helianthus* is *Heliopsis,* of which I have two cultivars, *H. helianthoides* 'Goldgrünherz' ('Gold Greenheart') and 'Karat'. These both grow three to six feet tall and have underground runners. They are so easily pulled out that I don't mind this (yet). Both bloom at the top of the plant with three-inch blossoms. 'Karat' has bright yellow flowers while 'Goldgrünherz' has a more golden flower with a greenish center.

The last composite I will write about is *Helenium autumnale,* which grows as a column about four feet tall with a mountain of small buttonlike flowers on top. I have 'Moerheim Beauty', which is a combination of brownish red and yellow petals around a black central disk. For some reason the insects much prefer this single plant to almost all the other composites I've planted. This certainly enhances its otherwise beautiful design. A negative quality of heleniums, of all the plants I've described so far, is that they tend to fall over if not staked. If you grow enough rank stuff around them, however, either they will not fall over or no one will notice if they do. This, by the way, is one secret of British gardening. They plant so much stuff that everything holds everything else up—there is no place for anything to fall.

Some of my rank plants are rank not because they are big (which they may well be), but because they are bountiful—exceedingly bountiful—in the crop of offspring they produce. Not a seed goes to waste. In fact, more seeds sprout than was mathematically possible for the plant to produce. *Linaria purpurea,* which I described earlier, is one such plant. Blooming from May until fall, it is an almost ideal plant except that it seeds itself silly. On the gravel pathway next to my two blooming plants are now hundreds of small seedlings, and I've been pulling them, transplanting them, and giving them away since last October. Not only that, but I used some compost from the pile into which I had tossed the spent branches from last year's plants, and now I have seedlings coming up in the woodland garden, the rock garden, the front garden, the side garden, and even the greenhouse. They are just like foxglove in that they seed readily everywhere, but unlike foxglove, which may sprout but not grow, *Linaria* has no problem growing. Fortunately, they pull easily!

Boltonia asteroides, much like *Linaria*, is another worthy plant, forming an upright column. But instead of the easy grace of *Linaria*, *Boltonia* is as stiff as a bundle of bamboo stakes. Which makes it damn near self-staking, and I admire that in a plant. This one blooms late, with the chrysanthemums, in September. It is a column of small white flowers (though there is a less-common pale pink one, too), which are exceptionally attractive to insects (yes, again).

An interesting foil for *Boltonia* is *Filipendula rubra* 'Venusta' (or 'Magnificum'), called queen-of-the-prairie though an eastern native. This eruption of astilbelike foliage is completely loose and informal compared with the ramrod stiff *Boltonia*. I've read that the plant can reach six to eight feet in moist soil, but in my drier garden it seems to peak at about four or five feet. It is, in essence, a big astilbe with pink flowers to match.

Another robust eastern native is *Eupatorium purpureum*, or joe-pye weed. This back-of-the-border plant reaches five to six feet with rough, dissected, purplish leaves and small purple flowers. It is coarse, to be certain, but not without merit: tall, rigid, self-staking, fall-blooming, tough, noninvasive.

So far about all I've mentioned are the tall rank plants, but there are a few intermediate and short rankish plants, too, in the two-to-three-foot range. I've planted *Filipendula palmata* 'Elegans' as a shorter echo of *Filipendula rubra* 'Venusta' except that its flowers are white. Another *Lysimachia*, this one called *punctata*, so far has proven more manageable than *L. clethroides*. It has small yellow flowers that look nothing at all like its weedy cousin. *Scabiosa columbaria* var. *ochroleuca* (sometimes treated as its own species or as a subspecies of *S. caucasica*) produces mounds of pale yellow pincushion flowers on top of randomly dissected foliage.

Pycnanthemum incanum, an eastern native mountain mint, is a fine, medium mound of dense, fresh green foliage, topped in early summer by hundreds of small white flowers. The leaves give off an odor of spearmint when crushed. The plant does not make much of a statement, but it is a good filler and understory plant for the big guys who often are a little threadbare at the base, having suspended most of their energy higher up in the sky. *Salvia officinalis,* in its golden form, is not grown for its flowers at all but for its lively foliage of yellow and chartreuse striping. *Tanacetum vulgare,* a ferny but invasive fellow, was introduced this year as an underplanting at the edge of the rank garden. Here it may run as it wishes. I've had its cousin, *T. vulgare* var. *crispum,* for years and found that it is not all that difficult to discourage errant runners.

I am not too worried about the invasiveness of these rank and rankish sorts of plants because their area is sharply delimited at the front by a gravel path and at the back by the ZOD. They may fight among themselves, and I will try to insure at least a fair fight. I don't want the entire garden to have a single grand champion. I hope eventually they will reach some form of equilibrium, and I won't have to be a referee for the rest of my life. But if worse comes to worse, I will simply flood the path with weed-killer and that will set them back at least a few months. Long enough to finalize my escape plans.

Week Three

In looking back over this week, I noticed one thing that has changed abruptly and without much fanfare: I've had to water parts of the garden every day. What has happened to the rain? Well, to be honest, there was 0.1 inch on Friday, but that scarcely counts as rain, I think. Then, too, looking back over my daily high/low temperature records, I find that most days hovered between 85 and 90 degrees. That is certainly hot enough to create a need for some artificial precipitation.

In an attempt to outguess the weather (always a desperate measure for gardeners who need to know, and an impossible task for weatherpeople), I planted out ten dozen well-rooted seedlings over the course of the week. Each afternoon when I arrived home from work, the air had the sultry feel of a thunderstorm about it, and I thought if I could just get a couple dozen more plants out, they would bask in the storm's wondrous water. (I am absolutely positive that rainwater is much better for plants than tap water.) No such luck. Each evening I'd plant out a new batch of seedlings, water them in, and then try to find the seedlings I'd set out the night before to rewater them. By the end of the week, I needed a map to find all the stuff I'd put out. And still no rain (to speak of).

As if the routine acts of gardening weren't enough to take care of this week, not to mention additional watering and a dinner function for relatives, my favorite gardening companion, Bruno, became ill and had to be ferried back and forth between home and the veterinarian over a five-day period. There were injections, two white pills twice a day, one blue pill twice a day, eyedroppers of vitamins, tubes of food supplement, and aqueous injections. This was some sick cat! I thought he was a goner at least once, but he survived his ordeal in spite of all the prodding and poking, loss of appetite for six days, and nearly constant immobility. Seems he had a problem with his liver or pancreas, but he is doing much better now. For most of the week, however, he's opted to remain in the house rather than help me work in the yard.

Well, actually, working in the yard never was Bruno's forte. He is more the supervisor-type. He generally finds a vantage point several feet from where I'm working, watches me intently for several minutes to make certain I'm doing the job correctly, then promptly falls asleep. If I should happen to move ten feet to some other project, Bruno immediately wakes up, walks over to inspect the new site (and to be petted), then finds a new vantage point from which to critique my work. It's not a bad job, really, and I'm just a bit jealous that he thought of it first. If I'd been just a little sharper, I might have been the supervisor.

I mentioned planting out seedlings this week, but that was not all. My order of a dozen dahlia tubers arrived, as did some cannas and caladiums, and all needed to be planted out. These plants are normally tender under our winter conditions, so I don't rely on them coming up in the spring. Rarely the dahlias might come up but never the cannas or the caladiums. Well, this year the cannas and the dahlias both came up! And therein lies the dilemma, for if I wait for spring to see what is coming up or not (which is usually not), then I will have missed out on ordering their replacements, which are not readily available in the local nurseries. But if I purchase the tubers in anticipation of their not coming up, and they do (as they did), then what do I do with a bunch of extra tubers?

With the cannas the problem was not difficult. I simply ripped out the old ones, threw them in the compost pile, and planted the new ones. I like to grow the varieties with purple leaves, and none of the ones I'd planted last year turned out to have purple leaves even though they were supposed to. I suspect the tubers got mixed up somehow at the nursery. The fact that they came back this year, almost a miracle by any standard, was not enough to make me want to continue growing them.

Every single dahlia that I planted last year came up again this year, and the ones I ordered were the same as last year's, so I will simply have to find new places for the new tubers. As with cannas, I also like purple-leaved dahlias. Because it takes these plants a long time to bloom in our climate—they might (or might not) be blooming in August—it is nice to get double duty from their foliage for several months. The two varieties I've been growing are 'Japanese Bishop' and 'Fascination', the former with brilliant crimson flowers and the latter with fluorescent pink. I do not plant them together (though that would create a vibrant, head-bashing attraction). I plant the 'Bishop' out back in the purple-leaved patch with the cannas and red-leaved mustard and 'Fascination' in the pink garden out front. The dark foliage takes an edge off the vibrant colors, but there are still enough edges to go all around.

While on the subject of color, I would like to mention a few color combinations of plants that have worked out well this spring and one that didn't. Combining colors is relatively easy when you're dealing with charts, but when working with living plants and the natural environment, good results are as much luck as they are good planning. For example, last fall's planting of tulips should have been at least acceptable this spring but turned out to be completely ugly—hound-dog ugly, as a matter of fact. This cannot happen, we are told, because tulips have the flowers built right into the bulb, and if anything is a certainty, it ought to be a tulip.

My planting consisted of ten bulbs each of white, pink, and "blue" (in tulip colors, blue means light purple) in two wide-spaced clusters. The bulbs were top-sized, so that they, per se, should not have been the problem. Only one of the blue tulips flowered, and it was a diminutive, worthless object if I ever saw one. All the pink and white bulbs flowered, but the white ones were at about ten different heights. Almost a mathematical impossibility. They were not the least bit attractive. The pink flowers were nice, full, and even-heighted by themselves, but their beauty was overcome by the distraction of the other varieties. I cannot explain the reason(s) for this failure with tulips, but it does add further diplomatic complications to my already uneasy truce with them.

Tulips demonstrate that even in foolproof plants there is no certainty in planning color combinations. Luck, however, is not always elusive, even for foolish gardeners, and this year I've achieved a few acceptable effects in spite of long, hard hours of planning. One of the most arresting (and I'm surprised I wasn't) is a combination of the brick red bearded iris called 'Danger' (any brick red iris would do, and I am sure there are dozens of them), a six-foot-tall-by-four-foot-wide tower of the brick-red-with-yellow-marked flowers of Burkwood's broom, *Cytisus* 'Burkwoodii', and the deciduous azalea 'Gibraltar' with flame red petals tinted yellow in the center. Without 'Gibraltar', the broom and iris would have been stunning but subdued in their effect. But with a little neon flame red added, the whole area exploded into a shameless mass of look-at-me hysteria. Pastel-lover that I am, I was almost embarrassed by the spectacle.

A more subtle, more stylish combination was an accident of seeding. Near the large pond is a yard-square mass of pale pink *Dianthus* (whose name I've long since forgotten), and thirty feet away in the terrace rock garden is a low-mounded lilac blue pincushion flower (*Scabiosa* sp.) that seeds about with some abandon. It seeded itself in the gravel path next to the *Dianthus*, and the two go so well together you'd think I planned it that way. In this case, I take credit for the combination because I could easily have pulled up the pincushion flowers as weeds. Some gardeners are opposed to plants growing in pathways, but I encourage them by selective weeding.

A somewhat startling combination was made by the front hedge of 'English Roseum' rhododendron, the rich pink flowers overhung by the saturated yellow drooping racemes of pealike flowers of *Laburnum* × *watereri* 'Vossii'. I've always found it difficult to believe that pink and yellow go together, even when I see that they do. It seems like one of those juxtapositions that shouldn't work.

Another combination that involves neon pink is that of *Paeonia* 'Largo', an anemone-type single-petaled cultivar against a backdrop of *Clematis* 'Ramona', with its lavender-blue flowers. Either one alone is an eyeful. Together they're two eyefuls. A similar intermingling of colors, though more subdued, is created by two clumps of pink columbine sur-rounded by three plants of a catmint, *Nepeta mussinii*, with its gray foliage and pale lavender flowers. The columbine started blooming about six weeks ago, and after about two weeks the catmint caught up with it. They bloomed together for about three weeks, and now the columbine is gone but the catmint will look fresh and new for many more weeks to come.

Creating harmonious combinations of color (as well as texture and form) is, I think, one of the great joys of gardening. I can say, with-out shame, that I have seen mixes of color that have caught my breath and brought me to the edge of tears. This has not happened often. But often enough to make the waiting between times well worthwhile.

Week Four

Did I say that last week was hot and sultry? Well, what I really meant was that it was cool and foggy—compared with this week. Again, four days in the nineties and no rain. Shades of high summer. Neither the gardener nor the garden is quite acclimated to this sudden switch in temperature (and humidity). The basic routine in this sort of weather, in so far as is possible, is to do the chores that need to be done when the shade gets around to them. This is the opposite of a month ago when I was tracking chores in the sun trying to keep warm. There is no trying to keep warm now.

It has been a while since I spoke of failures, except for the tulips, and everyone needs a good dose of reality now and again. One failure

harks back to last fall when I explained how little I knew about overwintering tropical water lilies. I tried two ways: with the reproductive
nodules packed in moist peat moss and placed in the refrigerator (my
own invented method) and with the nodules placed in a container of
moist sand and kept in the basement. About a month ago I brought out
both groups and placed them in distilled water according to one recommended treatment.

The refrigerated nodules rotted almost immediately. The others
have been in some kind of limbo. Although the thin, potatolike outside
skin of the nodules has deteriorated somewhat, they are still as firm as
when they began treatment. They do not appear to be growing, nor do
they appear to be dying. I cannot label the project an abject failure, because it is entirely possible, now that some hot weather has arrived, that
the nodules will go berserk and grow a foot a week. It is possible, but not
terribly probable. I will just keep the nodules in water until they either
put out a plant or two or fall into rotten pieces. I should be able to tell by
the end of summer.

Another failure has been the new white garden I seeded to the left
of the entrance to the house. This endeavor was supposed to be a quick
solution to a small area that I didn't have time to plan out. I scattered
three prepackaged mixtures of size-graded white annual seeds in the prepared bed, but nothing much came up. Not enough to call a garden,
anyway. It is odd how readily seeds sprout throughout my system of hot,
dry gravel pathways, yet when a bed of soil is specially prepared for direct
sowing, the results are almost always negative. Needless to say, I am disappointed that yet another attempt at easy gardening has gone astray.
Direct sowing is so much easier, when it works, than transplanting seedlings several times.

I've decided that my excess dahlia tubers will take the place of the
failed white garden. I will add some pink snapdragons and pink portulaca and extend the pink garden all across the front of the house. Unfortunately, pink portulaca reminds me of another failure. My seed-grown
moss rose (as well as some other newly emerged seedlings) were mowed
to the ground by a slug (or maybe two or three) that happened to get into
the seed flat. Thus, there will be no home-grown seedlings for me. Some-

times it is just easier to face facts and buy a few things. In this case, store-bought portulaca and snapdragons will not only save time and energy but will also be blooming a lot sooner than if I'd grown them myself.

My attempts to grow roses are always failures, and for that reason I am taking out three plants I've had for years. This will reduce my total collection to one plant. The first is a so-called historical rose given to me by Art Tucker, a professional studier of old plants at Delaware State College. Three years ago he insisted I take this rose, even though I told him I didn't much like roses. I planted it out front where it has managed to sneak around to spots five feet away. In the spring, however, just as it is in bloom, the entire plant is eaten to its veins by mysterious beasties. One year it was rose slugs, which are not slugs at all but the larvae of sawflies, which are not flies at all, but wasps. Then, too, I think slugs, which really are slugs, eat the rose. Whatever else might attack the rose is open to speculation, but the plant is worthless as a garden subject unless it is sprayed to death, and I simply refuse to grow plants that must be sprayed every ten minutes as roses are.

The other rose, of which I have two, is the climbing form of 'Dainty Bess', a single pink spring-flowered beauty. It is a beauty, if it blooms, that is, but my plants have probably had about twenty flowers in four years and have been continually loosing their leaves to black spot and mildew. These plants were grown over an arched trellis that a friend and I built and were, quite frankly, a disgrace to the trellis. I decided to replace the roses with two clematises and a fiveleaf akebia, *Akebia quinata*. Clematises are grown for their flowers, of course, but most of them have awful foliage. The akebia has beautiful foliage, but the flowers are not much to write to your senator about. They are beautiful if you can see them. In addition to these plants, I always grow a couple of 'Heavenly Blue' morning glories and evening-blooming moon vines on the trellis for late summer color. The morning glories bloom in the a.m., and I see them as well as the moon vines, which are still open from the night before, when I go off to work. The flowers of moon vine have a pleasing fragrance, too, always an added benefit in a flowering plant.

Some failures are simply the result of changing times. Many years ago, before the garden was very far along, I laid out a system of underground PVC pipe and some taps to take water to the furthest reaches of the garden-yet-to-be. Although I appeared to be laying pipes to imaginary destinations, the garden was sketched out on paper, and there really was some notion that advance planning was on my side. But time has a way of changing things around, and plants have a way of ignoring plans. The result is that several of my taps are now in rather odd places. The one I fixed over the past two days, for example, ended up in the middle of the holly hedge (*Ilex crenata* var. *compacta*) where it was becoming more and more difficult to reach. Not to mention the fact that once you reached it, it was becoming increasingly more difficult to snake the hose around to any part of the garden where it was needed. Something had to be done.

The project required only a simple reconfiguration of the single dead-end pipe now nestled in the center of the hedge. I would dig a trench, cut the pipe back to the hedge's south side, and then put in a **T** that would divert the water two ways: one to the hedge's north side and one straight up. I didn't even need much pipe, really, six inches going up and ten feet to go north. The biggest obstacle to my plan, it seemed, was that I couldn't go north under the hedge, I first had to go west around it, then north. But this would be a breeze compared to the original labor involved in putting the system in, and the end result would be two taps where there had been one. Two hours and *voilà*, instant water. Weeeell, maybe.

Fortunately, PVC pipe is one of the easiest materials to work with. It cuts with a hacksaw and glues with solvent to form a solid bond. The material is what they call forgiving (idiotproof, in my case) because you can make any number of stupid mistakes and still get it right in the end. Try that with galvanized pipe!

The addition of the northern pipeline, the most involved, complicated, and difficult part of the job (for the three-dimensionally challenged, that is), surprisingly posed little problem. It was made of all new materials that fit together properly, except for the old tap that I wanted to reuse. This had been cut off the old PVC line, and I was simply going to unscrew the old tap from the galvanized pipe riser and screw it into a new galvanized pipe riser. The old tap had been in the ground so long, however, and become so corroded that it wouldn't unscrew from its fitting. After fussing with it for the better part of fifteen minutes, and mangling one finger between a pipe wrench and a wrought iron chair (tools are in the mind of the beholder), it suddenly occurred to me that I didn't have to take it apart. The whole assembly still had a short piece of PVC pipe attached where I'd cut it off the main line. I could simply get a straight PVC pipe connector and connect the old faucet and galvanized pipe to the new PVC line. As usual, though, I had connectors for every angle except straight, so I had to drive to the hardware store to buy a twenty-cent connector—only the third trip so far.

New connector in hand, I had no difficulty (itself a dangerous sign) getting the old faucet and galvanized fittings assembled. Then it was on to the easy part: assembling the new tap with its PVC L, PVC-to-galvanized connectors, double-ended galvanized pipe, and galvanized L. Piece of cake. Now all that was necessary was to wait until next morning for everything to harden up, turn on the water, and make certain the line didn't leak before backfilling the trenches I'd dug. It really wasn't necessary, you know, just a precaution.

True to form, the PVC pipe really was idiotproof. Not a leak in sight. The newly assembled tap, however, had erupted Old Faithfuls at every joint in the galvanized pipe parts. Fortunately for me, the galvanized pipe assembly simply screwed into the PVC-to-galvanized pipe fitting, and I could take the thing out of the ground to work with it. Which I did. For about half an hour. I disconnected the fittings, cleaned them, put pipe compound on the threads, and reunited them all, tightening with compound leverage from two pipe wrenches. Then, when it came time to put the pipe back in the ground, I discovered that I could not screw it back into the fitting so that the faucet pointed straight out toward the garden as it did when I first put it together. Instead it pointed directly back into the holly hedge. This would not do.

After trying several different points of insertion into the threads of the connector with no luck, I decided I'd have to muscle the galvanized sections beyond the nearly impossibly tight fit I'd already made to keep the thing from leaking in the first place. So using pipe wrenches, my feet, some bricks, and every possible principal of leverage known to me, I was able to swing the tap around. I didn't know how far, however, since all my energy was going into making the thing move in sixteenth-inch increments. Apparently it was not sufficient, because when I screwed the pipe back into its fitting, I could only swing the faucet until it was parallel with the hedge. I was tempted to take the thing out, re-wrench it, and put it back in the ground, but I knew one thing for cer-tain—I didn't have enough strength left to wind an electric clock. Then there was the problem of overtightening, a procedure that usually re-sults in ruptured fittings (among other things). The tap actually was functional, I decided. It wasn't in the middle of the hedge any more, and who cared if it was parallel or perpendicular to the hedge? I didn't.

I learned long ago that one of the most difficult tasks in fix-it pro-jects is to learn when a job is finished. As far as I was concerned, this job was done.

Week Five _____

Having just come off an eleven-day run of 90-degree-plus record-breaking weather and no rain for three weeks, I am sorry I ever brought up the subject of too much rain. This past week witnessed the death of spring with a vengeance not anticipated and an unnecessary suddenness. Someone ought to be giving a little more consideration to gardeners and their plants. After all, we are doing the best we can to increase beauty and serenity in this poor world of ours. It's far too early in the gardening year to break the gardener's spirit with travail and torment of this magni-tude. You'd think the gods would hold off at least until July.

The final blow to spring came with the premature withering of the foxgloves. There is almost nothing more spectacular than a patch of five-foot-tall foxgloves in full bloom, and almost nothing worse than their subsequent vertical stalks of brown death. The plants, being biennial, look simply ghastly the moment they begin going to seed. The gardener has the choice of leaving them alone so that s/he will have seedlings com-ing up next year (by the billions) or of yanking them out before they set seed and sowing the store-bought kind. The chances are much better when there are tens of thousands of seeds being self-sown than when you shake out a few hundred seeds from the package. I've tried both.

In past years I've let all the foxgloves go to seed, then cut the stalks, rattled them all about the places I wanted plants to grow, and then carted them to the compost pile. Now I find seedlings coming up all along the pathways leading to the compost heap. Not surprising, really, as the seeds are minuscule. Interestingly and not unexpectedly, I also find seedlings coming up in all the places to which I've moved the compost. None has been more effective than the fifteen-foot-long raised planter I built in the former container garden behind the hedge of *Ilex crenata* var. *compacta* that provided so much enjoyment last week. I filled the box with compost and quickly realized that foxgloves were going to be the predominant weeds. They started sprouting almost immediately, and planted as they were at a one-foot elevation, they now stick up a good two feet above the holly hedge, which is only four feet tall. All told, the foxgloves appear to be giants this year—giant spires of brown. Planting them in pure compost did not stunt their growth much, but hot weather put an end to their spring reign.

The heat being what it has been, I've had to spend an inordinate amount of time watering. This I do by hand and by sprinkler. Watering is not all that bad a job in the searing heat—a lot nicer job, say, than laying asphalt. It does not require much energy, and you can always spray yourself in the face to liven things up a bit. Still, it is one of those jobs that is irritating because there is so much else that needs to be done and so little time to do it. Standing around doing an imitation of a hose-holder is not the best use of time, in my opinion.

On the other hand, one doesn't chose to do the heavy, earth-moving jobs, either, if one can avoid them. In the past, I've always had so much earth, rocks, gravel, and mulch to move that I could not be choosy in timing their movements. I had to work when the supplies demanded, usually to clear room for the next round of materials. Now, I do no routine moving, although I really do need to order about ten cubic yards of mulch. Once that arrives it can stay in the driveway for weeks, months even, until I feel like moving it. There will be nothing else to take its place this year.

Because there is no heavy work to do I now spend more time on cleanup, and the best sort of cleanup, in hot weather at least, is to weed. To sit or squat or kneel or lay in the shade and weed. My gravel pathways have become swards of seedlings needing constant removal or transplanting, in the case of good weeds. The most prominent weedy things now are columbine, if you can believe it. They come up by the thousands from mother plants that dropped their seeds last year. They are difficult to pull, too, because they've obviously been growing taproots for the past year before they put up a couple of feeble leaves. There is nothing much to grab on to, and when you pull, the foliage comes off in your hand, leaving the crown and root in the soil. The trick, I've found, is to let the plants grow two or three inches tall, but then they make a mess of the path when they come out.

An even better trick, I've found, is to cut the flower stalks off before they go to seed. This is not easy, however, because there are always some flowers still coming into bloom when the first seedpod starts to burst its seams. One must be ruthless and simply cut the flowering stalks just before the first pod splits. Normally, neither am I that ruthless nor are my interventions that timely. In the past I've cut the stalks off just after every pod has split. You can hear the seeds raining down as each stalk is cut—a veritable thunderstorm.

My entire garden of columbines began with half a dozen seedlings, the names of which are now lost to the antiquities, not to mention unbridled hybridization. Over the years I have let many seedlings grow where they will—and they gladly will—thinning them only enough to allow the chosen seedlings room to grow and to prevent the entire garden from becoming a single sheet of columbine, for that is all it would be in a few years. That and foxglove. My early attitude toward self-seeders was to pull them all because they were not coming up where I put them. And after all, I was the boss. Now I realize that I am nothing of the sort, I am simply a caretaker. By allowing certain plants to come up on their own initiative, where they want to be, I am acting as a selection broker, selecting the preferable plants from among the competing plants. It is not always as I would want, but maybe the plants know what's best for them, after all.

For example, on the west side of the house, between the oil tank and the driveway, there is a narrow, sloped strip of gravel that is hot, dry, impossible to water, and nearly pointless to try to landscape. It is one of those places where the mind simply stops functioning and creativity dries up. For several years I kept the place weeded of the noxious things, but lately good weeds are starting to creep in. Some columbine, as yet unbloomed, has reached the space. The great, self-sowing black-eyed Susan has found a home there from fifty feet away, where they were planted in the front border. Sweet williams from ten feet away, next to the greenhouse, have washed down the slope and seeded in. Yellow-foliaged feverfew and *Linaria* have made themselves at home. I doubt that I would have planted any of these in that particular spot or in the combination that is arising. But by accepting what wants to be there, I am at least assured that they will grow. I have never watered the space, and the only aid I have rendered is to take out a walnut that some squirrel stored there and to remove the few seedlings of chickweed or sour grass that pop up. In truth, surprisingly few bad weeds show up in this space; they are all being outcompeted by the good ones of my own selection.

Generally I practice the philosophy of live and let live in the garden. I do not go out of my way to dispose of life forms that conventional wisdom deems less important than I. I feel queasy, for example, when I accidentally cut a worm in half or when I mangle a dung beetle grub or especially when I move a stone and discover I've killed endless members of an ant society that was minding its own business. At times like these I feel like an intruder as well as a murderer.

I am even docile enough to coexist with life forms that can and do fight back. The social wasps, of which my garden is home to several species, are an example. Last year there was an underground yellow jacket nest located at the main entrance to the back garden. It was just to the left, between some stones, as you came down the driveway. For months, visitors had, unknown to them, funneled past the nest. Visitors generally become hysterical when you mention the word wasp, so I never do.

The wasps did not bother me in the least as I rumbled past their nest with cart and shovel, buckets of weeds, tarps of spent herbaceous vegetation, and the lawn mower. Only two feet away, and they could have cared less. Even watering didn't agitate them too much. You had to get right up to the nest entrance before they'd attack, and since even I am not that stupid, we lived in harmony for the entire year.

There are basically three sorts of social wasps that may be found in the garden or near the house: hornets, yellow jackets, and paper wasps. Each of these makes a paper comb from chewed bark or fence posts or even teak benches. The hornets make big paper bags that they hang up in trees. Yellow jackets usually nest in the ground or in cavities (like walls) but occasionally make free-hanging nests. Paper wasps often nest under the eves of houses where they suspend an open paper comb. The energy of each wasp, regardless of species, is devoted to increasing the colony's membership. In harsher, colder climates all nest members die at year's end, except for a new batch of queens created in the fall. The queens overwinter to begin a new colony in the spring. Until fall, all members of a colony are female, which is noteworthy for humans, because only females can sting. Thus, a wasp nest may be viewed by the pessimistic as a solid mass of pain waiting to happen. In milder, warmer climates colonies increase in numbers over several year's time. This fact is often not mentioned in retirement literature and is one reason why I no longer live in the South.

Of the three wasp types, paper wasps are the most docile and least vicious when disturbed. You practically have to beat them over the head to make them mad. People, for some reason, are generally willing to do that, and thus get themselves in trouble. These wasps make a simple one-layer, downward-hanging paper comb about two or three inches across. These colonies rarely have more than a dozen or two females. I've never seen their nests anywhere but under roof eves. In fact, you most often encounter them when painting the house and find their nests hanging in your way. What to do? Well, you could give their nest a square-foot holiday when you're painting. Not much of a problem, really. They will sit defiantly on their nest, turning toward you in a feeble attempt to stare you down, but do not be fooled. They look fierce but will do nothing until you get very, very close. Much closer than you would normally want to get. My father, who was a professional house-painter, used to slap the nest down with his paintbrush, but I do not recommend this approach. What I do recommend is that you paint your house in the early spring before the queen begins building her nest or in the late fall after the first frost. Cold knocks the nest occupants out, and winter finishes off all but the queens. (Queens, by the way, are rarely seen and are not very aggressive.) If you live in the South, I would suggest aluminum soffits as the easiest solution to the problem of paper wasps.

Hornets are the next least problematic, not because they aren't killers, which they most certainly are, but because they generally nest up high enough that they won't even be seen, let alone brushed up against. These are big black wasps with white markings, and they nest in colonies consisting of hundreds to thousands of females. A single female, though intimidating, does not seem to be particularly aggressive by herself. They do not seem to be as curious about human food, for example, as are the smaller yellow jackets, which seem to prefer barbecues to their normal insect diet. Size notwithstanding, however, I can think of no more painful way to die than to stumble into a sizable nest of hornets and be repeatedly stung into oblivion. Just thinking about it makes me glad they nest in trees.

Yellow jackets are arguably the worst of all the wasps. These little yellow-and-black critters fly in your face at the office picnic or drink from your soda can. They are not to be riled, these vixens, for they have a shortcoming all too common in today's world: an evil, wicked temper. Once they are agitated, you will know it. They are small, fast, silent, and deadly. They take no prisoners. There is no amnesty. You run or you die. This is doubly disconcerting because, of all the wasps, yellow jackets are most likely to build their nests in stupid places where people will fall into them. Holes in the ground are a particular favorite. They hollow out a cavity and build a paper nest like that of the paper wasp, only bigger. They increase the diameter of the comb as the colony grows. There can be thousands of females in a nest. Because they nest in the ground, yellow jackets are often inadvertently stumbled across by children, and occasionally adults, with unfavorable results.

Even I do not like yellow jackets, but as I say, I do not automatically destroy life forms in the garden simply because I do not like them. All these wasps are beneficial, although, I admit, it is difficult to believe this at times. As I mentioned in April, social wasps, and most solitary ones as well, feed on caterpillars and insects of various sorts. Social wasps chew up these insects and feed them to their young. To have a colony in the garden is not the end of the world necessarily, though at times it might appear to be.

Given my attitude toward bees and wasps, it came as no great shock to me while out weeding a few weeks ago to find the startup of a new colony of yellow jackets in the rhododendron hedge. With its mass underplanting of evergreen perennial candytuft, which requires scarcely any maintenance, it was not a bad place, I decided, to conceal a nest. A person would have to be pretty darn stupid, indeed, to be messing about in the hedge where he didn't belong. Any such person should be stung, I thought. I just didn't think it would be me.

I am a research entomologist, after all, and have worked for over twenty-five years specifically on wasps, although most of that time has been spent with the parasitic species, not the social ones. These wasps, which number in the thousands of species, are virtually everywhere and cause not the least bit of harm to humans because they can't sting. In fact, they are wondrously beneficial because they parasitize many kinds of plant-feeding insects. With these wasps I can truthfully say that I know what I'm doing, and for some reason, I thought this was true of social wasps as well.

It came to pass that late last week I was out deadheading the rhododendrons. My mind was preoccupied with thoughts of interstellar space, quarks, gravitational pull, and why rhododendrons had evolved such sticky flowers, when I noticed that something was not quite right. I had put my foot into an open space at the base of one plant, while the other remained firmly on the path at some distance from it. The stance was definitely spread-eagle, you might say, and I was off balance, and this damn stick kept poking me in the leg. In fact it was poking awfully hard and was starting to hurt like sticks shouldn't ought to hurt.

I looked down at my leg at the same time a wasp found the exact spot she was looking for. In the millisecond between the injection and the time the pain reached my brain, I had a chance to survey the situation. I felt obligated to let out a curse of some magnitude because not only did my leg hurt, but also I could see a swarm of ten to twenty wasps (or possibly 6,000, I wasn't taking a real accurate inventory) hovering near my widespread spindly white legs. Of some concern was that I had on a pair of especially baggy shorts, and an agonizing amount of damage could be done if I didn't get the hell out of there and fast.

The mind is a wonderful computer. It takes into account mountains of data, analyzes it in split seconds, and puts the old butt into gear even when all your gears were stripped years ago. Wasps, on the other hand, having nothing to think about in such situations, just do their job. Their computer has one simple order: search and sting. This they do well.

It was difficult, I found, trying to run with my thighs clapped together, but run I did. I took a hit on the knee, another on the ankle, and one on the earlobe. It did not feel especially good. I could imagine things feeling even worse though, as I dashed around the corner of the house, arms flailing. I could still hear buzzing noises in my ear, possibly from the same female who just nailed me. But I did not sense any more immediate danger. I was well out of visual sight of the nest. And I had avoided the stings that I feared the most.

For anyone interested in aerobic exercise, this is a fairly effective method to get your heartrate up to about 335 beats per minute. It stays that way for quite a while, too. My guess is that the rate goes up proportionally in relation to the size of the colony, the distance to the nearest cover, and how much clothing you have on (or off).

Later that same night, under shroud of darkness, I went out with my net (yes, all reasonable gardeners have butterfly nets) and looked for the nest. Amazingly, it was not underground, as is usually the case, but was constructed at ankle level on a small limb of a rhododendron. It was about four inches in diameter. At night there is no external activity at a nest, but its movement will still result in females spilling out to the attack. Taking care not to hit the nest, I slowly slid my net under it, then, pruners in my left hand, net handle in my right, I clipped the limb and pulled the net upward. The nest fell in, and I flipped the net bag over the wire frame to close it off. The specimens are now in the U.S. National Museum of Natural History.

As I said before, I believe in live and let live in the garden. In this case, I voted in favor of myself.

8

JUNE

Week One _____

    I'm certain we all have those times when we feel that the garden is overwhelming us. That there is far too much work and far too little time. That the plants all look like hell and—not surprisingly—the weeds all look great. That it finally *is* time to abandon the garden and take that trip we've been putting off for over twenty years. That maybe Father *was* right, after all, there is no justice in this world. That juggling razor blades would be far more rewarding, not to mention more pleasant, than gardening. That . . . but I think you get the point.

    Well, this week was one of *those.*

    Monday is never a good day under any circumstances. About the only decent thing that can be said is that it beats the alternative. The way I figure it, though, Monday sets the tone for the rest of the week. Off to a good start, then it's a good week; off to a bad start, and it's normal. This week started with an interruption and stayed that way, so I never felt like I got anything done until about 2:30 on Friday afternoon, and by then it was too late. It's not as if anything really bad happened on Monday, it's just that except for the interruptions, nothing much happened at all. That, in itself, is bad enough.

Tuesday was staff-meeting day. After the meeting I typed up a letter of resignation as lead scientist of my research unit, a position I have held for almost six years. I think it's time to step down. One's mind becomes musty after a while, and it's better to let some new-thinking person take a position of authority. Not that my position has any real authority. It is just a buffer zone between those higher up the food chain and the remaining plankton, including my own expendable self. I take the bad news from above and pass it down to the troops, in my case, five other scientists and two technicians. Then I take the gripes from the troops and pass them up to administration, who promptly ignores them. It was decided among the lead scientists (myself the minority vote) to have a two-day powwow to determine a plan of action by which to live in these troubled times. I've already been to two, or possibly three, of these tête-à-têtes, and I would as soon poke a finger in my eye. Two maybe. I'd rather work than play politics. Not that it isn't necessary, because it is—it's the way things get done in government. But I've already contributed my share to the betterment of the laboratory, and I need to get some real work done. So, as I said, I typed up a letter of resignation as lead scientist. I haven't turned it in for several reasons, not the least of which is that I promised to remain in the position until my boss, Dug, quit. I am still debating whether or not to break my promise.

Normally after such a day, rushing home to the garden would be a pleasure. Fifteen minutes of gardening is better for all that ails me than any other therapy known to humankind. Better even than half a dozen gin and tonics. But Tuesday I could barely face the garden. Nevertheless, I forced myself outside and edged part of the lawn, running sprinklers all the while. I'd be better off, I thought, moving back to an apartment.

In spite of constant watering, everything looked bloody well exhausted. Spring wasn't even officially over yet, and it felt like fall. It was far too early for the garden to look so poorly. It has now been over five weeks since we've had more than a trace of rain, and the plants have a dry, bony look. The look of tough, weather-beaten, adult, old foliage.

Foliage that's been around for a while—that's streetwise. Not the supple, fresh, innocent, soft look of spring.

As the proprietor of this place, I was sorely distressed at the apparent quality of my nurturing. If anyone from the County Office of Garden Abuse should come around, I'd be hauled off to court, slapped in solitary confinement for ten years, and have all my plants put in foster homes.

I water, honest, I do. That's about all I've been able to do for weeks (that and weed; of course, weeds don't need water to grow). But the only benefit of artificial irrigation has been to keep the plants in stasis. No matter how long or how hard I water, the relative dryness of all the surrounding soil (and don't forget the great depth of soil beneath the garden, extending at least to China) simply wicks the moisture away. It might help if I could flood the place once a week, but that's tough when you live on a slope.

The only encouraging news along the weather front was that the 90-degree weather broke on Sunday. Since then it's been anywhere from the fifties at night to the eighties in the day—much better, at this time of year at least, for the plants. Although they still need water, now when I water it doesn't turn to steam before hitting the ground.

Wednesday at work was slightly better than Tuesday but not much. When I arrived home I forced myself to tackle a job that didn't need tackling and, in so doing, made a botch of it. This is always good for the ego, and it pretty much summed up the rest of the week, too.

The job, actually, was rather interesting, having to do with a wildlife problem. A bird's nest was plugging up the stainless steel chimney of my wood-burning stove. I added the stove after I moved in and connected it to a twenty-six-foot-tall outdoor chimney. I built the chimney with an outdoor T at its base so that I could clean it by removing the base plate and shoving a chimney brush up from below. This brush is attached to a three-foot fiberglass rod to which more threaded rods are added as the brush is forced higher and higher in the chimney.

How could those birds get a nest started in what is, in essence, an eight-inch-diameter bottomless hole? Not only that, it is slippery on the inside. Normally they can't. I leave the base plate off in the summer, and the nesting material usually falls straight down and out the bottom of the chimney onto the ground.

I knew the chimney was plugged up several weeks ago because I could see the birds flying in and out of the gaps in the chimney cap. At that time I tried to get the nest out with my chimney brush, but it didn't work. The big-headed brush just pushed the nest higher up in the chimney. I was surprised, then, about a week ago to find a three-foot-long, eight-inch-diameter tubular nest lying on the ground beneath the clean-out T. It had fallen out of its own weight.

Wednesday I noticed that the birds were back (they appear to be sparrows) plugging up the chimney again. Rather than risk an impacted chimney pipe, I decided to fasten a hook to my chimney rods, ram them up the pipe, and pull the newly laid nesting material down. Better I should have stayed at work.

Pushing the rod up the chimney pipe was no problem. Without the brush attached to it, there was no resistance at all (with the brush it is a very tight fit, which, of course, is the purpose of pushing the brush up the pipe). In fact it was too easy. I pushed the rod up, up, up until the whole thing was as far as my arm could possibly go up the pipe, and then I pushed just a tad too exuberantly. The hook slipped over something in the pipe, possibly the opening in the chimney cap, and hung itself up. The rod is now hanging in the chimney pipe, barely out of fingers' reach. I cannot grab onto it, let alone get enough leverage to push it or pull it out of harm's way. As the roof is far too high and steep for me to attempt rescue, I suppose I shall have to call in a chimney sweep to get my rod out. It will not be easy to explain how all this happened.

Thursday appeared to be a kinder, gentler day all around, but that was because I was in total ignorance of what the real world was up to.

By Friday, if I hadn't been reading the newspapers, I wouldn't have had any idea that half the arsenal of the known free world was landing on the mall in our nation's capital in preparation for the celebration of our victory in the Persian Gulf. From my office I could have a perfectly fine view of the mall except for two factors: the windows, such as they are, are opaque, and my office faces an inner court of rooftop machinery.

I consider war to be a distinctly human endeavor, one that separates us from the higher forms of life such as bacteria, pond scum, and metamorphic rock. Humankind's propensity for self-destruction in the name of some ill-defined, higher moral ground is slightly beyond my grasp, and I find its irrationality irritating. To kill, let us say, tens or hundreds of thousands of people because we are too moral to assassinate one leader seems the epitome of moral self-deception. But then, I have dedicated my life to understanding insects, not humans. Insects have no morality, which, when you think about it, is interesting, because they will be here long after we are gone. The amoral shall inherit the earth. Not the sort of thing we humans care to think about.

For the better (or worse) part of the week, the machinery of war has been building up on the mall. It has been, of course, the number one topic of conversation among the local life forms, and I have been impressed (or depressed) by how easily the exact and specific names of tanks and personnel carriers and helicopters and jets and guns and ammo and other military stuff roll off the tongues of people who, to my knowledge, have never previously had any experience with military hardware.

On Friday, curiosity got the better of reason, and I, being partly human after all, decided to go out and see what all the hubbub was about.

It was a public love affair, as near as I could figure.

There were dozens of helicopters and dozens of tanks surrounded by men, women, and children all agape at such stuff as human suffering is made of. It was like a car show, with everyone looking for his or her favorite model. Or maybe even worse, a carnival. Children were climbing in and out of tanks that weeks before conceivably had blown the heads off fathers of other children. It was all such a great incongruity that for a moment I thought perhaps I was in a Fellini movie. A really bad Fellini movie.

I traversed the entire show down one side then crossed over and walked back the way I'd come. By the time I reached the end of "The Greatest Show on Earth," I had also reached the end of my wits. My mind was numbed by the enormity of it all. Not just the show, but the war and the reasons for the war and the need to have a victory show at all.

Most distressing for me was that the public was buying this celebration of belligerence as if it were our finest hour. I could buy none of it; not one cent's worth.

Then a sliver of sanity flashed across my mind. I recalled the topiary dinosaur that the Smithsonian's horticulture department had built on the east end of the mall at the side of the Museum of Natural History. I had been wanting to see how it had overwintered, and this was a perfect opportunity. I had to go past it to get back to my office in the Natural History building. It was not as I recalled from last year, but then, what ever is?

The saur stands about seven feet tall and is fifteen feet in length, not counting the part of the tail that curves around and comes back on itself. The skeleton is made of reinforcing bar (or something very similar) covered with chicken wire and stuffed with potting soil, sphagnum moss, and space filler. Of course, you're not supposed to know this because the whole thing is planted over with ivy. Well, that's the idea, anyway. Today the old thing was looking a little threadbare. Lots of ivy had died so that patches of skeleton showed. Its feet were surrounded with weeds, and a weedy vine of some sort, stems covered in velcrolike hooks, had ridden up its haunches—a sign of certain neglect. Its tail was melting away. That is, the ivy was mostly dead and the filling was washing out to reveal dinosaur innards. In truth, it was not only a mess but a singularly disgusting display to grace the corner of the nation's Museum of Natural History.

The dinosaur was quite a contrast, too, to what it had been last year. When new, it was the idol of every boy, and nearly every other girl, who walked by the museum. It was my idol, as well. I am a sucker for topiary, even the quick and dirty kind built upon wire bones. So fresh and green and imposingly big, I wanted it in my own garden. Peering over a hedge, perhaps. What right-thinking boy wouldn't? (I've even been looking for some heavy-duty wire to make my own topiary, maybe a scaled-down version of the dinosaur.)

Today no children were within a hundred yards of the place. They were all down looking at the hundred-thousand-dollar missiles, the million-dollar tanks, and the billions of dollars of metallic monsters out there on the mall. No one, except me, was giving the saur even a second glance. You'd think with the incredible amounts of money being thrown about that day that a country like this could keep its dinosaurs patched up. It could have been, too, for the price of a tank nut.

It all depends, I suppose, on where your priorities lie. Mine, I realized, are with the bare-boned dinosaurs of the world. As I walked back to my office, I dwelled more and more on the inherent beauty in that dinosaur and less and less on the fantasy on the mall.

By the time I got home that evening, it was into the garden and back to renewal. The world may want to grovel at the altar of war, but I knew where I'd rather be groveling.

Week Two

Yet another week without rain. I forgot to mention that last week it didn't rain either. Still, this week has turned out much better than last. In fact, I am going to brag about some successes and then relate a tale of gardening discovery.

The first success is now thriving so well that next year I may classify it as a weed. A good weed, but one needing thinning, nonetheless. For many years I have tried to grow the common red poppy, or corn poppy, *Papaver rhoeas*, with little or no success. This is the bloody-red-flowered poppy sometimes referred to as the poppy of Flanders Field. I don't know why, exactly, I've wanted to grow it, but I suppose it is because of the striking red flowers. Last year I managed to get one insignificant plant to bloom—my first ever. Now this year the seedlings from that plant are coming up all over.

Poppies are one of those plants you are supposed to seed in place because they resent transplanting. I have always taken this to mean that the seedlings are delicate weaklings that must be pampered. I have broadcast many a packet of seed not only of the corn poppy, but also of Iceland, Shirley, and opium poppies (which, by the way, you can buy quite legally from seed companies) with no success. Even though I sowed them into my best-kept beds, they never sprouted. Similarly, I've wasted many a packet of seed in seed flats, ignoring the advice about transplanting.

Occasionally I've gotten a half dozen or so seedlings of which anywhere from one to none has survived the transplanting.

This has always seemed strange to me because as a kid my parents had a border of opium poppies in a narrow dog-run of a space between the house and the fence. Here, with no help from anyone, or even water, it seemed, these poppies made a showing to rival any in the known universe. Once they finished blooming, my job was to harvest the seed. This I did by carefully picking off the seed heads so that they remained absolutely vertical and then pouring the hundreds or thousands of seeds from each head into a quart jar to save for next year. They rained out of little archways between the cap and the cup, and you could hear them pour just like salt from a shaker. I easily filled the quart jar, and if you've ever seen a poppy seed, you know it is nothing to brag about in the size department.

From these early experiences I presumed that growing poppies from seed would be no trouble at all. Apparently it isn't, if you learn one secret, which I will get to in a minute.

Last year, after my success with the one seedling of *Papaver rhoeas*, I did not have a chance to collect seed from the plant. I returned home from a trip only to find a dead, seedless little heap of foliage about twelve inches high. These are annuals, after all, and they tend to quit blooming and die early in the season (about June in these parts). And that, I figured, was that.

I was somewhat surprised, then, early this year, to find what appeared to be poppy seedlings coming up in some profusion near where the mother poppy had been. They were coming up in the hot, dry, packed gravel pathway beneath the carefully prepared bed where I'd put the mother. She'd been planted in pure compost and had grown scarcely a foot. Her children were voluntarily growing in what amounts to loose-packed cement. None came up in the mother's bed. This, I think, tells us something. If you want to grow poppies from seed, put them in the absolutely worst place you've got. Next year I am going to sprinkle seeds of Iceland and opium poppies all about the edges of my gravel pathways and see what happens (besides going to jail, I mean).

(Just an aside about opium poppies, *Papaver somniferum*. I've read various statements about the propriety of growing this plant, and from what I've read, it seems that while it is legal to buy the seeds, it is not legal to plant them. I find this hard to believe since even first-rate horticultural magazines show photographs of gardens with opium poppies growing in them and label them as such. I don't know if ignorance of the law is an excuse in this case, but that's what I shall plead when the feds come swooping down on my garden next year.)

My second success is a case of serendipity resulting in an interesting little focal point using water. The story starts a few years ago, when I planted a dreadful weed called *Houttuynia cordata* 'Chameleon'. This was one of those plants that was picked up by the trade as some sort of wonderplant and sold to thousands of unsuspecting customers (like me). The thing is nice to look at with its multicolored leaves, but it can be invasive and noxiously so. I took my plant out the second year after seeing examples of it growing in a display garden where it was the only thing left on display (after smothering out the entire rest of the garden). It looked like a dwarf kudzu. It took two years to eradicate my single plant from its limited site, but I potted up several pieces of the thing on the theory that I could always use it in a pot. I'd just paid for it a year ago, so it didn't seem right to throw it away so soon. These plants sat around in pots for several years, and I even gave some away—with stern warnings of their danger. Then I read an article somewhere that said houttuynia would grow in water. So I plunked my pot in a cachepot of water, and sure enough, it grew just fine. Better, even, than in the ground. And the garden was safe because it couldn't go anywhere.

I have several glazed pots without drainage holes in which I grow water-loving plants to set about the garden or on the balcony for a little spot of color or just plain decoration. Houttuynia is one of these plants, and others include red-leaved aquatic cannas, variegated Japanese iris, dwarf cattails, and variegated sedges. The pots themselves cannot sit out all winter without breaking, so I bring them, plants and all, into the greenhouse then trot them back out in the spring. This spring I removed the houttuynia from its cachepot and stuck its plastic pot temporarily in a much bigger cachepot with the aquatic canna. Here it filled up the base of the pot with its foliage and covered the thin little ankles of the canna. Not only that, but the foliage color combinations were quite pleasing. The canna's leaves are mostly deep red, but its herringbone veins each are margined by a little chartreuse. The houttuynia's leaves are mostly deep green, but they have margins of yellow blending into chartreuse, orange, and red. The pot itself is terra-cotta (with a glazed interior), blending well with the overall reddish effect.

These pots, then, without any flower color, are an exceptionally colorful and portable garden that can be put anywhere, even on a temporary basis. They combine water, an attractive container, and the architectural quality of the plants. Right now these water pots sit on my balcony and the terrace. They can be admired whenever I go out to read or just to sit and think (or sit and drink). Because they are constantly wet, the leaves do not get that desiccated look of plants in the ground that may have missed a watering or two. Therefore, the plantings are fresh and colorful almost all summer, and the water adds a touch of coolness to any composition.

Gardens do not have to be big—or floriferous—to give pleasure.

Occasionally the gardener makes a little discovery that is both unexpected and gratifying. A nice combination of colors or textures, a beautiful container in a junk shop, or a plant of special interest among the weedy fare of a nursery bed. This story is about a plant discovery several years back that was brought to mind this week as I planted out its progeny.

In the fall of 1989, I believe it was (or possibly the spring of 1924, you know how gardeners are at keeping track of time), I was visiting the nursery of Andre Viette in Fishersville, Virginia, with my friend Dee. As usual, we toured the display garden first to see what was in bloom. Often, after examining (and coveting) the plants on display, you can find smaller examples for sale in the nursery area.

This particular day we found a small shrublet about two feet in height and spread composed of emerald green glossy foliage. The leaves were oblong, about two inches in length, and crisscrossed with veins. The areas between the veins were puckered, giving the leaf a beaded texture. (Some hostas have such puckery leaves.) There was no label for the plant, so we marked its spot in the display garden for future reference.

Once back at the sales area, we asked a worker if she knew what the plant was. She didn't, but we described its salient features and location, and the girl went off to check on it. She came back, eventually, and told us it was a species of *Digitalis*. Well, I know a little about plants, I thought, and this has as much chance of being a foxglove as I have of being the next vice president of the United States. Well, OK, maybe there was a chance it was a foxglove, but just a slim one.

With the pronouncement of "*Digitalis*", I abandoned hope of finding out what the real name of the plant was and began browsing among the nursery stock looking for other potential plant gems to put in my garden. I walked up and down the aisles, selecting plants as I went until I came to a pot of leopard's bane (*Doronicum*), which looked rather odd. I don't care much for this plant, largely, I suspect, because it goes dormant in early summer. The flower of the plant on the bench was typical for the genus (yellow daisies), but the foliage was totally wrong. It was, in fact, the foliage of the plant we had seen in the garden. Apparently it had self-seeded into the leopard's bane and was in the process of outcompeting it. I certainly didn't want to buy the bane, but I grabbed the plant and ran off to show Dee my newly acquired "what's-its-name." We still didn't know what it was (maybe a cross between *Digitalis* and *Doronicum*!), but we had a plant.

Although Dee, as I have said, is a gardening saint, she is not without some degree of covetousness. It was clear that she wanted the plant, too, and it was equally clear that I was not about to part with mine. Fortunately, it all ended for the best, because Dee, with her sharp eyes, managed to find another plant growing in a pot of something it wasn't supposed to be in either.

It was Dee, in fact, who eventually unraveled the mystery of the plant's name. She found it growing at a relatively new botanical garden in Richmond, the Lewis Gintner Botanical Garden. And well worth a visit, but that is another story. The plant is called *Boehmeria biloba*, and it is a member of the nettle family. It does not have stinging hairs, although the leaves are hirsute, feeling somewhat like a three-day-old beard. A close relative, *Boehmeria nivea*, is called the Chinese silk plant, or ramie, and is cultivated for its long, silky fibers. I don't know if *B. biloba* is grown for any utilitarian reason, but it is a handsome foliage plant for the herbaceous or shrub border. In my climate it is best grown in the shade where it retains its lush greenness. In full sun it becomes tough and yellowish. It is not reliably hardy in this area, but I haven't lost it in the past two years. Those years haven't been much of a real test, but the plants have died back to the ground each year. When grown in a proper environment, the plant is supposed to behave as a shrublike perennial.

Because of its borderline hardiness, I take cuttings of the plant in late summer, just as insurance, to overwinter in the greenhouse. Last year Dee collected seed of the plant and grew hundreds of seedlings, of which she gave me several dozen. The bloom, by the way, is typically nettlelike—a long, greenish white cluster of tiny nondescript flowers. Certainly not the reason you'd grow *Boehmeria*. They produce an abundance of seed and apparently as we saw at Viette's nursery, seed themselves at will. My plant has never flowered, perhaps it is in a spot that is too shady or receives too much root competition from surrounding trees. Perhaps I am fortunate, and the plant is really a self-seeding weed in the right environment.

This week I planted out the seedlings Dee gave me in a dry, shady spot that needs just a touch of green foliage and nothing more. It is possible that *Boehmeria* will do the job, but now I will just have to wait and see.

I guess if there is any moral to this tale, it is to keep your eyes open whenever you go nursery shopping, and don't always pay attention to the labels. Just the other day at a nursery I saw a pot of *Dianthus* for sale that looked suspiciously like the violet I pull out of my garden by the pound. Mislabeled pots have the potential for either good or evil, and one never quite knows whether to take the risk or not. Unfortunately, one seldom knows if a plant is mislabeled until it is too late.

In the case of *Boehmeria* the story has a happy ending. So far.

Week Three _____

It is a Sunday afternoon and raining. Even though nearly the entire weekend was rained out, I'll not complain about it again as I did in the spring. I've learned my lesson! At that time, when the gardener in me cried out for relief from winter, I never imagined times would turn so precarious.

But now it's been six weeks since we've had a half inch of rain and almost eight weeks since an inch has fallen. We are well below our normal for this time of year, and on top of that, May was the hottest on record. Not a good mix of conditions for the garden or the gardener. The ground has become dust dry even with endless watering (fortunately, we do not yet suffer from water shortages), and the plants are beginning to toughen up and stop growing. In addition to that, the early heat has caused plants that normally bloom in July or even August to rush headfirst into unexpected flower. Crape myrtles and butterfly bush are two such plants, and even some chrysanthemums have decided it's time to think about blooming. Although these latter have been pinched back and are only four inches tall, several varieties have set buds already.

This week on Tuesday there were 1.6 inches of rain, yesterday another 0.3 inch, and today 0.5 inch, bringing us almost 2.5 inches this week and still not enough in my opinion. It appears that the rain will continue on into the evening, so perhaps we will get 3 inches in all for the week. That is a goodly amount, no doubt, but the ground is in such severe water debt that it may have come too late. Most lawns in the area have turned into dormant hayfields, and their recovery until fall is questionable. Now it is better for them to stay dormant until that time. If we can believe what the weather diviners say (an improbable likelihood at best), we are in for a week of 90-degree, rainless weather.

How will the plants respond to this mixture of good (rain) and bad (heat) news? Have they already set their biological clocks for fall? Stiffened up their foliage, hardened their cell walls? Will they break new foliage or simply sit and sulk? Well, I guess we will have to wait to find out where this will lead. There is little to be done about the random acts of nature.

I spent yesterday morning transplanting to the garden in an attempt to take advantage of the expected rain. There is no telling what will really happen. I have had a number of rock garden plants sitting around in pots either growing up from recent divisions or hardening off from their overwinter stay in the greenhouse. Yes, I am still trotting plants out of the greenhouse from last year's propagations. In addition, I am still putting out seedlings started earlier this year: lychnis, violas, and sunflowers. I might note that in spite of this week's rain, the ground is surprisingly dry.

When it rains I try to catch up on the never-ending job of weeding. Again this week I went over the gravel paths for what must be the fourth or fifth time already this year. Considering how hot, dry, compacted, and inhospitable gravel seems to be for plants, an awful lot of stuff sprouts in it. Most of the weeding consisted of taking out columbine, yellow-leaved feverfew, toadflax, and even a few real weeds like sourgrass.

I noticed a newcomer sprouting in the gravel and decided to leave the four little seedlings in place for a while. I'll probably end up transplanting them later. They are *Calamintha nepeta* (also called *Calamintha nepetoides*) and appear to be growing just as nicely in the gravel as the parent plant does in its bed. This is a member of the mint family, but by no means an invasive one. Clausen and Ekstrom, in their book *Perennials for American Gardens*, say that it should be planted alongside paths, "where a passing touch will release the delightful scent of the foliage." They didn't say anything about growing it *in* the pathway, but that seems to be where it wants to grow. The fragrance is a bit like catnip, but Bruno sees very little sense in disturbing *Calamintha* when he can have nearly the real thing in *Nepeta mussinii* growing only yards away.

In spite of the heat and general lack of rain (or maybe because of it), some plants are doing quite nicely. The notable bloomers this week are daylilies, most of which I've grown from hybrid seed, and real lilies. There is no plant like a daylily, in my opinion, and to be without them would be akin to moral bankruptcy. Although normally thought of as full-sun plants, one of my named cultivars ('Commandment') is planted in full shade and blooms with enough exuberance to just about kill itself every year. But it doesn't. Other plants in partial shade bloom just as well as those in full sun. The current lack of water has not bothered them a bit (it seems), and they are all striving to outdo each other. I bought a new variety this week at Behnke's, the local plant palace. This cultivar, 'Charvel', has a large, deep yellow flower of heavy substance—like lemon peel. I think the ranks of daylily cultivars are vastly overpopulated, and I would expect that no one could find this variety even if s/he looked for it. That is why I do not go into an exhaustive listing of the varieties I grow. Many of them I selected sight unseen from catalogs based entirely upon descriptions, and others, as I say, I grew from seed. I think it is nearly impossible to grow a bad daylily. While it is preferable to see what you are going to get beforehand, it is not absolutely necessary.

Real lilies are a bit more difficult for me to handle. For one thing, they are not as easy to grow as daylilies. I know this for a fact. Daylilies grow no matter what, but lilies grow only if they damn well want to. Another reason is that lilies come in a vast, complicated assortment of sizes, shapes, colors, bloom times, and cultural necessities. I have to think long and hard about what, where, and how I'm going to plant them. Daylilies just go in the ground and that's that. Almost any combination will do.

My favorite lilies are the oriental sorts because they have a fragrance that knocks my socks off even when I'm barefoot. *Lilium regale* is one of the easiest, cheapest, and best, I think. This is a perfumer, flooding the evening air with a heavy, dense cloud that overwhelms the senses. They are an added incentive to throw myself on the ground near them to weed until it becomes too dark to see, all the while smelling the great fragrance. If I were less inhibited, I would roll around in the lily patch much as Bruno rolls in his catmint. I see the point in it!

Another lily I greatly admire is 'Green Magic', which looks like a regale lily with a few extra feet of height and flowers tinged with green where the yellow would be. This is classified as a trumpet-type Aurelian lily and is apparently derived from species not including *L. regale*. So, although they look essentially the same, they aren't. (I find lily classification as idiotic as that for roses, but I like lilies so I simply ignore their classification. Roses I ignore completely.)

Last fall I planted out some bulbs of *Lilium candidum* and was sorely disappointed this spring. It wasn't that they didn't come up, because they did quite nicely. But about the time they started to bloom they were stripped to absolutely nothing overnight. The slugs liked the lilies better even than the hostas next to them. Total overnight destruction is not something I can handle. I don't move that fast. Maybe if the slugs had eaten only half the plant, I could have responded. But when the whole thing is gone in the blink of an eye, I say what's the point of growing it? Not even seedlings go that fast. This lily tastes too good to slugs and so must go. Contrary to rumor, this is not a slug farm.

Another lily that does exceedingly well is an Asiatic one called 'Ming Yellow', which is a rich golden yellow. I've had the same plants for eight or ten years and have treated them about as badly as anything could be treated, and yet they come back every year. They never need staking or watering or anything. About six years ago, when I was thinking of building the new rock garden, I decided they were expendable and buried the site in a foot of dirt and some sand. The next year they came up as if nothing had happened and bloomed just as happily as if they liked being buried an extra foot. Then five years ago, after rethinking the rock garden a bit, I planted ornamental grasses right over the top of the lilies. As the grasses slowly filled in over the years, I just assumed they would crowd out the lilies. Not so. The lilies squeeze up between the narrow grass stalks and emerge as if they loved it. I keep meaning to plant more lilies in the grass hedge, but I haven't gotten around to it yet. Maybe next year.

OK. I guess that's enough on lilies. Well, maybe one more item. Last November I told you about repotting my three bulbs of *Lilium* 'Casa Blanca'. This is their second year in the ten-inch pot. The plants are just as healthy looking as they were last year, but each bulb is going to produce just a single flower instead of the fifteen-to-twenty six-inch-diameter blooms of last July. I think they would have been better off if I'd planted them out in the garden instead of repotting them. The insurance policy I took out on them last fall, three bulbs of an Asiatic hybrid called 'Sterling Star', turned out to be a disaster. They bloomed early, perhaps because of the heat, and the flowers are a dirty white—there is almost nothing worse in flowers than a muddy white color—and have brown spots in the throat. Not a pretty sight at all. Perhaps the heat also affected the whiteness. Whatever the problem, I will most likely plant them out in some awful place, hoping they will die of shame.

I've already placed my order for three more bulbs of 'Casa Blanca' to pot up this fall for next summer. Then they will go into the garden to join this year's bulbs.

And speaking of bulbs, I have been inundated by catalogs. It is far, far too early to be forced to think about next spring. Every year around April or May, when the catalogs start descending like acid rain, I say to myself, "Self, there will be no more bulbs bought. No how. No way." And then, instead of dumping all the catalogs in the recycling bin, I dump them where I am most likely to be tempted by their seductive pictures—the living room couch. Here, night after night, as I watch television, I pour over them trying to find just the right combination of bulbs at a fair price. It is not easy, and my heart really is not in any mood to worry about next year so soon. Can't someone make it a capital crime to disperse bulb catalogs before September?

As I grow older and with each pass through the gauntlet of the catalog season, I become more steadfast in my ability to withstand seduction. But who's perfect? And so I will order a few things this year, as always. So far my list includes *Eremurus*, or foxtail lilies, which are not bulbs at all but thick, fleshy roots sold in their dormant state. I greatly admire these members of the lily family for they shoot straight up and produce a succession of flowers from bottom to top. I've had mixed success in the past with these overwhelming plants. Mostly the roots appear not to make it through the winter, which is not the least bit surprising because they grow in warm, arid regions in dry, sandy, stony soil. You wouldn't think they could grow an inch in our sticky clay. For two years, though, I've had three plants of the garden variety called 'Shelford hybrids' that have made it through the winter and into bloom. These are planted between the large rock garden and the grass hedge in soil that has been heavily amended with sand. Here their lemon yellow flowers are attractively highlighted by the deep green of tall switch grass (*Panicum virgatum* 'Strictum'). When the foxtail lilies stop blooming they disappear from view—both literally and figuratively. They die down almost immediately after flowering and are invisible when not in bloom.

Also on the list are some fall-blooming crocus, including *C. speciosus* and *C. sativus*, the saffron crocus. I've grown both, but the color form of my *C. speciosus* was not good, and the plants scarcely ever bloomed, so I will try them again and hope for better results. Of *C. sativus* there is never enough, so more seems in order.

I've decided not to buy any more daffodils, except maybe some dwarf species for the rock garden. And I decided several weeks ago absolutely, positively not to buy any more tulips, so I stopped looking at their marvelous pictures. Today, however, in a new bulb catalog, I saw a picture of an assortment of pink tulips that would be positively, absolutely perfect in my front garden next spring. Someday, if I try long enough, maybe I'll be able to grow the damn things.

Week Four

Each gardening year has its own unique character, or personality, and often its own set of associated characters as well. By characters, I mean living beings other than the plants, but not counting the gardener or his friends and visitors. By the end of spring I can usually surmise what is likely to be the most abundant creature in the garden, and I practice the Chinese system of associating each year with animals. Unlike the Chinese, however, I label my year with the most abundant pestilence or sometimes, the most striking presence in the garden. For example, last year was the Year of the Earwig. In thirteen years I had scarcely seen an earwig, and last year they were everywhere and in everything. This year nothing!

Several years ago it was sowbugs that came from nowhere and were into and under every conceivable container in the garden. The yard has seen slug years several times. Japanese beetles were devastating only once. One year it was cicadas, not that they did much damage, but their invasion elevated the general populace (and the media) to near hysteria. Another year it was fleas, but that was largely Bruno's problem, and mine only indirectly.

I had not known what to label this year until only recently. Neither the sowbugs nor the slugs nor the despised gypsy moth have amounted to a pittance. There have been more ticks than I've ever seen before, but not enough to have a year named after them. The mosquitoes, too, have been worse than I can ever remember, which is odd because it has been so dry that there is no free-standing water in which they can breed. It may be that my numerous water sources attract them, for I have a large pond behind the house, a small pond in the large rock garden, a dolphin fountain on the wall, three water containers on the balcony, a half-barrel buried near the grass hedge, several cachepots in hidden spots, a birdbath, and a rain barrel. The mosquitoes may come to the water, but they cannot breed in these places for several reasons. For one thing, the ponds and half-barrel have fish, and as anyone who keeps fish can tell you, nothing escapes their ever-searching mouths. The birdbath and balcony containers dry up too quickly to allow breeding or are easily flushed when I replenish their water. I flush the wall basin and cachepots every few days so that anything living in there ends up as water and nourishment for the plants beneath it. And finally, the rain barrel is drained into the pond once a week (when it rains, that is), but if it isn't, I put a slight film of vegetable oil on the surface to kill the larvae. Oddly enough, mosquitoes are pests only down at the north end of the garden, which is where the least amount of water is. They are most annoying when I stand in one place watering or squat for a time weeding. I guess the answer is just to give up weeding.

I will not call it the Year of the Mosquito, though, for they have not been as numerous as the chipmunks. These spunky little rascals have been so common that I'm starting to see them everywhere and every day. Today I saw several run across the lawn. Yesterday, two ran up the drainpipes. Several times I've seen one in the driveway as I've driven in. They can't all be the same one, either, as I've already found two dead bodies in the garden. These were the work of my companion, Bruno, who is more interested in meat on the hoof than tuna in a can. I do not blame him in the least, nor do I consider this some sort of unholy cat crime against nature.

We humans have so botched up the natural world around us that one chipmunk (or 100) more or less is totally insignificant in the scheme of things. I genuinely do not like to see death, but then I remind myself many times over that I did not make life's rules. The addition of one cat to the property pales in comparison to the wholesale destruction caused by the customary building practices around here. A one- or two-hundred-acre tract is bulldozed with the loss of the entire fauna (a microecosystem) to a six-inch depth, and the topsoil is sold. Then the entire area is graded to control water runoff, thus altering streams, water tables, and who knows what else. Then the entire area is built over, four or five houses to the acre, plus asphalt roads, and the final affront is to sod the entire subdivision with introduced grasses and plant silver maples, yews, and azaleas. To add a cat, or even a hundred cats, to this holocaust does not add a whit to the destruction.

A garden can be a haven for animals, of course, and mine appears to be one. Fortunately, several acres of the properties behind mine form part of a drainage that is undeveloped. It is by no means a bastion of native vegetation, consisting, as it does, of introduced plants, but it forms a shelter belt of sorts. (It is apparently too small an area to house deer, a circumstance for which I am most grateful.) My guess is that the reason my garden is relatively full of animals is because the garden, in its complexity of plantings and water features, has created a sanctuary that compliments the much larger shelter area. It would not be bragging (I hope) to say that the garden that exists today is a thousand times more ecologically complex than when I took the place over. Then there was lawn, the silver maple, the wisteria, the two Japanese maples, the tulip poplar, a few apple trees, and that was about all. Now there is free-standing water in many forms, tall shelter, thick shelter, woodpiles, brush piles, rock piles, woodsy soils, sandy soils, and food of all kinds in seeds, flowers, and even bulbs. Not only that, but I scarcely use any chemicals (even fertilizer) in the garden and none on the lawn. (I can only guess how many chemicals were drenched on the soils over the very long period that this area was in apple production. A much scarier thought, really, than chipmunk body counts.)

In spite of the chipmunks, I think this is not the Year of the Chipmunk. Nor is it the Year of the Frog, although they have been extremely abundant as well. One morning I counted seven large green frogs (the species) sitting at the edge of my big pond. Every time I walk by the pond, I hear frantic *kerplunks* as they dive headfirst for their watery safety. Not only do I have green frogs but tree frogs and leopard frogs as well. (One year, I recall, was christened the Year of the Toad. They were everywhere, and it was impossible to do anything without accidentally killing some. I really felt bad about that, but once again, I did not create the problem of toad overpopulation. I just helped solve it.) The frogs are present, in part, because of the aforementioned drainage. Apparently almost any pond will attract frogs from places unknown. Several of my friends have ponds in built-up subdivisions, and these became frog-havens within a year of construction.

Nor is it the Year of the Mouse, though there have been a few of those around in spite of Bruno. If you've read my previous book, you may remember the distinctive mouse varieties I've identified: the stove mouse, the aquatic mouse, the wall mouse, the sunflower mouse. To these may now be added the lawn mower mouse and the dashboard mouse.

The lawn mower mouse is an almost fortnightly occurrence. I can be fairly certain that every time I attempt to mow the lawn, I will find a mouse nest in the motor housing of the mower. It is a pain for both the mouse and myself that I have to remove a nest every time I want to use the mower. If I don't, the choke gets stuck on high, and I am at full throttle for the entire job. I prefer to adjust the mower to as slow a speed as will get the job done. No more. The mouse and I fight over this, and I'm sorry to say that the mouse loses—every time. Usually she scurries out as soon as I pull the mower from the shed. Several times there has been a rapid exodus upon starting the engine. On a few occasions I've removed dead mice and mouse babies. The life of a gardener (or a mouse, for that matter) is not easy, and no one ever claimed it would be.

The dashboard mouse has just struck this week, and I'm afraid I may be in for either an expensive mouse-removal bill or a smelly car.

Neither one will be pleasant. One day I noticed the rather pungent odor of mouse in my car. As you might guess after my many run-ins with mice, I can smell them a yard away. They saturate their living environment with this odor, which I suppose is urine but really don't care to know. After the smell came the nesting material when I turned on the vent fan one morning. Mice use whatever is at hand to construct their nest, and in this instance it was foam-rubber gasketing and what appeared to be wood shavings (I still can't figure out where they came from). Luckily, I could see a wad of nest when I looked into the vent grill, so it was just a matter of prying off the cover and removing the nest. Which I did. Then I turned on the fan to blow out what I could, which then required that I vacuum the car. End of story? Nope! Not on your life.

This morning when I got into the car I could smell mouse—larger than life. I turned on the fan and out blew clouds of dust, foam bits, and wood shavings. Apparently, the mouse is firmly entrenched in the dashboard and there to stay. I can't get at any other parts than I've already gotten to. The area is completely shielded from the engine compartment by a steel wall. I guess the mouse gets in and out from underneath the car, but I don't see why it goes to all that trouble. I turned the heat up full blast this morning and let it blow for about five minutes (it was 93 degrees outside so I stayed out of the car, naturally). I don't know if this will do any good. As I said, the car could be a little smelly this week.

But back to the year. This is definitely the Year of the Bird. They are by far the most populous invading organisms here. Not that they are bad, mind you, except when they plug up the chimney or when too many of them land on things that can't support their weight, such as dahlias. There has been a lot of breakage this year, which I take in stride (mostly because I don't have a gun). Regardless of this slightly negative bird behavior, never in my long and incredibly boring, overworked life have I seen so many birds doing so much work and having so much fun while at it.

I am not an avid birder, so you will have to forgive me if I can't get the names just right, especially on the sparrows and finches. They all look alike to me. But there has been an assortment of odd birds this year, and combined with the quantities, this has provoked the taxonomist in me to better standards of observation.

I've already told you about the chimney birds, who, by the way, are doing just fine. They've got the chimney nicely, totally impacted once again. (Another bill to add to that when I have to have the dead mouse removed from the dashboard.) But that is only the beginning.

Early on this year, I noticed birds doing an awful lot of investigating about the place. At first it was some doves in the juniper right outside my living room window. It is not unusual at all to have a pair around the place for most of the year, but they've never been so bold before. On some days I could have reached out and touched them (with a three-foot pole) if the window weren't in the way. They didn't nest in the juniper, but they seemed to be rather partial to it. The juniper was attractive in turn to a small, finchlike pair and then to some robins.

I noticed that many of the other conifers suddenly sprang to life whenever I walked by. This had not happened before, so I was genuinely startled every time a bird came barging out of a nest. A lot of damage could be done if a bird bashes you full throttle in the face. (Well, OK, maybe not in my case.) These nesting birds are all finches, I believe, judging from the reddish markings on the males, who stay close to the nest.

One fine day I noticed an enormous woodpecker on my maple stump and was surprised to say the least. It was a pileated woodpecker. I've scarcely seen half a handful in my life. Then not much later a common flicker was pecking around the same stump. There are many good reasons to leave dead and dying stuff in your yard rather than being too tidy. Surprises such as these are one of them.

The water sources I provide are great attractions for birds, and often the smaller the source, the better the birds like it. Not many days ago there was a flock of six or eight goldfinches all bathing in the pond in the large rockery. These are one of my favorite birds because of their bright sunflower yellow color. Goldfinches are attracted to the seeds of composites, especially rudbeckias, and I prefer to let them go to seed rather than keeping the garden tidy by cutting back the spent flowers when they've finished blooming.

Even more spectacular in coloration were the northern oriole and his mate who came to bathe in the sprinklers one hot and otherwise dusty evening. The males of this species are burnt orange and soot black with white markings and are easily the most brilliant birds to visit my yard. This is only the second pair I've seen; the first nested in the tulip poplar overhanging my deck.

Returning to the rockery pond for a moment, I met another pair of birds there that I'd never seen in the garden before. This pond can't be seen from the pathway as I built a steep embankment to hide it from view. Sometimes, when I'm adventurous, I sneak up on the pond to see what birds are bathing. This can be a two-way surprise because the birds frequenting the pond can't see me and I can't see them. Then suddenly we both see each other and anything might happen. One day last week I was walking down to the shed to get something, when suddenly there was a great commotion near the rockery pond. The air erupted in unaccustomed sounds, and I wasn't certain but that the end of the earth was at hand. I was surprised—no, I think scared witless is putting it more accurately—when two great black shadows lumbered out of the depression and took off with great fright. Mostly mine. The birds were only crows, but being surprised out of a stupor by big, black, flapping objects is always good for an accelerated heartbeat or two. Or three.

One bird I haven't seen this year but that occasionally stops by for a fish fry is the green heron. This bird is majestic in its wily stalking, and I once watched, completely captivated for half an hour, while one slowly approached the big pond. When it grabbed one of my large goldfish, I jumped up and started casting aspersions on its heritage. It came back several more times that week, and I've seen others in ensuing years. For some reason they have not been about the place this year. Which is odd because one would think that a fishing bird would be on the lookout for aquatic habitats. Mine is one of the few in the area.

All things considered, I have decided to call this the Year of the Bird. Their presence has been more noticeable than in any year I can remember, and this despite a cat who lurks about the place, taking as hors d'oeuvres any nestlings that fall to the ground. In fact, I can tell where the nests are by the birds' raucous chastising of Bruno as he walks innocently past a nest he never suspected. Sometimes nature exists in spite of humans and their domesticated animals. Maybe it exists just *to* spite them.

9

JULY

This has been a waffling week, a week of pendulous swings; much more like spring than the summer we are supposed to be in. First cool, then hot; slightly wet, but mostly dry; gratuitously depressing, then slightly uplifting; the rejection of all things gardening, then acceptance of reality; progress and regress. In short, a week as typical as almost all the others since the beginning of time—only precipitously closer.

The heat this summer seems, on the whole, to be more bothersome than in most years, and in talking to other gardeners, I've openly wondered if its effect has been the same for them—or if it's just me approaching the intolerance of old age. The consensus seems to be that the heat is the most oppressive factor this summer, followed by the lack of rain. Perhaps we sense the stress under which our gardens have come.

When the garden received 0.3 inch of rain early in the week, the world seemed almost fine. There were cool days and overcast skies to help. The plants seemed to perk up, turn green, and look like real plants.

Gardening might be worth it after all, or so it seemed. Then back up to the nineties. Bright apple green turned to dull dry-grass green, and we began to wonder again. Is this the beginning of the end of the garden?

Stress due to lack of moisture. Stress for the plants and for the gardener.

One theory has it that the heat arrived so early (we had, after all, the hottest May on record), that there was no period of acclimatization for either the plants or the gardener. From 50-degree late-winter weather to 90-degree summer heat: a slap in the face with a hot washrag and that was that. There wasn't even enough time for iced tea to thin the blood.

Stress due to heat, pure and simple.

Another theory is that our eastern biorhythms are totally disrupted due to lack of rain. Whereas we would normally be working in the garden doing garden things, we are now all tied up in watering—a problem about which we scarcely ever have to worry. Now we must fret about alternatives that western gardeners respond to automatically. Do we water in the morning or the evening? If we are supposed to water in the morning is it all right to water at night because we are already at work by sunup? On the weekend can we water at midday even if the sun is shining? How much do we water? The obligatory one inch a week? A half inch twice a week? If we water one inch a week and the soil is bone dry in two days, do we not water for five more days? Why are there so many rules about watering anyway? Nature waters whenever it wants to, and the plants seem to do just fine. You see, the decisions soon become overwhelming to the poor gardener who just wants to pull weeds and think pleasant thoughts about the world around him.

Stress due to deviation from the normal!

I suppose the unrest among us eastern gardeners is a combination of all these factors: lack of rainfall, heat, deviation from the normal way of life. Whatever the cause, unrest because of our physical environment has been the topic of conversation among most people I know, both gardeners and nongardeners alike.

Supposedly, this year's weather has been some sort of unnatural act, an abnormality of inhuman proportion. The real problem, I surmise, is that there is no such thing as normality when it comes to the weather or to nature in general. Somehow we humans perceive a weather pattern and then convince ourselves that this is the normal state of things. Ever after, weather is judged by this self-determined yardstick.

Let me give you an example from my own simple background. My first two winters in the Washington, D.C., area are so strongly identified with freezing cold, icy winds, and bouts of snow that my idea of a normal winter here suggests something intermediate between Iceland and Siberia. Since then there have been many more mild winters than severe, but because my first were severe, that is my idea of how they all should be. I've been amazed, then, by the last few winters. Somehow it doesn't seem natural for the temperature to be in the forties when it ought to be hovering between 30 degrees below zero and cryogenic.

As a transplanted northern Californian who has also spent five years in Florida, my gardening psyche is somewhat confused as to what constitutes normal weather. I lived in San Francisco from age three to nine, and my entire concept of that area is of cool, drippy fog interrupted by occasional sunny, cheerful, magnificent days. This is my San Francisco memory bank of what normal is. Then we moved across the bay to San Anselmo with its Mediterranean climate of hot, dry summers and mild, wet winters. This is my San Anselmo memory bank. When I travel to California, most often at Christmas, I still expect, after forty years, that San Francisco will be foggy and cool and that San Anselmo will be mild and damp. Invariably, they are both sunny and beautiful. I should know by now that glorious weather is normal for December in the San Francisco Bay Area, but I always expect the weather I recall from childhood.

Occasionally, reality strikes as during my visit this past Christmas when winter was not the weather of anyone's childhood. The week I was there it reached a balmy 13 degrees Fahrenheit, curling everyone's socks—not to mention the water pipes! Surely this must have been an abnormally cold December just as our recent eastern May was an abnormally hot one. Then again, maybe not.

In the overall scheme of nature and recorded weather, we humans have not been around for much time at all. Maybe we have decent records for a hundred years. Most likely we don't. Even if we had records for a thousand years, it wouldn't help any of us figure out climate patterns, because, as I say, we tend to judge all elapsed time by when we individually started thinking about the weather. When we moved to a new house or town for example. Or when we planted our first garden at age forty-seven and a half. Whatever the stimulus, the weather for that memorable year is our point of reference, and from that time on, no matter how many facts challenge our perception, winters are either harsh or mild, summers either wet or dry, all relative to our starting point.

I'm certain that hundreds of studies must have been done on this phenomenon—that millions of dollars have been spent on our perception of the past as it relates to every known aspect of life. I can't cite any of them, however, because the feeling that everything has been studied is just another point of reference picked up during a lifetime. Occasionally I'm reminded as I travel through life's little maze that reference points are simply to get me where I'm going. That is, they shouldn't be taken too seriously. There's a tendency, I find, to believe that the reference point is always the same point no matter where you are.

Nothing could be further from the point.

A lot of gardening (and life) verges on the expected—some sort of idealized optimum—and when this fails to transpire, then we sometimes become a bit petulant and out of sorts. But the garden is, after all, indifferent to itself, and only the gardener perceives its indifference as a personal affront. When the garden lets me down, I try to remember that I do not live in a picture book where some photographer's split-second timing dictates reality, but it is far from easy.

To my mind there are too many pictures and picture books showing the garden in magnificent repose. Although meant to be inspiring, these opulent photographs of even more opulent gardens instill in our imaginations a very unreal expectation of what a garden ought to look like. A pseudopoint of reference, as it were.

A photograph of a garden is a surprisingly limited view, even with a wide-angle lens. If the view is close-up, of course, it is only natural that it would seem limited because it actually is. Nothing difficult to understand here. But rarely do we accept how truly limited such a view is. For one thing, you see only what the photographer wants you to see, and you see it only the way s/he wants you to. Pristine, dew-dropped, well-lit, saturated in color. The photo lacks the richly vibrant overtones of the garden surrounding the subject. Such as weeds, slugs, damaged foliage, blank, empty places in the border, knocked-over dahlias, places where the dog made a few mistakes, places where the lawn mower leaped the bounds a bit. The photo is peripherally vacant.

An overview of the garden can be just as deceiving, if not more so, as a close-up. A camera lens does marvelous things for a garden if you know how to use one (which I don't, by the way). From certain angles a shot can extract all the empty space from a garden and cram the plants into a sea of uniform beauty. Sort of like condensed soup. Or, if you're far enough away, the rich "overtones" again can be lost to view. Lighting can so dramatize a two-dimensional photograph (or slide) that you might be surprised to know that you were standing in the same place the photo was shot.

I say these things not to disparage photography nor to malign fine gardens but to suggest that just because you see a fantastically glorious, completely breathtakingly stunning garden in a photograph does not mean that it really exists as such on God's earth. Trying to imitate these sights, which I have been doing for years, by the way (with total frustration), is one of the biggest and most confounding point-of-reference mistakes you could ever make. It is like trying to create an exquisite wine by aging window cleaner in an oak cask.

I am frequently discouraged when I see pictures of plants or gardens in books, especially when I can compare the photos directly to my own garden. I bemoan the fact that the garden doesn't look anything like it ought to according to such books, nor would it ever grace pages designed to epitomize the height of gardening endeavor. But I am probably wrong about this, as most of us are in our self-appraisals. With dramatic lighting, the proper moment, and some skill, it is probable that an expert photographer could make a silk purse even from my garden.

I try to believe this, anyway, when the garden disappoints me. I squint my eyes to enhance my tunnel vision, narrowing in on the good views, excluding the peripheral claptrap. I envision select vistas as a photographer might and say to myself that with the correct lens and maybe a low angle I could extract a certain degree of beauty from the garden. Sometimes this psychological approach doesn't work and I quit the garden for a few days, stomping off in ungrateful rage or resignation. But sometimes the approach does succeed, and then I am inspired to work even harder in an attempt to achieve the ultimate in the picturesque garden style.

The trick to gardening is to develop your own sense of focus when viewing the garden.

Week Two

If you are one of those people who loves to dwell on the pain and suffering of others, then you should enjoy the following story very much. It is a sequel to the adventure with wasps I related only too short a while ago. It is not much of a garden story, but if you dine alfresco it might give you some pause for caution. I call this story, "Man Bites Wasp, Sort Of."

Three of us were dining on the rooftop terrace of a friend who rents in the old part of Georgetown. The ambience was that of a secluded tree house or an exclusive club—dining in the treetops with the squirrels and birds. It was a balmy, warm evening as we began our feast of smoked chicken and ratatouille.

As I placed the first succulent morsel of chicken in my mouth, I noticed a shape rapidly descending toward the gaping abyss. The shape was just to the corner of my eye, but I knew instinctively what it was because there had been several yellow jackets circling about for nearly an hour while the chicken cooked. If anything, they were probably hungrier than I. This, I sensed of the approaching engagement, was not going to end well.

At first I couldn't tell if the wasp actually met the chicken in my mouth or if it took a last-second fade to the left after examining my tonsils at close range.

Then I knew.

The chicken started fighting back. Some decision as to what to do next had to be made and rather quickly.

Knowing something of the behavior of wasps, I reckoned that if I closed my mouth to spit the wasp out, I risked irritating her. One does not do that to a wasp who's sitting on one's tongue having a seemingly quiet dinner. Better to leave the mouth open and flick the wasp out with a finger. Since it would have been bad manners to ask for the use of someone else's finger, I used my own. Sadly, my tongue, in its own involuntary manner, rose to the occasion by twisting just as my finger flicked and the result was not unexpected:

Wasp: one point (in the tongue); finger: zero. OUCH!

A new strategy was called for. I gave the marching orders: Mouth, close and spit like bloody hell. Results:

Wasp: two points (in the lower lip); brain: zero.

Eyes water. Tears form. No more. Involuntary prayers begin to well up. Result:

Wasp: three (lip, again); prayer: zero.

And then, with a mighty "phooo—toooo—oot," the wasp was finally winging her way at the speed of sound, crashing headfirst, I hoped, into the nearest brick wall. Unfortunately, in my haste, I had relatively little ability to aim, and so the lucky wasp flew off to relate her version of the story to any nestmate who might be in need of a cheer-up.

Meanwhile, back at the dinner party, I continued to bravely eat on, the lip a little numb and starting to swell, the tongue just sort of apically twitchy. The feeling was the numbness of Novocain surrounding small areas of pain. I was not so much worried about the pain, however, as the possible swelling up of my throat followed by slow asphyxiation. My dining companions, both entomologists who professed some degree of sympathy, kept watch for the remainder of the evening in case I should drop over in a lifeless heap. Under the circumstances, I was anxious to get to the dessert before it was too late.

Surprisingly, the slight pain lasted only through the next afternoon; the swelling, too. By Sunday all was nearly normal except for the inside of my lower lip, which looked as if it might fall off. Unlike the stings of several weeks ago, which itched for almost a week before they let up, there was no itching, just a general sloughing off of skin much as in a blister. Apparently, yellow jacket stings in the mouth are no worse than elsewhere, maybe even better.

My advice to all would-be outdoor diners is to remember that wasps eat, too, and let the biter beware.

I had to face the evidence today and finally admit that my tropical water lily, the nodules of which still reside in a bowl of water on the terrace table, did not make it through the winter. They are still hard, still healthy looking, but I guess if they haven't sprouted by now, it is no use waiting any longer. Even if they were alive, it is too late for them to do any good this year.

That firmly established, there was naught to do but visit Lilypons and pay an exorbitant price for yet another plant. Even though I convinced myself last year that it was well worth the thirty-five-dollar expense to have a tropical water lily, I still have reservations. For the same amount, I could purchase a wonderfully extravagant specimen of *Chamaecyparis* or even a new shirt, but neither, I suppose, would look as good sitting in the middle of the large pond. I've reserved a big space there for the tropical lily, and it will look bare if I don't get one.

If it weren't for the fact that it has become a gardening challenge to overwinter the plant, I probably wouldn't bother. I'd move one of the hardy lilies over to the blank space and make do. But I have another scheme for saving thirty-five dollars (annually), and by Jove if it takes me ten years and four hundred dollars (allowing for inflation) to overwinter one, I am going to do it. This year's scheme is to take my thirty-gallon aquarium—the one that has sat empty for thirteen years—buy a cheap water heater, and put the plant, the aquarium, and the heated water under fluorescent lights. If I keep the nodules at about 70 degrees, I think they might survive. Either that or die. You can never tell with plants, but it's the challenge of the thing, you see. It probably won't cost more than about sixty dollars in parts and electricity the first year to overwinter the thing, and think of all the money I'll be saving. Eventually. If I don't live too long.

So it was with light heart and heavy wallet that yesterday my friend Dee and I drove the thirty miles or so to Lilypons. If you've never been to an aquatic garden, or nursery, it is a unique experience, even if you don't have an interest in water plants. Especially Lilypons. I generally visit the place at least once a year just for an outing.

Lilypons has recently created a display area of formal and informal pools that is attractive and instructive. There are also numerous large earthen growing ponds that hold hardy and tropical water lilies as well as marginal plants. Additionally, and perhaps best of all, are the large ponds of free-ranging lotus, which were in flower in this week of early July. If I had a larger pond I would grow these giants of the flower world, but I have to make do with the small variety 'Momo Botan', that grows only about two to three feet tall. Amazingly, these monstrous, tropical-looking giants are entirely hardy in my area (USDA Zone 6B).

Lilypons first began selling mail-order in 1930 as Three Springs Fisheries. In 1934 it renamed itself after the opera singer Lily Pons. The original business is situated on several hundred acres (not all cultivated) next to the Monocacy River in Frederick County, Maryland, and a smaller nursery is located in Brookshire, Texas. Presumably this is where the tropical water lilies come from for it is much too cold to overwinter them outdoors here.

It was somewhere in the nineties as Dee and I wandered around the growing grounds. Just the right temperature for water lilies. And after giving the place the once-over, we ordered our various and assorted desires. Rather, I should say Dee's order was assorted, I simply bought another 'Red Flare', for which I turned over my eating money for the next two weeks. As this variety worked so well last year, and as I saw nothing I liked better, I decided to stick with the familiar and not try something different. One of the advantages of waiting until rather late in the season to make a selection is that you can see the plant in leaf and bloom.

After placing our orders, we waited in the shade for them to be pulled up from the growing ponds. That's essentially what you get, here, when you buy a water lily—a plant, pulled from the mud, washed, and put in a big plastic bag. They will plant it in a container, but that's extra. I was silently amused (and distressed) by one lady who was handed a very small cardboard box with a bill for almost eighty dollars. She had a great big look of disappointment on her face. Most of her plants were the submerged sorts, and they don't look like anything when you first get them.

A word of warning about water gardening: it becomes rather expensive if you should catch the infamous water bug. I mean there is no end to the ways you can spend money on this sort of gardening. From the construction of the pond itself to the water lilies, lotuses, submerged plants, bog plants, fish, snails, fish food, fish medicine, fertilizer tablets, planting buckets, algicides (and many other water-altering chemicals), filters, pumps, fountains, and books. Of course, if you know an aquatic gardener, s/he will be able to give you all the plants you could ever want because, with the exception of tropical lilies, once you get a water plant you spend the rest of your life removing it from your pond. Remember, you don't have to water these things. They are automatically watered twenty-four hours a day. When the weather is 80 or 90 degrees, water plants have nothing better to do than grow. And grow. And grow.

I guess if you look at water plants as a long-term investment, the initial cost is rather meager. Unless, of course, you just have to have tropical water lilies. Then you'd better be happy with some really good short-term returns.

Week Three_____

It was another dry week. Hot and humid, but dry. No rain whatsoever. I was weeding (the weeds seem to grow fine in this steamy weather) down by what I call Viburnum Walk, which is a grand name for half a dozen doublefile viburnums that I planted three or four years ago. I was weeding with one hand, fending off mosquitoes with the other, and all the while dreaming of falling snow. Ten feet of snow. Snow in July. So that I could sit in the house in perfect peace dreaming of what a decent garden I could make if only I knew how. (Sometimes when reality becomes too real I do these things.)

I was aware, as I weeded, that something was not quite right. (No, it was not snowing.) It's the sort of feeling you get when you're concentrating on something with every ounce of your ability (like killing mosquitoes) and suddenly you feel like someone is standing behind you. Someone maybe with an ice cream cone or more likely an axe. Suddenly you are startled and find that someone really is standing behind you. And you wish *you* had the axe.

I had that feeling as I weeded. But when I looked around there was no one—not even peeking at me through the brush. It's a funny thing, I thought to myself, that someone could be peeking at me through that brush, because there isn't suppose to be any brush there. That is where the wisteria is supposed to be.

It was at this point that I discovered what the problem was. A ten-inch-diameter branch from a nearby mulberry tree had twisted itself out of its crotch and was supported on top of the wisteria. The top of the wisteria at this point could more accurately be called the bottom, though, because it couldn't get much lower. Unless maybe if I cut it off. Even then I would have to dig a hole to do it.

The mulberry tree is one of those neighborly sorts. It started at the eastern fence line long before I moved here and buried the wire fence midway within its trunk. Mulberries are worthless trees in my opinion and are grown only for their growth, if you get my meaning. Some trees are that way, such as silver maples. They grow fast, so people grow them. My neighbor Margaret would have pulled the mulberry up when it was a seedling, she informs me, except that her husband, Jim, wanted it left there. This apparently was before the days when women had anything to say about the garden.

Whatever the past history of the tree, the present history is that it is being cut down the day after tomorrow. Which means, of course, that another shade garden welcomes in the sun. The tree is tall—twenty to thirty feet—and casts a lot of shade. It will not do so much longer.

The cost of removal hovers between two hundred seventy-five and seven hundred twenty-five dollars, depending upon the obviously differing points of view of several tree specialists. And this wonderfully good news is the simple result of not pulling the seedling up twenty or thirty years ago when it wouldn't have cost a dime. The thing about trees is that all are not created equal, and your garden should not become a masterpiece of chance events of the seedy sort—nor a monument to bird doo, either. Some exercise of judgment should be made when trees first appear as seedlings in the garden, and most of them should be pulled up. Gardens are no place for trees unless you happen to have a big garden. At least, that is my view.

When it doesn't rain it really pours around here. Not two days after the first mulberry broke I was in the bathroom when I heard a sound like exploding firecrackers. At first numerous small poppings, then a tearing sound, and then a very long tearing, fall-down-go-boom sound. All humans, you know, lead lives of quiet desperation. In some cases the quiet is deafening. So, as I sat there quietly contemplating the universe, humankind, and all things bright and beautiful, I said aloud so that Bruno could hear (he was outside, by the way): "What the hell is it this time?" Actually I said some other things as well, but that was the essence of what I said.

I didn't find out what happened until later that day. Not that I didn't go out and look. My first impression was that the remainder of the fallen mulberry tree had become unbalanced, given up the fight, and decided to fall over, too. I went to look at it, but it was still standing. No problem.

Since I had been rebuilding some of the soil in Viburnum Walk anyway, now that it was to become a sun-filled garden, I decided to cart a few more loads of compost over from the pile at the opposite end of the garden. I would obviously need some more room in the compost area for all the dead and dying garden that was resulting from the drought and the fallen tree. I wheeled my cart over into the compost compound and began filling it up with nice, dry, crusty compost.

I was aware, as I shoveled from the pile, that something was not quite right. You know, the sort of feeling you get when you are concentrating on something with every ounce of your ability and suddenly you feel like someone is standing behind you. Someone maybe with a cold bottle of beer or more likely a chain saw. Suddenly you are startled and find that someone really is standing behind you.

When I looked around to see who was there, there was no one. Not even peeking at me through the brush. It's a funny thing, I thought to myself, that anyone would be peeking at me through that brush because that is where another mulberry tree used to be. And sure enough— without making this up—half of the mulberry tree that sits on the boundary between my neighbor to the north and me was laying on the ground, sort of. This was a twelve-inch-diameter branch laying as flat on the ground as it could, considering that it had fallen on top of an old apple tree.

The first thing that occurred to me was where I could get the name of a good lawyer. The way I figured it, since at least two inches of the trunk of the tree grew on my property, I was in for another "halfsy" on the tree removal. But such was not the case. Several days later I discovered that the limb had been sawed into lengths and all the refuse removed. I think it was a do-it-yourself job because my neighbor is quite handy with mechanical devices.

Now if I could just get him to cut down the remainder of the tree to the east, this story might eventually have a happy ending.

I finally broke out of the lethargy and stupor induced by the hot, humid, rainless days we've been having. Normally during these periods I'm active, at least I have been in the past, even carting soil and mulch all about the place and generally enjoying it immensely. That's in a normal year, though, when the garden looks halfway decent. This year the garden looks mostly indecent, and putting a lot of back-breaking, bone-crunching, finger-cutting work into it seems mostly like a waste of time. Who wants to put out fresh, tender, young seedlings into a stew pot? It doesn't seem right somehow.

The days I chose to work were certainly no different from any other days in the week. No hotter and no cooler. I somehow managed to break through the inertia and charge off into the abyss without really knowing why. This happens often in the course of the gardening year, and sometimes the tireder I am when I get home the faster I get out and start working. It doesn't make much sense, really. Some days, by the time I finish my day job, I can scarcely believe I'll live to see the next day. Other days I do not even care to. My eyes are bleeding from microscope work and manuscript reading, my mind is numb, my fingers are torn with paper cuts from reading the endless (and mindless) memos that circulate throughout all branches of the federal government. My fervent desire is only to get home so that I can say good-bye to Bruno and end it all.

But then I get home, pay my respects to Bruno, and suddenly feel as if the garden is calling for help. "Just a little work," it sighs, "just a weed or some watering, maybe a little mulch, move a plant, trim the lawn, deadhead. Anything," it says to me. "Just do something to make me look a little nicer." I must be a sucker for this plea, because as soon as I change into my shorts, I'm off to do its bidding.

This week it was refurbishing the bearded irises. Last spring (or was it fifty years ago?) I remarked upon the interesting combination of color made by Burkwood's broom and the brick-colored bearded iris called 'Danger'. The effect worked well, and when this happens, the gardener should do one of two things: (1) pull everything out and try again, because it is a well-known garden axiom that anything that works well is a mistake and will never happen again, or (2) fool him or herself into thinking that if a little worked well, then more will work even better.

With the irises I chose the latter, probably because of heat stroke, but who really knows. Right after 'Danger' bloomed, I went out and marked it with string to distinguish it from several other varieties of pink irises that were blooming at the same time and that had all grown together. This was amazing foresight on my part, for little did I know that I would actually get around to doing anything with the irises this year. It's unusual to say the least when I think of something and do it, all in the same year.

This week, after work one night, I went out in the 90-degree heat, dug up the irises (there were six varieties in all), lumped them by color, divided them, cut out the iris borers from the tubers that were infested (and some always are), and replanted a big patch of 'Danger' in front of the broom. Next spring the patch should be about two feet deep and four feet across and maybe have one flower, but the year after they will be much better. I hope. There's just no telling with bearded irises.

Gardening sometimes requires the skill of a plastic surgeon, and the project I undertook today was just such a piece of delicate surgery.

First came the selection of all the proper tools, laid out in precise rows: axe, spade, spading fork, hammer, trowel, pruning shears, buckets (no, not for the blood), burlap, crowbar (just in case, you never know when you're going to need a crowbar during surgery), garden cart (to carry off the pieces), and a will of iron.

The job: a stolonectomy, somewhat like a nose job only on the other end. Removal of 50 percent of the below-ground roots and above-ground foliage.

The reason: *Panicum virgatum* has become wayward; obsessively demanding—and aggressively taking—more space than it deserves.

The grass hedge is definitely becoming too much of a good thing. Back in March I began mentally wrestling with its expansiveness and the amount of labor involved in removing the spent winter foliage and in keeping its summer growth upright. No matter how much of it I stake, portions still fall over at the least amount of rain. I've been pondering how to retain the hedgelike character of the grasses while taking some out and increasing the diversity associated with it. The bed is essentially sixty-five by four feet of vertical undulations. Removing some of it would not hurt, I reasoned, if I could leave the overall character of the hedge intact.

The structure of the hedge, on a west-to-east diagonal, is as follows: a cluster of five variegated Japanese silver grasses, two parallel ten-foot rows of switch grasses (red switch in front, tall switch in back), a cluster of three silver grasses, another ten-foot row of switch grasses, a cluster of three more silver grasses, a ten-foot row of feather reed grasses with white-flowering fountain grass in front, and finally, another cluster of three silver grasses.

The restructuring, I decided, would take place on the westernmost section of red switch grasses, from which I would remove an eighteen-inch strip. The vertical dark green stems and leaves of this five-foot-tall grass would make a nice backdrop for a planting of lemon yellow daylilies and regular lilies (or lilylilies, as I sometimes call them to avoid confusion). Already, on the eastern end, was the clump of 'Ming Yellow' lilies that I'd tried to bury to death years back. They are attractive, blooming as they do in the hedge; then, when the flowers are gone, the lily's stems disappear into the greenness of the grass. New lilylilies would add a touch of color to the western part of the hedge in June, and the leaves of the daylilies would compliment the color and shape of the grass. Then they would bloom from late June into mid-July. The addition of four to six weeks of color, backed by the grasses, might not detract too much from the even-handed greenness of the hedge. If I get really ambitious I might even dig in a few dozen daffodils for color in April or May. These would be placed between the grasses and the daylilies. They would come up and bloom before the grass even thought of emerging, and about the time they died back, the grasses, daylilies, and lilylilies would cover over their crummy tops. I've used daylilies elsewhere with daffodils, and it is a good combination.

I admit that this is not the correct time to divide grasses, but then that is the reason for the elaborate surgery, which is not so much a division as an expulsion of parts of the plant. Normally, in the early spring after last year's dead tops are removed and just about the time this season's tops start to emerge, I dig up the grass clump's root mass, divide it into chunks, and put a chunk of it back in the same spot. But I don't really want to wait until next spring to start the project, and I've just managed to purchase half a dozen more daylilies on sale. They may as well be growing in their chosen ground all winter long as sitting in their pots. And besides, it is the correct time to divide daylilies. (Actually, anytime is the correct time to divide them.)

Panicum virgatum, in any of its varieties, is a vertical grass, but it does not stay vertical if more than two drops of water or more than one Japanese beetle alights on its foliage. Even though I staked the plants earlier in the year to allow for such contingencies, they are fairly well splayed out by now. My surgery today required cutting the front two-foot-wide row of red switch grass into a one-foot-wide row, moving the stakes inward to keep the patients' insides from falling outside, and then axing out the roots. A simple procedure, really. It was made only slightly more difficult by a pesky yellow jacket that wanted to be in the plants at the same time as I, and I must admit that I am still a little shell-shocked, if you know what I mean. I was taking no chances today and that made the job take longer.

The job was done with a minimum of effort (except for the darting glances every few seconds). I cut down the foliage, removed the roots, turned the soil, added a cartload of compost, and planted the daylilies (the lilylilies are on order and will not arrive until fall). For the daylilies I chose more of 'Charvel', which I'd seen in bloom only a few weeks ago when I bought a single plant. It is tall and blooms from late June into early July. I placed that cultivar in the back row, and a shorter, later-blooming variety called 'Yellow Cheerfulness' in the front. Both flower colors are identical, and the choice of the two varieties was to increase diversity of both bloom height and duration. A little trick I might offer in picking out daylilies at a nursery is to buy the plants with the most individual fans. Each fan can be cut or pulled apart to make another plant. The ones I saw last week were either single or double fanned, so I purchased the double fans and received twice as many plants for my money. And since the nursery had a one-third-off sale, I saved a lot.

By the time I finished today, the grasses looked as if they had not been touched and the bed in front of them looked fresh and new. It is important, I think, when you do cosmetic surgery in the garden to take a little extra care of appearances. Especially when it is still the middle of the gardening year. It doesn't matter so much in spring or fall, but open wounds in the middle of the season might make visitors a little squeamish.

Week Four

May Sarton, in her *Journal of a Solitude*, writes of "that waiting-for-rain tension." The tension here is inescapable. Today capped the seventh continuous day of 95-degree-plus temperatures with nary a touch of rain for sixteen days. It was 100 degrees earlier this afternoon, and the air is now so humid that if I could find a way to wring it out, there would be plenty of water for the garden. I can't and it is totally frustrating.

A horrendous storm that was expected to drown us between 7 and 10 p.m. skirted right around the garden, raining to the east and west (up to five inches, according to the late reports). As they pass through, purportedly hellacious winds are grinding off trees. The weather radar tonight displayed my area as the handle of a dumbbell. Others got rain, wind even, but not me. Just enough breeze to slam the doors shut as it brushed by the house on its way to more important places.

I have been so anxious about the failing health of the garden and its daily dose of sunburn that I am emotionally wrung out. Then a gardening friend went away and asked me to take care of his garden for two weeks. Even if I watered all day long I could not keep both gardens going. I do not really feel up to it. But it was I or nothing, so I will do what I must. Even though I watered my garden all day Saturday and most of Sunday, two days later it looks more like a suburb of the Sahara than an eastern U.S. garden. No amount of water helps when the basic underlying soil is as dry as dust. Even my clay has been sucked dry.

When will this gardening thing ever become easy? Will it ever be at all pleasing? Or is it simply eternal work? Eternal struggle for its own sake? I don't know, but I do grow as weary and discouraged as I have ever been with the gardening life.

Last week I worked in the compost area, and, as usual, the process gave me enough time to ponder a bit and get a tad cranky. Mostly my thoughts have to do with all this infernal racket about landfills, waste, and recycling. It seems to me that if everyone pulled his or her own weight, we wouldn't have a lot of these problems that don't seem to get any better—just worse.

The way life is these days, you'd think everyone is in some kind of hurry to get somewhere and that no one has any time to take care of the business of cleaning up after him- or herself. Apparently the solution to all life's challenges is a big plastic bag and the convenient trashing of anything inconvenient that gets in the way.

Now I am no great fanatic of organic gardening or even of home-grown produce. I grow none myself. Nor do I propose that each and every person becomes a professionally dedicated composter of the highest order. What I *am* proposing is that we don't need to send so much organic material to the landfill where it will become mummified heaps of space-filling, nondecomposing matter. We are going to need more landfills for all the inorganic crap we humans generate (mostly because we keep generating more humans), so the least we can do is handle our own organic material efficiently. There is no point in stressing the land any more than we already do.

I do not consider myself a proponent of the fine art of composting because I am not. It is a great big pain in the pitooty to follow all those directions about layering, fertilizing, achieving meltdown, and so on. I am what you would call an organic recycler—most assuredly not a composter. I simply arrange organic matter in piles, shovel over a few shovelfuls of stuff from the working end of my recycling efforts, and that is that.

I make it a point that no organic matter leaves the property with three exceptions: anything that goes in the toilet (understandably, I hope); brambles such as greenbriar, blackberry, and wild rose; and the native weedy onion and garlic that abound in nearly all gardens in this area. The brambles grow on the wire fences between my neighbors to the west, east, and north. They are part of the reason I've had to establish the various defense lines around the property. Essentially they are narrow hedgerows, or fencerows, that reach out laterally, and, as with the ground runners (ivy, honeysuckle, wisteria, smilax), form the basis of my eternal hacking programs. Without the defense lines, all this greenery would meet in a tangle in the middle of my garden.

I do not compost the brambles because I use my bare hands to sift compost, to work the soil, and for general cleanup. I do not like getting ripped to shreds when I garden, nor do I like kneeling down to find I've put all the weight of my knee on a rose cane. It makes me grouchy. Even so, I find that more and more I use this material, chopped, as mulch for my rough paths where I'm learning not to kneel down. The native onions and garlic I do not compost because they won't compost, they simply grow and multiply by the thousands. If I used such compost, I would be reinfecting the garden every time I improved it.

Although I am reluctant to dispose of this material, it does not amount to more than a compressed bagful of organic matter a year, so I do not consider myself some sort of hypocritical infidel. I certainly do more than 99 percent of my human compatriots, and I aim to tell you about it so you, too, can become an asset to society instead of a liability. The awful sad truth here is that you probably already do all the things I am going to talk about, so I am preaching to the converted. But then again, maybe you are not. I can't afford to take any chances. Even if you do, maybe you could pass this chapter on to people you know who put all their organic matter in plastic bags to be taken away to the landfill. Even better, buy them a copy of this book. They obviously need it.

You're probably thinking that I have very little organic matter to get rid of, and that it's no big accomplishment to hide it under a bush. Well, you're wrong. I've only got a third of an acre, after all, but I am surrounded by trees on three sides, not to mention all the trees I've had taken down. In addition, half the garden is herbaceous perennials (some to five and six feet tall), and all that must be taken down once a year and put somewhere. Then there are the defense lines to contend with and their endless growth. My estimate is that I have at least one pickup truck-load of mashed limbs and heavy stems a year and three truckloads of herbaceous stuff including leaves.

Behind my shed is a space about ten by fifteen feet that used to be a dog pen in the days before I moved here. It is fenced in with chain link, which I detest, but it does the job and is made invisible by the shed, by a planting in front of mixed deciduous shrubs, and by Japanese honeysuckle that weaves all about the place. Even honeysuckle becomes compost at certain times of the year. I do not have fancy structural bins even though I would like to have them. I am much too lazy to build fences to keep compost contained. Instead, I either just pile things up until the law of gravity takes effect, or I store material (rotted fence pickets, stumps, broken stakes, and the like) that needs to be gotten rid of but is organic. The best place to store this type of material is at the bottom of a compost heap, but this requires some forethought. Some of this stuff is stored under the service paths around the perimeter of the property. It is covered in duff and eventually turns to dust.

Right now, for example, part of my pen is lined with four-foot-diameter eighteen-inch-thick wheels of stump from the silver maple. I used most of the tree in my wood-burning stove, but I couldn't split these huge wheels with the sledge and wedges. In fact, I couldn't even move them for a year because they were so heavy. Finally, however, I was able to flip them on edge and roll them over into the compost area to line the inside of the fence. Now, after four years, they are falling apart into the compost and adding a great amount of organic matter. Soon I will have to find other liners for my compost area.

Early on, when I arrived here, I had access to lots of tree limbs and unsplit logs. This was because the trees that were here kept falling over. Since I had no wood-burning stove at the time, I used these logs and branches to hold up my compost piles, but they have long since turned to humus and been redistributed to the garden. I point this out to any of you who have heavy tree parts and even light limbs. Wood rots, too. Especially in hot, humid areas such as I live in. In dry areas your approach would probably be different, but on the other hand, such areas probably produce proportionately less biomass. Considerably less than the incredible amount of growth we see here in our wet eastern deciduous forests and meadows (which become forests in no short order).

One more comment on heavy wood, and then I'll move on to branches. Once I read that the English search out a product called "willow wood" that forms in the crotches of dead limbs and trunks of willow. There was a big old willow on the property when I first moved here, and over the years it has slowly broken and fallen and shattered and shredded itself into nothing but a rotten stump. During many of those years I gathered the willow compost from its crotches and used it in potting soil. Now the stump is all that is left, and it forms one corner of my compost heap—one prop that the maple wheels butt up against. The stump is a melting testimony to decay and enrichment. All the tree's punky and rotten limbs have gone straight into the compost pile to disappear forever—except when they recycle themselves as hostas or daylilies. I point this out simply to emphasize the fact that big organic matter rots just as does the lesser stuff, and there's no sense dumping such materials in a landfill where it won't rot or be any good at all. You may as well find a good use for it; I'm certain you'll be surprised how fast it disappears. Soon you will be going door to door asking, nay begging, folks for logs and chunks of limbs and will have a fine reputation throughout your neighborhood.

Now to branches and limbs and lesser stalks. If turned into a brush pile, itself a good garden oasis for animals, these piles seem to take their time decomposing. I think this is because most of the branches are constantly bathed in fresh, relatively dry air, and little of the pile's organic material is in direct contact with the ground-dwelling microorganisms that aid in decomposition. To speed the process of decomposition, once or twice a year I cut up all such articles into small pieces. The big ones I saw up and use as kindling in the wood-burning stove. When dry it makes a fine quick-to-light fire-starter. Smaller materials are cut with loppers or hand pruners into short lengths and used as mulch on the service paths that parallel the fences and serve as my access to the backs of the beds. Why buy expensive, aesthetic, professionally shredded mulch for the working paths when you can make it yourself? (I still buy yards of the pretty stuff for the front of the beds.)

I suppose you are thinking to yourself, "What a moron he is to spend all that time cutting and lopping when he could buy an expensive chipper/shredder that would do the job efficiently." Well, you are right in a way, I am a moron, but that is in spite of the fact that I don't have a chipper/shredder, not because of it.

I have been reading about chipper/shredders for years and years, but I'm reluctant to invest in one for several reasons. First, because I would be the thing shredded. I, or at least part of me. And I am rather fond of almost all of me, at least at this time in my life. I also do not like the infernal noise or the oily, gassy smell—of machinery, that is. A chipper/shredder is just like a lawn mower, the only difference being that I could never fall headfirst into a lawn mower. At least I don't think so.

When I work I do not always do so to get a job done. Sometimes it is to relax that I take on a job in the garden. Limb-lopping is a good fall chore. When the temperature drops to the forties or fifties and I need a warming-up kind of job, lopping is it. I go into the garden to cut and hack and get my mind back on track. If I am lucky, my mind stays on the track of the limb. Occasionally it doesn't, and I end up thinking a lot about bandages. But I find that a few half hours of cutting now and again reduces almost any pile to matches. I have been putting these bits on my rough paths for thirteen years, and they are still only two inches high. The thing about organic matter is that it's mostly empty space. Once you start treading on it, it all squeezes out and you're left with almost nothing.

Now to the compost pile itself. Mine is simply a pile in which I stack everything that will eventually decompose. Usually I start on the bottom with tree limbs and branches if I want to get rid of them without chopping them up. If not that, then I use some coarse, branchy material like composite stems, ivy trimmings, or Japanese honeysuckle. Then I layer on all the organic matter I can get my hands on (except as noted above), and since my garden is mostly perennials and weeds, there is much material that goes in each and every year. Oddly enough, garden writers do not warn you about trash when they advise you to plant the all-purpose, never-needs-work perennial. It annually needs to be cut, removed, and composted, which amounts to about as much work as growing the same quantity of annuals. But I digress.

My pile is built in the shape of a U. Sometimes it leans more toward a V, and occasionally a Q, but this is only occasionally. The big U allows me to take recycled organic matter (compost) off one end, thus creating a new place to start laying down organic matter. Over the course of a year or two (or six), I slowly move around the U, working with my body positioned in the center, taking out cartloads of stuff to put in the garden and adding new matter as it accumulates to the places I've emptied. When a foot-high layer of new organic matter is in place, I simply take a few shovelfuls of compost from the pile in front, cover the new organic matter with it, and add more organic material on top of that. I generally get to about four feet high at the new place, while the oldest place in the U has shrunk to only two feet. With this system I create a constantly moving organic pile somewhat like a snake eating its own tail. I do not have to flip things from one bin to another.

Another boon is that I work the open face of the pile like a quarry, slicing down through it with the spade. Often I do not cut up elongate herbaceous stems (such as ornamental grasses) when I take them from the garden but simply lay their three-or-four-foot lengths in the pile. In six months, when they are partially rotted, the spade slices through them producing bite-size pieces. This creates a lot of twiggy material in the finished compost, and I used to sift it all through a screen. Now, however, I just shovel it into the cart and every few minutes use my hands as rakes to snag out the most offensive material, which I throw back into the newly cleared area. Eventually, it all wears out. Except for the clam shells and rocks that I've been recycling for about twelve years that haven't worn a speck.

My compost heap is, not to put too fine a point on it, a heap. It is uncovered and in constant shade. It is moistened only by rain. I rarely put fertilizer in it, and then only when I've got an excess cupful that I don't want to bother storing. I scarcely ever turn the pile, relying on the constantly shifting U-shape configuration to shake it up a bit at best. As suggested above, I put nearly all the garden's wastes into it, and from the house I dump old eggs, shriveled potatoes, watermelon rinds (and seeds), paper coffee filters, vegetable parings, dried-up bagels, tea bags (with strings and tags), scrapings from inside the refrigerator, year-old leftovers, excelsior and shredded paper from packages, ashes from the wood stove, leftovers found under the wood stove, and on and on. (Any really good book will tell you what not to put in a compost heap, and there are a lot of such books around.)

I hope I have convinced those few of you who don't already recycle your organic matter that it is worthwhile, simple, efficient, thrifty, healthy, cleanly, practical, stimulating, exciting, and patriotic to do so. It is better than paying someone to cart it away. If it all sounds like too much work, it really isn't, and besides, few of us have anything better to do.

I learned a long time ago that life is what you do while you're waiting to be recycled. So pitch in there and do your share.

10

AUGUST

Week One ————————————————————————————

Thus does one month end and another begin. If July was like August in the reality of weather, then August should be like September. Senescent leaves fall from the tulip poplar and crab apple, and already I have begun to rake them. Panic has set in, for when leaves fall, is autumn not close at hand? I am not ready even to think about it. Summer is not yet a third over!

We are now, according to Washington-area authorities, into our tenth month of above-average temperatures and our third of below-average rainfall. Is this global warming? Or just plain normal weather? I would guess the latter, for as I said only weeks ago, we do not really know what normal is based upon our own brief periods of record keeping.

Earlier in the week we had a half inch of rain that did, if I may be frank and cranky, not a whit's worth of good. It came down in the morning and evaporated in the hot soil. Again, this a.m. a few passing drops hit the ground, immediately turned to steam, and went directly up again. This is not the stuff that gardens are made of.

Begrudgingly, I began watering yesterday, realizing that rain was not waiting in the clouds. It was already too late for a few plants in the rock garden. A lot of these have small needlelike leaves, and it is not always easy to detect when they are under stress. Some plants, such as *Saponaria, Marrubium,* and *Aethionema,* have broad circular leaves (relatively speaking, of course), and if they look happy, I just presume that the narrow-leaved sorts are doing as well. Not so. I have lost the middles (and possibly entireties) of several phloxes, silenes, and pinks. Lost them before I even knew there was a problem. Overnight. This is my fault, of course, for believing that a half inch of steam on Monday would hold the rockery until Saturday. It didn't. So yesterday I laid down an inch of water, and now await the predicted 95-degree weather. The heat and new moisture will now most likely combine to rot out half of the healthy-looking specimens that haven't succumbed to drought. The good point in all this is, I suppose, that next year I can try a lot of new plants.

While on the subject of the rock garden, I have a recurring problem that few, if any, gardeners have to contend with. In fact, most gardeners will think I am quite mad when I explain the problem. It is, nevertheless, a particularly difficult dilemma in the rockery and especially for me because of my innate acceptance of most animals in the garden.

The problem is an annual one that began about five or six years ago when I first started the large rock garden. To explain the problem I must momentarily return to that time and explain the construction of the garden. About twenty cubic yards of heavy clay soil had just been excavated for the foundation of the new addition to my house. The soil was dumped in my driveway, and as anyone who uses a driveway knows, it is tough to park a car on a mountain of dirt. As a double-pronged solution to both removing the soil from the driveway and creating topography for the new rock garden, I moved it to the designated area and mounded and sculpted it over a roughly twenty-by-forty-foot area. Clay soil is not the preferred growing medium for rock plants because of its slow (or nonexistent) drainage. Many such plants come from well-drained deposits of gravel and grit, and their crowns, or necks, thus never become waterlogged. This is an essential fact for growing many alpine plants, and it should come as little surprise that a rockery built solely of clay is the antithesis of the gardener's art.

My plan for the rock garden was to work several inches of sand into the clay, to cover this with four inches of sand, to cover the sand with several inches of gravel, and finally to work the rocks into these prepared mounds. Since I didn't have any sand or gravel or rocks, and because I am usually slower than Congress when it comes to big projects, the bare clay soil sat for nearly a year before I covered it with anything except doubt. During this time certain creatures were taking advantage of my inattention, and a life form had taken up residence beneath the surface of the barren earth.

I did not discover this until one day in July the following year when all the construction had been completed. I noticed a large mound of what appeared to be finely sifted earth on top of the well-manicured gravel top dressing I'd just installed. There was a quart or more of soil. It gave the rockery a messy appearance, and I cleaned it off immediately. Next to the pile was a hole that went straight into the ground. Ah! Chipmunks, I figured. Baby chipmunks. Their parents are all over the rest of the garden, and now I'd created a nursery for their children.

The next day there was another mound of soil, and as the days passed, even more. The place was turning into a bloody mine field of holes and dirt mounds. A prairie dog colony would have felt at home here. As much as I like animals in the garden, my mind was fiendishly working overtime to find a method of chipmunk extermination.

Then I discovered it was not chipmunks. While working in the rockery one morning, I noticed a huge (and I do mean big) wasp giving me the once-over. It was our common cicada killer, which comes in at about 1.5 to 2 inches. This type of solitary wasp is not the least bit aggressive (thank the gods of nature for this one), but they are territorial and investigate anything that is not normal. Not unexpectedly then, the wasp took a great interest in me. I, too, took a suspicious view of her (or him, it's hard to tell on the wing).

I watched as the wasp flew erratically to the ground and disappeared into a burrow. A she, after all, because only females dig burrows. Now this posed a problem for me. I like wasps (and still do, in spite of my recent misadventures with them), especially the solitary sorts. I've even written scientific papers on their behaviors and biologies. Therefore, they have always been generally welcome in my garden. The cicada killers, however, being so large and such prodigious diggers, were ruining the rock garden. A quart of soil on top of a half-inch-tall plant is tantamount to death. In the perennial border wasps would have been no problem, nor in the ivy bed tucked safely away under a Japanese maple, but in the rockery they were a problem.

What to do?

I did essentially nothing. Instead, each day I cleaned up after the wasps, removing the excavated soil from the tops of plants so that they wouldn't die and trying to keep the place looking halfway decent. Eventually, the wasps stopped digging and that ended that. Until the next year. And the next. And now.

The reason these wasps dig is to make underground chambers in which to place paralyzed cicadas. On these cicadas they lay eggs which, in only a short year, give rise to new cicada killers. These then come spilling forth from the ground to repeat the cycle. Because the female wasp produces more progeny than simply her own replacement value of one, the population of wasps at a nesting site can become quite large over several years' time. In the hundreds at a good nesting site.

The term *good,* I suppose, is relative. Many people would consider this a bad nesting site, and it was not too long ago, near my own workplace in downtown Washington, D.C., that a colony of several hundred wasps was wiped out due to their proximity to walkways. Humans do not like walking alongside big, buzzing, potentially stinging things. It scares them. But unlike the yellow jacket, which actually enjoys flying directly into your mouth just for the fun of it, the cicada killer wants no more to do with you than you want with it.

This year the population of cicada killers in the rockery has built to the aesthetically objectionable point. I've let several females make nests to insure the survival of the species, then netted them in my net, and released them out in front of the property. The desire was that they would be disoriented and fly off somewhere else to build more nests.

Actually, my neighbor across the street has a huge pile of dirt in his front yard. It could sit there for weeks or years for all I know. It would be nice if the females I let go would set up housekeeping in that pile where they wouldn't do any damage.

Some weeks ago I mentioned the unfortunate ivy-covered dinosaur that resides outside the Museum of Natural History. At that time it was rapidly crumbling into disrepair with no help in sight. Now, however, the story takes a turn for the happy ending. It appears that the horticulture department is giving the old thing a reprieve from the compost heap and is refurbishing its bones from the bottom up.

In a recent newspaper article I read that the dinosaur's creator, Walter Howell, is being allowed to replant the framed topiary after its move from the mall side of the museum to the street side. This is a good move because the mall side is the south side and, it appears, is much too hot and exposed for ivy-hided dinosaurs. The north side of the building offers better growing conditions.

I saw the renovated topiary this week in its new setting, and it is 100 percent improved. Newly replanted, it looks prosperous and healthy, and the setting is a vast improvement as well. The dinosaur now stands serenely in a bed of lush ferns under the overhang of a majestic elm. It appears to have been grazing there for years, like some huge, well-contented cow. I am pleased that this magnificent piece of gardening art has arisen from such a dry, dusty, weed-encrusted hulk. I am ever more convinced that some such folly will join my garden in the near future.

Somehow, in spite of my dehydrated lethargy, I managed to get out and clean up the western fencerow. This is a wire fence that over the years has become enmeshed in seedling wisteria (some now two inches in diameter), Japanese honeysuckle, sassafras, greenbriar, ivy, Virginia creeper, multiflora rose, and mulberry. Sometimes, also, I discover too late the rampant foliage of poison ivy. This and Virginia creeper look so similar to the intently hacking eye that I sometimes get in trouble before I know it.

All this exuberant life exists on my neighbor's side of the fence, but if I do not maintain some sort of demarcation (the Maginot Line in this case) at the fencerow, it won't be long before the surge of green sweeps over my garden like a tidal wave. I leave as much as I can of the pleasant green backdrop, but still one must be ruthless at times for the sake of the garden.

In keeping with my principles of organic recycling, I simply cut everything off (except I paint systemic weed-killer on the poison ivy), chop it into pieces, and let it drop in the two-foot-wide pathway that parallels the fence. No muss, little fuss, and in a week you can scarcely tell I've done any work there.

I am glad that my neighbor allows the fencerow to remain because it would be all too easy, in the typical nongardening way of things, for him to cut down the brush and plant wall-to-wall lawn. People often feel that anything hinting of a wild or uncontrolled look in their yards is tantamount to slovenly housekeeping and must be cleaned up in all haste. They remove a relatively dense and varied canopy of vegetation enjoyed by birds, squirrels, and bugs and replace it with a theoretically neat lawn that is essentially a nearly sterile blanket. This, supposedly, is required if one is to have a civilized yard.

My own prejudices are that if you want to live in a house surrounded by land then you should either let it go back to nature or create a garden or both. If you want to be surrounded by endless expanses of scalped lawn, then you ought to live in an apartment on a golf course. That would leave more land for those of us who care for it and less work for those of us who don't.

Week Two _____

For my birthday this year I received 1.5 inches of rain. Can't complain about that! Well, I could . . . but I won't. No sense complaining when good things happen because it takes the edge off when you really need a sympathetic ear.

To celebrate, I was rendezvousing with my friend Dee at Andre Viette's nursery down in Fishersville, Virginia. It's a pleasant day trip from here, and I need to get away from my own garden now and again just to see how gardens should be made.

The day began at 5:00 a.m., which is a bit too early for my taste, but sacrifices must occasionally be made for the garden's sake. The trip is about 150 miles one way, so to get there and back and have time to visit requires an early start. Once beyond the greater (or lesser) D.C. area, I take a comfortable back road that has little traffic. Usually. This particular morning, however, did not seem to be terribly usual.

About twenty minutes before I reached Gainesville, a tractor-trailer had had a little race with a freight train across the center of town. The truck lost and the trailer was sliced in half. Luckily, no one was hurt. Normally, this might have been exciting, but today the main intersection was entirely blocked not only with train but also with trailer parts and hundreds of cases of broken glass coffee pots. These reminded me that I needed a cup of coffee and, I decided, it wouldn't hurt to get directions on some other way out of town. Any way out, as a matter of fact, because I sure wasn't going anywhere this way.

Fortunately, it was just a matter of a side street and a three-mile detour. Fortunately, too, I was heading south and all the traffic in the world was heading north. My three-mile detour on a two-lane road was simple. I was nearly the only car going that way. The other lane, however, was backed up the three miles plus two additional miles once I got back out to the main road. This would have been a serious deterrent had the traffic been southbound. In fact, I probably would have turned around and gone home. I am not one for adversity, especially at 6:00 in the morning and not yet having finished a cup of coffee.

The remainder of the trip down went without incident. A singularly pleasant statement of fact. I do not count the half cup of take-out coffee I spilled in my lap as an incident. That was an accident and just plain stupid. I arrived at Charlottesville only ten minutes late, which is twenty minutes late for me as I am always too early for any appointment I make. Even with the dentist.

At Charlottesville I abandoned my car and switched to Dee's truck for the forty-minute ride over to Fishersville. As anyone who visits nurseries knows, a truck is really the only appropriate vehicle. Anything else is just second rate. A tractor-trailer would have been better, but the one I'd planned to rent was still up in Gainesville rearranging itself. Sometime around 9 a.m. we reached our destination.

If I were any good at describing things, I would go on for hours about the Viette growing grounds, the display gardens, and so on, but I have a general bias against reading such stuff and a positive inability to produce it. Therefore, I will only say that the house and demonstration gardens sit below the rim of a gentle valley that runs approximately north and south (either that or east and west, I didn't have my compass with me and the sky was overcast). The sales area is at the top of the ridge above the house. The hill overlooks the growing beds some distance below in the bottomlands of the valley. In this atmosphere of rural green fields, well-watered by recent and frequent rains (much to my envy), and undulating terrain with few houses to be seen, a picnic lunch would not have been out of place if one were given to forethought and had an overly organized life.

Our normal routine during one of these visits (of which we've made four) is to skim over the sales area quickly, tour the display gardens for several hours, dash off to lunch, then return and buy, buy, buy. Well, usually I simply buy. I watch Dee as she buy, buy, buys because she has two acres, after all, and I have only a third of an acre. If we prorated purchases based upon garden size, then I might be the extravagant one. But I am in good company and do not feel the least bit guilty about spending my paltry sixty or seventy-five bucks while Dee's bill goes into triple digits.

I must say, reluctantly, that this trip did not yield anything spectacularly, unbearably wonderful. I suppose, in part, it had to do with the general malaise the garden and the gardener have fallen into this year with its uninspiring weather. I have not been my normal gardening self.

Another difficulty was that upon arriving at the nursery, Dee called her vet to check on the health of Marylou, one of her dogs, only to discover that she had died during the night. This was like losing a child, and we came close to calling the day off, then thought better of it. It is best to be in the garden, even someone else's, in time of sorrow. There is something remarkably restorative in contemplating the hustle and bustle of a garden as it goes about its business. The butterflies and bees, wasps and hoverflies, birds, and even dogs. Of which there were several varieties at the nursery. Dee paid particular attention to the dogs this day.

We did not vary our normal routine except to leave an hour or so earlier than usual. Neither of us had made the gardening find of the decade as usually happens, but we packed up the truck with enough ordinary stuff to make the trip worthwhile. Nursery trips are always worth the effort, even if you return home empty-handed.

The trouble with living too long is that your mistakes eventually catch up with you. This is certainly coming true in my garden, and more so every year. This seemed like a good week to catch up on correcting ten years of gardening errors. I suppose someone had to do it, but I would have been better off doing what any right-thinking person does . . . moving. (This is the most expedient way, I have found, to correct most house and garden mistakes; it is far easier to accept a new challenge than to correct an old mistake.)

And so this week was devoted to replanning my paths. Many gardeners think that plants define a garden, but I reckon it's the paths. After all, if there are no pathways, your garden might as well be a field. My garden *was* a field when I moved in: no paths, no flowers, no shrubs . . . just a few trees and a lawn. (A lawn is just a field that's been shortened.) Before planting anything, I thought it best to know were the paths would be so that I wouldn't be stepping on plants for years to come. Therefore, it was necessary to have a plan.

It was a firm plan on firm paper, though the paper is wearing tragically thin in some spots from so many erasures. My plans, you see, seldom work, so I am continually at liberty to attempt new and even more physically debilitating ways to garden than I'd previously thought possible. Although the garden's design has changed as often as I've looked at it, the garden's pathways have remained as I originally laid them out years ago. As a result, the garden is reaching path-illogical anarchy: there are paths that go nowhere, paths that are stopped by vegetation, paths with forked crossings that cause schizophrenic confusion (which way to the garden?), paths formed from too many disparate elements (stone, brick, grass, gravel, mulch, logs), and paths that don't know if they are paths or lawn or flower bed. Something had to be corrected before I could get on with the secondary purpose of gardening, which has something to do with plants as I recall.

Without going into untidy and never-ending detail, I offer the following simple solutions that I used to correct my years of path mistakes. On the paths that went nowhere, I simply heaped soil and will create new flower beds as the inspiration arises. Paths stopped up with vegetation were corrected by one of two methods: move the path or move the vegetation. (I did both.) For the forked pathways, I closed off one fork, thus creating one path that went somewhere and one path that went nowhere. (The latter is called reinventing a mistake: see above.) Of the paths made of many differing elements, I simply followed Germany's lead . . . I unified them. At one point, I took out a mulch path, moved it three feet to the left, then four feet to the right, then six feet to the left, and finally, in disgust, I just threw it down in the middle of the garden. And in another path I took up the brick and replaced it with . . . with . . . well, with different brick. (It seemed reasonable at the time, but for some reason I don't think I quite know why. Let's just say that it *had* to be done.)

As to the paths that didn't know what they wanted to be, we have reached an understanding. Yes, paths do communicate with us, and we would do well to listen to them on occasion. For example, whenever you see a well-worn rut across the corner of your lawn or through one of your flower beds, the path is saying, "Here is where I am needed." It is useless to put up a chain-link fence (criminal, actually), brick wall, or barberry hedge. Admit that you are wrong and the path is right and correct your mistake. In the case of my paths, I listened particularly well because they had been trying to get my attention for a number of years. We decided it would be best for one of the paths to be a garden for a while. You know, test it out; see if it was up to the job. Another undecided path will remain a path, but with tentative modifications. I am changing its surface from grass to mulch, becoming a little tentative along the edges, and adding a few plants. It has decided to check out this garden-mystique business before completely converting over. (I have some sympathy with this approach—being tentative, that is.)

All told, this week I managed to move just about every object any-where near, in, on, over, or under a path that needed moving, and in some cases, even if it didn't. When I correct mistakes, I don't aim shy of the job. I redo everything in my path.

Week Three

I suppose the third week of August is too early to proclaim that fall is officially here, but if you reckon time by the labor of the week rather than by the calendar or the temperature, then fall it is. Raking leaves is a fall chore in my way of thinking, and I've already had to rake a sheet of dried crab apple leaves and roly-poly grape-sized fruit from the driveway. This is undoubtedly drought-induced stress, but the result is the same as if Old Man Fall had told the tree to drop its leaves. Similarly, I've started laying in firewood for the winter—not because the cold is upon us but because the eastern mulberry tree that broke apart in late July was fi-nally cut down this week, and the wood needed to be put somewhere. The woodpile seemed about as good a place as any. Only too soon the piling will begin in earnest.

This week has been a busy one in gardening terms, but I'm not certain why. Perhaps because the weather let up a bit and 85 degrees is preferable working weather to 95 degrees. Or maybe the garden grew tired of my finding excuses not to go near it and began demanding resti-tution. The belated felling of the mulberry tree created a mess on both sides of the fence, and it may have been this disarray that set me off. Then again, I had relatives over for dinner one night and was shocked during the obligatory garden tour at just how shabby the garden had be-come. I will also be off in several weeks' time for an unexpected insect-collecting trip to Arizona. This means a fourteen-day absence that I will have to make up for either before I go or after I return.

All these factors contributed to the business of the week, as did the realization that winter is almost here. The garden needs to be tidied up so that fall planting can proceed with a minimum of distraction. I began, probably too late, last Sunday by sowing biennials for next year's bloom —Canterbury bells, sweet williams, and wallflowers. I take my cue for sowing biennials from what is happening in the garden. Self-sown fox-glove seed began sprouting about two weeks ago, which means I am about three weeks late in sowing my seed. I can't think of everything, and even when I do, it sometimes takes three or four weeks to actually do something with the thought. After five days most of the seed sown ear-lier in the week has sprouted. Now I hope I can find the time to trans-plant it.

I sowed climbing nasturtiums directly into the greenhouse planter box and trellis that I built some time ago. This planter has been largely a staging area for a series of ineffective attempts at gardening. The green-house is cold all winter (generally between 32 and 50 degrees Fahren-heit), so tropical vines will not grow. Cold-adapted vines for winter should be amenable, but I haven't yet found any that are. Sweet peas grew and grew all winter and put out about six flower stalks on fifty pounds of vegetation (not to mention a hundred pounds of aphids), so I will not try them again. The purple bell vine, *Rhodochiton atrosan-guineum*, grew fine and even flowered, but the plant's structure was less than desirable—a pencil-thin stalk with scarcely any leaves except for some eight feet off the ground. The striking flowers you needed binoc-ulars to see. I am looking for something that makes nice, lush foliage as well as produces respectable flowers during the winter. Nasturtiums adapt well to cool weather and are somewhat hardy, so I'll give 'em a try and see what develops.

I also sowed three varieties of pansies for late fall, winter, and spring bloom. Amazingly, pansies flower sporadically in the cold months when-ever there is enough heat to stir their souls. By March they have so much pent up bloom fever that they blow apart with excitement at the first op-portunity. They bloom ferociously in the cool spring months, then calm down as soon as really hot weather hits. Just last week I pulled up the re-mains of last year's bedraggled plants. They could scarcely be called living, but still there were a few, small, misshapen flowers clinging to the mis-taken notion that summer was not really a setback. In the past I have not had much luck growing pansies from seed, but this year I am following Dee Wilder's suggestion and placing the seed pots in the refrigerator until the seeds sprout. If they don't, I can always fall back on the more expensive option of buying plants at the nursery. Pansies, along with chrysanthemums, are one of the big-ticket items for fall sale around here.

Seed pots of ornamental kales and cabbages also went into the refrigerator, at least for a few weeks. I have never grown these before and am probably too late in sowing, but even if I can't get them into the garden in time, I can always use a few potted plants in my greenhouse. Because my garden is composed of a great many herbaceous perennials, the winter months expose a lot of brown earth (or mulch) as a result of everything's dying down. Although I generally do not much care for the garden in winter I thought that if anything could cheer up the ground a little, it would be ornamental cabbages. They are really quite good at it. Our local botanical garden, Brookside, has handsome and intricate plantings of these vegetables that are attractive well into winter. Even the streets of downtown Washington, D.C., have planters of these curious but colorful cabbages.

My final refrigerator-sown seeds are of *Primula obconica*. I have grown these from seed before, and they make a nice pot plant that blooms in the cold greenhouse all winter. They come in various shades of pink, rose, apricot, and blue, but I generally have luck germinating only the rose and pink varieties. In fact, I sometimes have no luck germinating them at all. With me it seems to be an all-or-nothing proposition. If the seeds sprout I generally have enough plants to line the entire greenhouse in four-inch pots. This is not bad, actually, as I give them away in full bloom in December, January, and February and appear to be quite the knowledgeable gardener. It is only luck, however, because one year out of two I have nothing to give away.

I've had a similar experience with the florists' cyclamen. One year I had half a dozen plants in the greenhouse, of which some were grown from seed by my friend Dug and others were purchased out of desperation for winter color. They do very well even in a greenhouse that reaches 30 degrees on occasion. The spring following the big cyclamen bash I noticed cyclamen seedlings coming up everywhere. In the gravel below the benches, in the pots of neighboring plants, in the pots of the cyclamens themselves. I potted up nearly four dozen plants and raised them through the next year, giving them away with great abandon. Never since then, however, have seedlings spontaneously erupted anywhere. One gains a false sense of ability when, in one year, a great whopping crop of primroses or cyclamens is at hand to give away to friends and strangers alike. Just as often the gift of growth is taken away and we are left to wonder what it is we did wrong. We never wonder what it was we did right in the first place. It is mistakenly believed that a good gardener can do anything at will. If true, I would be a very bad gardener, indeed.

The garden has taken on a new look with the felling of the second twenty-plus-foot mulberry tree in nearly as many weeks. Last week my neighbor to the north unilaterally decided to cut down the mulberry tree that grew slightly on my side of the property boundary. As the tree leaned in his direction and as there was nothing else in that direction except lawn, bamboo, and other trees, he simply cut the thing off at the base and let it fall. It now rests as a twenty-foot-wide pile of brown leaves awaiting further progress.

The tree on my eastern boundary, near Viburnum Walk, was done by professionals . . . though I'm not certain exactly what profession they might be in. Demolition perhaps. I was not home when the felling began, and that was good. I do not like to see destruction in action as there is little that can be done to stop it. According to my neighbor Margaret, even though the tree company had five employees on site who took the tree down in carefully roped and guided pieces, apparently some pieces got away from the guiders. It did not matter on Margaret's side of the fence as there is absolutely nothing you can do to harm ivy. But on my side several subjects are the worse for the experience. One of the four-year-old doublefile viburnums is now about five feet shorter than its neighbors. A planting of half a dozen patrinias in full bloom is now horizontal and will stay that way until they regrow next spring (if they regrow). And the old wisteria is now about a third of its former size.

Quite a few mulberry logs were lying all about the place when I got home, as well as pieces of dead branches that had exploded when they hit the ground after the twenty-foot fall. About the only consolation I had as I cleaned up was that it could have been worse. True, the viburnum now stands a towering two inches tall, but next year it will probably put out a good two to three feet of new growth. Especially now that the tree that had stunted its growth is gone. With the newly revealed sun, the removal of root competition, and some water, the viburnum will probably be much happier than it has ever been. This is usually not the case when a branch shortens a person to two inches. So I do not worry too much about the viburnum or the patrinia or the wisteria. They will recover. Before I can say "damn mulberry," I'll undoubtedly be hacking at the wisteria trying to keep its new growth in bounds.

Many of the logs were too long to use in my wood-burning stove, so I lined the back of the viburnum border with them. As on the west and north boundaries, I maintain a two-foot-wide cleared service path along which to monitor encroachment from my neighbors' property. The stove-sized pieces of wood were stacked in the driveway for use this winter. All the other bits were gathered up and distributed evenly over the service path where they will rapidly disappear.

A half-day's cleanup on both sides of the fence and everything looks neat, if not a little bit disturbed. The removal of a huge block of vegetation has given my garden a new feeling. Instead of the dark, black, dense wall of vegetation that formed the backdrop for my garden, the view is now open, bright, and cheery—as if my garden extended another thirty feet or so into the ivy-lined flatness of my neighbor's. I know for a fact that newly sprouting trees will be up three feet tall by this time next year. The pack will be lead by mulberry seedlings, followed closely in numbers by silver maples, wild cherries, sassafras, elms, and tulip poplar. The ever-present walnut will doubtless arise in quantity as the nuts from my neighbor's tree have fallen everywhere in abundance. The squirrels have had a vigorous time planting them in every conceivable (and ill-conceived, at that) place. Here in the East trees come up like mustard plants. It's not unusual to see rain gutters filled with maple seedlings, old buildings with a mulberry growing from between its bricks, or a walnut tree in the middle of a flower pot. Removing one tree is merely an open invitation to colonization by the fittest.

My neighbors are essentially nongardeners, waffling in indifference, willing to accept a squirrel's concept of where that walnut should be planted or letting the wind have its way with this silver maple's seed.

On all sides I am at the mercy of winds, birds, squirrels, and chance as to what comes up next in my neighbors' yards. Even more, I am at their mercy as to what stays—including myself. If they allow a woodlot to take over, or regrow, in the case of my eastern neighbor, then I might be forced to abandon my garden in favor of more open pastures.

Week Four_____

Beginning next week I will have to entrust the garden to a complete stranger. At least a stranger to me. It's not someone I dragged off the street, of course—that would be too simple. It is the graduate student of a friend of mine who teaches at the University of Maryland. I will be taking a two-week break from office work to do fieldwork in southeastern Arizona. Not a bad exchange, actually, because any week in the field is worth two in the lab.

I had not scheduled any fieldwork this year because I am in the middle of writing up a large research paper, and I wanted to put all my effort into finishing it. However, priorities are one thing and fieldwork in Arizona is another, and one must be practical, after all. Fortunately, I am well ahead of my research writing goals, so I do not feel guilty switching to the field for a week or two. In fact, I was just about to go permanently insane working on that manuscript, and a break from myself might just bring me back to my senses. Well, for two weeks at least.

In the old days, that is, B.G. (Before Garden), I spent a lot of time doing fieldwork related to my co-equal love and profession, the study of insects. I am an entomologist and that is what entomologists do. Study insects. My particular interest lies in parasitic wasps, about which I now know very little. It used to be that I knew a lot about them. But sometimes, after working with a subject for a very long while, say twenty-five years or so, one realizes that one knows a lot less than one thought one did in the distant past. The smugness of the expert decreases in proportion to the distance from graduate school. At least theoretically it should. Many experts believe they know more after twenty years of research than they did as graduate students, but they are mostly deceiving themselves.

Knowledge increases exponentially faster than our decreasing ability to absorb it. Thus, you can never know relatively more than you did when you left school.

A.G. (After Garden), I began slowing down the fieldwork a tad and spending more time at home and office. That is the responsible thing to do, is it not? One cannot create a garden then abandon it at the least distraction, can one? No, one can't. When one becomes the responsible parent then one assumes the responsibility for the child, or in my case, the garden and cats (a few have departed since I began the garden, leaving only Bruno). It is not easy going from the carefree, uninvolved wanderer to the protector of the garden, but then, no one said life would be easy. Or even fun, for that matter. Life just is.

The garden has proved something of a millstone with regard to my freedom to travel the world when and where I want. My profession poses few handicaps to travel, except for endless trails of paperwork involving justifications, expenses, and the like. I've been to China, India, Venezuela, the Greater and Lesser Antilles, England, Canada, Mexico, and the majority of the states in the Union in the quest for parasitic wasps.

But the garden says to me, "You have showered me with endless amounts of money and labor, endless hours of love and devotion, and you had better not leave me just for the sake of a good time. *I* am your good time, and you'd best not forget me or I might not be here when you return."

By this not-so-subtle approach I am warned of the consequences of dallying in the fields—in nature's garden. I, who grew up devoted to the natural world with the garden as occasional mistress, now find that the garden is the keeper, the cajoler, the master, that I am subservient to it, and that the natural world of the forest, the desert, the meadow is no longer the object of my devotion. It is an embarrassment to be thusly enslaved—brainwashed—by a creation of my own, and it becomes ever more painful to sneak away for the occasional indiscretion with my original love. What is a naturalist-turned-gardener to do?

The decision to leave the garden, even for two weeks, is never an easy one. True, in the dead of winter, there are few problems to contend with. Outside, the garden is asleep. No, I think dead drunk would be a better description. There is not the least chance it will awaken. The greenhouse is easily managed even by a novice. A perfect time to sneak off. But where? An overseas destination is not too difficult a choice . . . nearly any place in the Southern Hemisphere would do—Australia, New Zealand, sub-Saharan Africa, South America, New Guinea. All places I would like to study, but also places that are expensive to get to. (Regardless of people's perceptions, some sectors of government do not have endless amounts of money to spend, even if the research can be justified.) Eventually, if I live long enough, I may get to some of these areas without garden-linked regrets. Most likely after I retire.

There is not much satisfaction in winter travel within my natural range. If I am to study biological activity, especially the cold-blooded insects, conditions must be conducive. There must be warmth, there must be food (nectar) available for adults, and there must be suitable insect hosts for the parasites I study. Thus, in winter, I am limited to southern Florida, southern Texas, or Hawaii for nature's pleasure, and even these places are not assuredly productive in terms of research at that time of the year, nor am I particularly interested in studying their faunas, or are they assuredly natural any more. "Civilization" (a euphemism for too damn many people) has taken its toll, and the natural state of things in these places is becoming obscure as well as more and more difficult to find.

The problem is that all the places I do want to study are best visited while the garden has its hold on me. If I leave in the spring, for example, I miss the busiest time of the year as far as garden preparation is concerned. If one does not produce the seedlings and get the transplants into place, then the rest of the year is bound to be a disappointment. Then, too, spring weeds are the worst. They've had the entire winter to work their roots into all sorts of deep, dark places. They burst forth at the earliest moment, and this first heavy assault must be stopped or havoc will rule the rest of the year. Finally, as if it mattered at all, the spring garden is one I've been looking forward to all winter. It would not do to wait so patiently then scurry off to unknown places just the week before winter's grip breaks loose in glorious fulfillment. No, I cannot leave in spring unless someone quite unpleasant forces me to do so.

To leave in summer is to risk losing the entire garden. It does not make sense to plant a garden with untold treasures in spring only to abandon it later to a person who scarcely knows water from tar paper. The result would surely be the death of every ten-year-old focal point in the garden. Not to mention all the transplants put out just weeks before. Inevitably, I would return to a garden of lush weeds and dead specimen plants.

If I leave in fall, then I will miss the best planting season for next year's garden. Bulbs, of course, can be stuck in the ground any old time up to November or December if you plan ahead. But who does? It's tough to plan that far ahead when I can scarcely even remember I'm going on a trip next week. Therefore, bulbs must be planted as soon as I get them or they will be mislaid in the basement until some time next June when their season will have passed permanently. Then, too, fall is the best time to transplant evergreens, and I need to survey the garden, determine what evergreens to move, decide where to place them, and then move them—otherwise the planning isn't of much use. Fall is an advantageous time to buy nursery stock, especially evergreens, because it's frequently on sale. Around here no one shops for outdoor plants in winter. Nurseries need to deplete their stock quickly or be faced with the task of overwintering plants. Some great bargains may be found in the fall, but it helps if I've planned a bit as to where these gains might be placed. It does little good to save sacks of money only to discover that I don't have any space left to plant thirteen pines, each of which grows to fifty feet in height.

Already I have on order six dozen perennial and rock garden plants. Some of the plants may arrive while I'm away because I placed some orders before I knew I was going anywhere. The orders sent off in the past week or two will be fine, I hope, because I instructed the nurseries to ship after I return home. I hope they can read. Then there are the seeds potted up in the refrigerator. What if they sprout while I'm gone? Will someone think they are edible and use them in a tofu salad? And the seedlings that sprouted this week in the greenhouse, what will happen to them? I've transplanted twelve dozen sweet williams, Canterbury bells, and wallflowers, and they are sitting in the greenhouse just waiting for the overwaterer to arrive and give them all a good dose of damping-off. You can't trust your plants to just anyone, even though, when you travel, you often have to.

Well, as usual, I've just about convinced myself not to leave. In writing about the responsibilities of the garden I've made myself hysterical. How can I leave now that I've sanctified my anxieties in words?

Sitting at airports is certainly nothing I enjoy doing. Being surrounded by square miles of asphalt, enormous hulks of metal, billions of gallons of fossil fuels, cubic miles of exhaust fumes, and hordes of marauding people all going nowhere in particular does not make for an enjoyable time. I am in Detroit awaiting the plane that will take me to Phoenix. The current choice for entertainment is to read, people watch, or write. I have read about all I care to read on the trip from Baltimore to Detroit. I've seen about as many people as I care to see for a lifetime. So the choice seems to be made for me. Normally, I cannot think in a place that is so distractingly peopled, but I am falling slightly behind on my garden-writing deadlines. With the field trip at hand I will fall even further behind if I do not use time when I have it.

I've been up since 3:00 a.m., due in large part to two patrol cars and a helicopter with incredibly bright lights that spent about an hour circling overhead looking for who knows what. They centered for a while on the third house over, returning twice to that area, and it occurred to me that they might have heard rumors about a gardener abandoning his garden. Perhaps they were looking for such a scoundrel. As I had to meet my ride to the airport at 5:30, I thought I might as well get up anyway.

Now that I have escaped from the responsibilities of the garden, it seems as if they really might not exist after all. Perhaps it is a dream, and I am simply a fellow traveler in the universal brotherhood of airport passengers, merely Brownian motion on an uncharted scale of organization.

To escape the physical garden is to also escape the psychological garden and its need for constant attention. If I can abandon the garden for two weeks, then why can't I simply ignore it for two weeks when I am there?

Well, I do not know exactly. Perhaps it has to do with the work ethic I learned from a mother who as a child had to tend the family garden in order to survive. Or perhaps it has to do with striving toward some goal of unreachable perfection (although to look at my garden, no amount of work could possibly bring perfection). Or perhaps it is the need to expend the nervous energy generated by the daily stress of life. A replacement, perhaps, for biting one's toenails.

Gardening is a discipline wherein one has control over something in one's own life (at least in theory). A miniature kingdom in which one rules the earth: where an epilobium from 10,000 feet in elevation is commanded to grow at sea level, or a poppy from arid hillsides is expected to perform in wet eastern mud; where the gardener has illusions far grander than anything s/he might have in the real world. Could the garden be simply an escapist fantasy where social misfits—among whom I count myself—retire into anonymity cloaked with a touch of class? Possibly the garden represents our artistic, expressive self coming to the fore. Without expression we poor humans are simply animals, are we not?

At different times I have felt all these parts of the equation and to differing degrees. Sometimes I garden simply because I feel guilty, other times for joy. Sometimes for artistic reasons, other times for the sheer feeling of power over nature—to dominate. Or sometimes simply to escape from the world.

When I am self-banished from the garden, as I now am, I often ask myself if I even want to return. It is the perfect opportunity to escape forever. To become a wanderer. To become the naturalist I once was. But I always do return, eventually. Perhaps like a homing pigeon or a monarch butterfly, I must return to the garden simply because it is my genetic destiny. Or, more simply, because it is there.

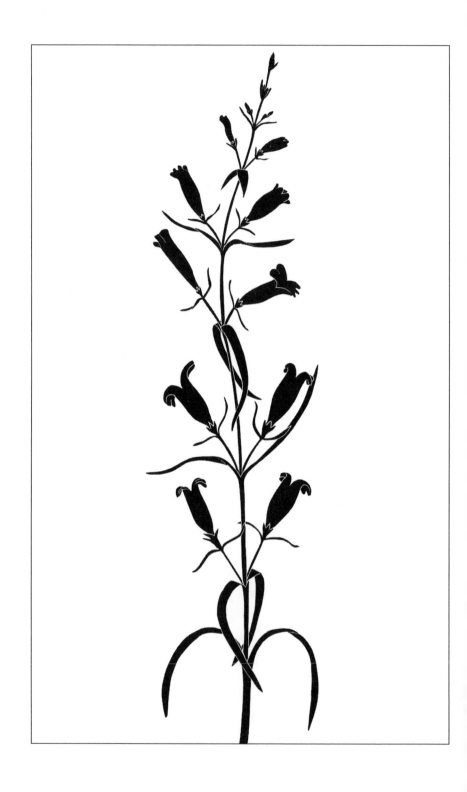

11

SEPTEMBER

Week One

The deserts of Arizona would appear to be as far from the garden as one could get, yet as I tracked through the state's southeastern washes, stony outcrops, and pine-covered mountains, I was never far from reminders of home. A lilac-colored *Verbena* turned up everywhere from mountaintop to desert wash, differing mainly in color from the pink-and-white cultivar that welcomes solicitors (and the odd guest) at my front door. Two wild wallflowers (*Erysimum*), one fiery orange and the other corn yellow, reminded me of the four dozen seedlings of cultivated wallflower (*Cheiranthus*) I'd just transplanted the week before leaving on my trip. 'Glasnost' is the variety's name, not so blazing in color as these sun-soaked native species, perhaps, but as topical as the vague headlines I'd caught about the splintering Soviet Union. Patches of a rose-colored *Sphaeralcea* reminded me in miniature of the hollyhock seed (*Althaea*) I'd harvested several weeks ago to bring to my friend Ellen in Tucson. This seed was returning to its Arizona homeland where, years before, I'd originally gotten it by answering a "seed-for-trade" add in a folksy garden magazine. *Helianthus annuus,* a nearly ubiquitous roadside wildflower of lower elevations, occurs in my garden as a pampered multi-hued hybrid, though it has seldom achieved the wondrous effects it exhibits naturally in the hard-packed, dry-baked habitats it elects to grow in. Several species of *Yucca* continually reminded me that I had just purchased the variegated form of the eastern *Y. filamentosa* and had left it in its pot awaiting planting out upon my return home. Mountain species of columbine, coral bells, phlox, and penstemon reminded me how much better plants do when they are happy in their wild state than when enslaved in my garden.

Southeastern Arizona consists not of one habitat but of many, ranging in elevation from about 2000 feet to over 10,000. I believe that the diversity of natural habitats here is greater than any to be found in a similar-sized area of the eastern United States (or perhaps even in the entire eastern United States), ranging from sun-drenched desert floor to Douglas-fir covered mountains. Its vegetation appears to be limited mostly by the inconsistent natural rainfall, which might be generous in any one storm but on average is fairly niggardly.

I took infrequent opportunities to view Arizona gardens as I drove by them on my way out of towns into the countryside. The availability of natural habitat alone, I found, is deceptive in terms of where people actually choose to live and build gardens. The higher, cooler reaches of the mountains surprisingly (and thankfully) have few houses, or none, with the exception of what appear to be mostly summer cottages, or heat retreats. These have no landscaping and sit among the trees and shrubs that naturally surround them. The vast majority of people live at the flatter, lower elevations where the heat is greater and the rainfall less—verging on nonexistent in some places. This is where the gardens are built, if they are built at all, that is.

Most of the noncity dwellers appear, on average, to be nongardeners and perhaps rightly so. The landscaping around rural houses is a borrowed one, consisting of native vegetation that was there when the house was built with the addition of a few junipers, cypresses, and acacias for height and shade. Local cacti are sometimes added or at least saved from the bulldozer.

I did not spend much time in cities, only long enough to get out of the Phoenix airport as fast as I could and a few evenings in Tucson, when it was generally too dark to see much of anything. My impression was that most gardens were of the xeric sort; that is, no intensive irrigation for lawns and no perennial borders. Instead there was a healthy reliance upon native cactus, palo verde, mesquite, acacia, mimosa, some creosote bush, and lots of drought-tolerent plants about which I haven't the slightest knowledge.

As a biologist I greatly admire deserts as places of extremes. Extremes of temperature and rainfall, extremes of adaptation in animals and plants, and perhaps most of all, extremes of human emotion and consciousness. You cannot be indifferent in the desert. You either hate it or love it. As much as I love the desert in my guise as biologist and almost rational, sometimes intelligent human, as a gardener I would have to completely change my garden aesthetic and develop an appreciation for the xeric way. I think I could do it, but it would be difficult. And I would cheat just a bit in the time-honored tradition of hot-weather countries.

I would first adopt the courtyard or true patio garden surrounded by walls of some sort, preferably adobe. This would be my oasis-garden. There would be a little dripping or falling water for sanity's sake and maybe even a reflective pool. I would have a cistern or two at the corner(s) of the house to catch rainwater. One of these could possibly double as the pool if I gave it a little extra water from time to time. I would have small areas of decorative tiles, either in the walls or in the patio floor, and benches, small tables, terra-cotta pottery, and even stone sculpture to remind me of my human side. Of course there would be heat- and drought-tolerant plants of all kinds, including herbs, to buoy the spirit. There would be no cacti in the courtyard as they are antihuman by nature. This would be my desert retreat, not re-creation.

Outside the wall the notion of the garden would, I think, become a matter of optimizing the dry outlook. That is, condensing the best aspects of the natural desertscape, which can be woefully spartan at times, into a more densely orchestrated effect. I would have native trees and shrubs (or perhaps, cheating just a bit, heat-adapted shrubs from other desert regions) grown for texture, foliage, and flower and structured into an outer perimeter wall or barrier. This would form a hedge of sorts, but it would not be formal in any sense. Between the inner adobe wall and the outer barrier, I would build a desert walk that incorporated, again in condensed fashion, as many native self-sowing annuals and perennials as I could adopt into an essentially waterless garden.

Having grown up in a Mediterranean climate, I can imagine using Mediterranean plants and those introduced from Australia and southern Africa, but I have little knowledge of truly heat-tolerant plants. I would first want to consider native southwestern plants. But then knowing how little we value our native vegetation, especially that immediately surrounding our home grounds, I would imagine that it is difficult to procure (legally, anyway). Therefore, one would have to become a nursery scout, attender of native-plant-society meetings, avid botanizer, or perhaps proprietor of a native-plant nursery to meet the needs of the garden.

It is possible that I shall put this plan to use someday, perhaps when I retire and move West. Tomorrow, however, I will return to my own garden, which deserves all the garden thoughts I can summon. As it now stands, my garden is by no means an outstanding example of the gentle art of garden thinking. It is easier, I know, to plan a garden than to execute one, and I should not be thinking thoughts of what I could do in the arid West when I could be doing something about my arid garden in the East.

Home again. Arriving at twilight I rush all about the place to see what can be seen in the failing light. Everything looks good—acceptable is perhaps a more accurate word—but it is obvious that heat and drought still persist. I am startled by the openness caused by the loss of the two mulberry trees. This will take some getting used to. Possibly during the winter, when all the leaves are off the trees, I will forget how densely wooded it appeared only weeks before. By spring the emptiness will seem as if it had always been there.

During my absence the first of many boxes of plants arrived and was placed between the front door and the screen door. There it sat, overlooked by my house sitter for possibly a week. It was not the sitter's fault. I told him a box was coming; I just forgot to tell him the delivery man often hides boxes between the doors. Oh, well. Most of the plants were cooked to mush, but a few survived and will be coddled for a while to see if they recover. If not, they will make good compost. The plants were in two-inch pots so I did not lose a whopping investment. Still, I would have liked the opportunity to kill them myself.

Several especially nice plant combinations are in full color now in the first week of September, having apparently doubled in size during my absence. One is a grouping of *Verbena* 'Apple Blossom', umbels of white and rose pink flowers, intermixed with the lavender-pink heads of *Gomphrena* 'Lavender Lady'. The gomphrena is about two feet tall and cascades along part of the front walkway while the verbena, at ten inches, is both spreading out across the path and climbing up into the gomphrena. The doorway is an adventure in lively stepping, and the result lets the wary visitor know that all is not normal at this household. Perhaps a gardener lives here after all. It is not readily apparent from much else.

A second effective combination relies on a half-dozen plants of *Verbascum* 'Arctic Summer', which are now basketballs of white felt underplanted with low-growing annual alyssum (*Lobularia*) in white and pale lilac and ajuga with various shades of white and purple leaves ('Burgundy Glow' is the cultivar). Although only the alyssum is in flower, the interplay of the various white, purple, and cream foliages is both unsettling and calming—as if nothing much is going on but something might explode at any minute—a pastel hysteria, perhaps.

Of the above-mentioned plants, only ajuga is a true perennial in this area (even so, it often dies out from fungal infection). The rest must be either propagated anew from seed each year (*Gomphrena, Verbascum,* alyssum) or restocked from overwintered cuttings (*Verbena*). One of my first duties upon returning is to take cuttings of the plants that don't reliably overwinter. In this category, in addition to *Verbena,* falls the genus *Diplacus,* half-hardy, sticky-leaved evergreens that have enormous mimuluslike flowers. This California native has been hybridized into some jazzy colors from its basic brilliant orange, but mine is the purest of whites. It stays in flower the entire summer—truly! In mild climates the plant becomes shrubby, and the ones I set out last spring are now beginning to show this habit. The winter will kill them, however, so I've taken cuttings to insure their repeated and predictable behavior next year. There is a luscious raspberry red form, too, that I will try to get next time I wander out California way.

Then, too, I must take cuttings of those marginally hardy plants that might pull through the winter on their own but then again might not. Although these plants usually make it through without problems, occasionally they just die out for no particular reason (that I know of, anyway). If they don't, then I have plenty of plants to give away come spring. The half-dozen hybrids of *Penstemon hartwegii* that my brother sent last December fall into this category, as do *Ruta graveolens* 'Blue Beauty' and *Senecio* 'Cirrus'. The latter two are grown for their foliage, the rue being glossy gray-green and the senecio nearly white. You can never have enough foliage plants, and I insure that this maxim is enforced by taking more cuttings than I can ever use. By spring I will regret not having taken more.

Week Two _____

Returning home after a trip, even a short one, rekindles the gardening spirit much like the onset of spring after a long winter's wait. Two factors, however, detracted from my return and its anticipated pleasures. For one thing, the evenings had grown noticeably, and regrettably, shorter in the two weeks I'd been gone. It is not good when the nights grow long—dark by 8:00 p.m., then by 7:45, then by 6:00. It is not good at all. Now it is impossible, without a headlamp, to work much beyond 7:30. This is a sign of the inexorable closing of the garden season. No more working into the late evening; no more arising in the early morning light to water the potted things. I cannot dwell too long on the subject of light, or I will not be fit for decent company.

The second disturbing factor is that after our unusually dry year, everything is so desiccated and hardened-off that it seems best simply to admit defeat and put the garden away for the winter. There seems little point in prolonging the agony of what many of my gardening friends admit has been a decidedly hard year. Not that we're sissies, mind you. We can take our lumps with the best of them, but the heat and lack of water are starting to tax even the natural vegetation, including large, deeply rooted native shrubs and trees. This is a bad sign. Good Lord, if we knew that we had to water to keep all this stuff alive, most of us would have planned our plantings better. We might even have thought about (shudder) drought-tolerant plants. The thought makes me wince after being only a week away from Arizona. The northeastern United States is no more in need of massive cactus plantings than Arizona needs lawns and bowling greens. What is the world coming to?

But still, still, . . . still, there beats the heart of hope and reason. Surely the year has been too short to be over so soon. Something must be done to save the year, maybe even to make next year's garden the best ever. But what?

Bulbs for the spring, perhaps? No, bulbs for the spring are almost gratuitous, especially when you've already put in so many you can't figure out where to put another new one. Bulbs for the fall might be more noteworthy, and more immediate, as well. Bulbs for next summer would show a little initiative. Luckily, I've covered these bases with my earlier orders for fall-blooming crocus, including *C. sativus* and *C. speciosus.* I've had both in various parts of the garden, but this year I've planted nearly a hundred in the rock garden. Then too, still on order, are a number of lilies, my bulbous hopes for next summer, which will keep me busy, but not until October or November.

Then, too, my flats of biennials, transplanted before I left for Arizona, need planting out. Certainly these are next year's hopes. Perhaps too few and maybe too late, but if even half the eight dozen wallflowers, Canterbury bells, and sweet williams survive the winter, that will be a start toward the new year. Include, too, the pansies just emerged from their refrigerator treatment that induced almost perfect germination. They will first need to be pricked out, then transplanted. Here is hope not only for next year but for this winter as well. I might even be able to coax some into bloom in the greenhouse by Christmas. I've never tried that before.

Two orders of plants arrived this week and must be looked after until a good planting-out time comes. They are most assuredly an investment in next year's garden. One order included extremes of garden-making—six-foot gawky giants and ground-hugging mosses. Our native ironweed, *Vernonia noveboracensis,* which reaches head height in moist soils, will be planted in the rank garden. Next year I plan to terrace that area slightly, berm it, mulch it, and flood it. I think this will work much better for watering than the overhead sprinkler method. I've never thought of using this approach as a standard form of watering, but it might be worth a try. Generally, my highly worked soil drains too well, even when compacted, so maybe I should add some dry cement to it to form a hardpan. Then again, maybe I'd just better take this terracing idea one step at a time.

I ordered five varieties of mosses (of which three were sent) to plant out in my moss path, which is a deeply shaded area on the east side of the house. The moss garden was, up until this year, a respectable patch of several square yards of whatever moss happened to grow there. It is a pathway, and I weeded out the other plants, including grasses and *Rhododendron* seedlings, so that the moss would not be outcompeted. But our early spring rains washed out a section of the path, and the moss has not respored its way back yet, although the remaining moss appears quite green in spite of the general lack of moisture. The three new mosses look no different to me than what is there naturally, but I figured a little new blood might spark the place up a bit. I've seen several moss gardens (on television and in books), and they appear quite restful, not to mention aesthetic in a Zenlike way. I would try to grow my own moss from spores, but I have not seen any for sale. It is only a matter of time, I suppose, before moss gardening becomes the next fad of the decade, and I will be able to buy moss in all the best places. Right now, however, I can only experiment with the few small plants that came in the mail. These were grown and shipped in small plastic market packs wrapped in moist newspaper. Moss, having only microscopic rootlets, needs scarcely any substrate upon which to establish itself.

The second box is dedicated to next year as the plants are so tiny as to be invisible in this year's garden. They will either die or put down a wad of roots during the winter and burst forth with great exuberance in the spring. Next summer they will help fill up the large rockery, which is still vastly underplanted with relatively great gravelly expanses between smallish, rather obscure specimens. Next year, though, they'll do some filling in, and maybe the large rock garden will begin to look like the mountain outcroppings it was modeled after. Many plants did well this year, in spite of the searing heat generated in that gravel pit. Thymes did especially well, and when you consider that they are growing best in the graveled pathways, they are almost like miracle plants. If anything can take poor dry soil, heat, and compacting foot traffic, thyme is it. Some of the plants begun last year from sections ripped out by their roots from a fellow rock gardener's rockery are at least a yard wide this year. I've had to cut a few plants back or they could easily have taken over several square yards of terrain.

Aside from eagerly awaiting next year's new plants and imagining just how wonderful they might be (*might*, mind you, not *will*), there is one other thing I am going to do to salvage what I can of the rest of this year: I'm reevaluating the garden from top to bottom. All right, so this wasn't the best year ever, and if I had it to do over again I wouldn't. But for my own sense of dignity, I am going to concentrate on the good parts (if I can find any) and redo everything else. As they say, "When in doubt, clear it out."

And that's just what I shall spend the next month or two doing. Taking stock, reassessing, criticizing, rethinking, planning, and doing everything I can during the short time remaining in this year to have the main show ready to go as soon as the first crocus croaks next spring. This shall be my theme for the remainder of the gardening year.

Reassessment is often a difficult thing. It means at least the thought of lots of work, for it is entirely possible that I will think up many more changes than I can possibly make in one year. Those changes that aren't made by next year will be rethought next fall, and perhaps I'll find that I've saved myself lots of time by doing nothing. It's entirely likely that the bits of garden I plan to change this year I'll decide next year to change back again, and if I don't get around to changing anything, I might be better off. I can think up a lot more mischief than I am generally capable of handling. Sometimes it pays to procrastinate.

In rethinking and making changes to various parts of the garden, about the only area that can be ignored is the rock garden, which seems to be going about as planned. Obviously, something must be wrong, but since I don't know what it is, I will ignore the rock garden for a few more years. Just add some new plants every season and fill in the blank places a bit. Everywhere else, however, could do with some change.

One thought I've had, for example, is to remove more of the ornamental grass hedge. The hedge itself is a study (not to mention a nearly three-hundred-dollar investment) in reassessing the flowering shrub border that it replaced. Well, which it would have replaced if I'd finished the shrub border, which I didn't. I realized about halfway through the planning phase that I did not want an entire border of shrubs, so I reassessed it nearly out of existence, retaining only one shrub—*Buddleia alternifolia* 'Argentea', a spring-blooming, gray-leaved butterfly bush. (If you can change your mind before you plant anything, it saves a lot of money and work in the long run). Anyway, if I removed most of the hedge, I'd have an additional sunny area in which to plant other perennials much as I did with the daylilies and lilylilies some weeks back. I've already begun an area of gray-foliaged plants around the base of the buddleia. I'd like to expand that and remove most of the plain green grasses that can scarcely stand on their own rhizomes.

Another remake will be the wisteria area. I started a group of purple-leaved plants near there but none has been satisfactory. The dark-leaved dahlias are slow to grow in the early part of the season, and even when they do put on growth in late summer, it has no mass or structure to it. The mulberry tree, which is now removed, provided too much shade, and the dahlias did not create the solid dark backdrop against which to plant the ember-colored flowers I envisioned. Because the dahlias are not reliably hardy, I've had to replant the area every year, so I might as well try to find an annual that will do the job. I may try a red-leaved castor oil plant (*Ricinus*) called 'Impala' that grows only three or four feet tall. The specifics may change, in fact, *will change* for a few years until I find the right combination of plants that does well together. Then I hope I can stay with the combination for at least a year or two before I change my mind again.

I'm also going to renovate the right front part of the pink garden. Last year I spaded the whole area to remove the roots of my neighbor's silver maple, fertilized and limed the soil, and planted cleomes, cosmos, and foxgloves, hoping everything would reseed itself so that I could escape having to plant anew each year from seed. I wanted a slightly wild, cottagey look. Last year it was fine, better than expected, actually, and wondrously exuberant. Then this year everything came back as hoped, grew six inches, and stopped as if by divine command. That was it. The right section was a disaster—a study in diminution. Even the slugs avoided it. The problem, I discovered when I replanted the iris a few months ago, was that the roots of the silver maple had grown back, and even shallow-rooted annuals could not compete with the tree's congested, thirsty root masses. Respading the area defeats the purpose of having a self-sowing, ongoing jungle because it disturbs the soil and the fallen seeds. The dilemma is whether to respade and replant on a yearly basis or to put the area back in lawn. I prefer to have a garden rather than a lawn but may fall victim to my practical side and resod the area. I will redo the entire right side this fall, try transplants again next spring, and see whether the results are worth the effort. Then I'll decide what to do. Sometimes it's best to put off making tough decisions as long a possible.

Another task I must undertake is to remove and divide perennials from a few overgrown areas (I planted them only five years ago, after all), incorporate a few inches of compost, and replace the divisions. My clay soil really tightens up if humus isn't added every few years or so.

Then, too, I need to prepare a bed for next spring's move of my six-foot-diameter specimen of *Hosta* 'Frances Williams'. This is possibly a mistake, but too much of a good thing in one place is the problem. And too little in another is an even bigger problem. It is best, I suppose, to try to right the inequities. Although I can't move the monster until spring, now at least I can plan the move, make the necessary incisions to root prune and encourage a smaller rootball, and prepare the soil at the new site. I seem to have plenty of time at present, and spring is always too busy to do everything that needs to get done.

Then there's the question of fifteen cubic yards of mulch that should be spread over the garden. I suppose now is as good a time as any—the best if you can believe everything you read. It is supposed to be good winter protection. Maybe so. I know the garden will look much better with a new top dressing of mulch. It won't have that threadbare dirt look. Two springs ago I put over twenty cubic yards of mulch on the garden, but you can't see as much as a toothpick now. If I'd mulched the garden last winter, as I should have, I probably wouldn't have had such severe water-stress problems this year. I've learned my lesson about dryness and mulch.

The problem is that one can think only so long and so hard before all this work actually becomes a chore. This summer was more of a chore than even I care to admit. The fault was mine for not preparing this year's garden last fall, which would have been the best time to start. Similarly, this fall is time to start next year's garden. I would much rather be preparing the garden for next year than brooding about closing the garden down in a month or so.

Much of gardening is cultivating a sense of perspective, and I am still working on this. It is possible that next year's garden, which could be the best ever, will have arisen because this year's was the worst ever.

Week Three

The world of summery heat and predictability has come to an abrupt end. After two (nearly three) days of record-breaking heat in the midnineties, the temperature fell fifty degrees in twenty-four hours to near record-breaking lows. Fall has fallen four days earlier than scheduled. Not to mention one-third of an inch of rain as well. Still, it is not enough rain. Earlier in the week, inches of rain pelted the surrounding countryside but again missed me completely. It is aggravating to drive the few scant miles to work only to find big, gleaming potholes of water standing all about the road when they could be doing some good back in the garden.

In spite of the weather I have begun to fulfill last week's call to action. One night after work, when the temperature was still bearable (over 90 degrees, that is), I removed three more clumps of *Panicum* from the grass border. In spite of being shallowly rooted, they did not want to be extracted from the concrete they were growing in. An otherwise simple job took some axe work and no little prying to bully the roots into submission. Well, into the compost heap, actually. I will remove at least three more clumps, leaving half a dozen. Also, I plan to take out another two clumps of variegated Japanese silver grass (*Miscanthus sinensis* 'Variegatus'). The remaining few clumps will lend a bit of structural stability to the border and will allow me to plant other treasures that might not require so darn much staking. Also, the amount of herbaceous foliage removed every year will be reduced substantially, and my compost heap won't look so much like a haystack. If you think a lawn produces a lot of clippings, then you should see the pile that six-foot-tall patches of grass make when you cut them off.

The question arises as to what I shall replace the grass with, and I admit that I do not know exactly. But I do have all winter to think the question through, and then perhaps several years to regret the choices I make. I've already replaced one patch of grass, as described earlier, with daylilies in shades of yellow. I still await the yellow lilylilies that will be planted with them. This planting has the background of several remaining clumps of *Panicum* and will, I believe, add a little variety and color into an otherwise dull wall of green.

The newly renovated areas now have a background of rock garden, but I will screen this off with suitable plantings as thoughts arise. One such planting already in place is the gray-foliaged perennials surrounding the buddleia, including cat mint (*Nepeta mussinii*), Russian sage (*Perovskia*), rue (*Ruta graveolens*), and several artemisias ('Powis Castle', 'Huntington', 'Silver Queen'). The artemisias can't seem to make up their collective minds whether to barely remain alive, to die, or to engulf the entire area in underground progeny that come up where least wanted or expected. Perhaps they will get their lives sorted out now that the grass does not shade them so much.

In another area the removal of several clumps of *Panicum* was actually built into the planning some years ago. The background already has been growing for four years. When I first built the ornamental grass hedge, I placed a small specimen of *Chamaecyparis pisifera* 'Filifera Aurea' as a background for the rock garden from one side and the background for some low-growing perennials from the other. Since the cypress was so small and could scarcely be the background to anything for a few years, I decided to use several panicums as a temporary visual barrier until the evergreen could do the job on its own. Now that it has grown to about four feet, it is time to release it from subservience and allow it to take its place in the scheme of things. I can pull the grass out without misgivings now that it has served its purpose, and I will ponder low-growing replacements this winter.

In addition to grass removal, I've demolished a patch of the dark-leaved dahlia 'Japanese Bishop' as proposed last week. The tubers were removed rather unceremoniously, considering their high-class status in life, and dumped on the compost heap. In a reciprocal agreement, I shoveled up a cartload of compost and turned it back into the spot from which the bishop was removed. If this all seems rather brutal, I suppose it is, but it is honorable to admit a mistake when you see it and even more honorable to do something about it. Gardeners can, and sometimes must, be ruthless. (In all likelihood, the dahlias will emerge next year from somewhere in the compost heap and grow into the most magnificent, bedazzling bishops ever seen by humankind. So much for ruthlessness!)

Today I transplanted eight dozen pansy seedlings, wondering all the while what I should do with them. It may already be too late to move them outdoors before it becomes too cold. Alternatively, they may grow so fast as to astound me, and frost may come so late as to astonish me. Occasionally, these things all work for the best, but there is no way to plan it in advance. I don't consider myself a gambler, but if a garden isn't an almost 100-percent gamble, I don't know what is.

In transplanting seedlings I prefer to use potting soil rather than compost because my compost has too many perennial seeds in it (remember, it's a recycling heap, not one of those seed-baking professional piles). In the process today I ran out of potting soil, so I had to make an emergency run to the nursery center. This is not a good idea because emergency runs to the nursery are about as easily accomplished as out-patient heart transplants.

The problem, of course, is temptation. Show me a gardener who can go to the nursery and get only what he or she needs, and I'll show you some serious lobotomy scars. I don't mean to be rude, but it is *im-*

possible for us gardeners to buy only what we go to buy because the minute we walk through the door, we immediately forget what we went there for in the first place. "Potting soil? What's potting soil? Say, wouldn't that variegated hibiscus with the black flowers look just right next to the 'Japanese Bishop'?"

Why, we've even forgotten momentarily that the bishop is laying prone on top of the compost heap. The hibiscus actually would look better in the compost heap, too, but we are in no condition to realize that as we move from must-have to must-have, forgetting each previous must-have as we go through the inventory. Many nurseries are aware of this problem, and that is why they put those carts near the entrance—just like in a supermarket. They know that if you take a cart, your must-have instinct will force you to load it up as you go along. That is why I do not get a cart until I'm finished looking. By then I've forgotten mostly everything I had to have and simply buy the last few dozen things still sticking in my mind.

At the first nursery (yes, I went to more than one) I saved the potting soil for last. Naturally. I didn't want it to interfere in any way with my unnecessary shopping. I pawed through the perennials on sale, the shrubs, the newly stocked chrysanthemums, the annuals now finally on sale (I should hope so!), the pansies, the aquatic plants all on sale, the houseplants, the flowerpots, the evergreens, the fountains, the Indian corn, the corn-stalk bundles, the bird seed (nothing quite as pretty as a barrel of ebony black sunflower seeds—I ran my hand through them much to the disgust of future bird diners), the tools, and, yes, finally, the potting soil.

But lo! Of this they were out. What to do? My mind was primed to buy, but suddenly the thing I needed most was gone. This was not good. It tends to dampen the must-have enthusiasm. There I was all charged up to charge, when suddenly it seemed pointless. What to do? Why, visit another nursery, of course, and do it all over again.

The second nursery was not as large as the first, so I scarcely bothered to look at the plants. There were some nice flowerpots outside, however, and I spent a goodly amount of time figuring which of them fell into the must-have category. Then I went inside the greenhouse/sales area where there were houseplants, more pots, potting soil, and parrots. Yes, parrots. Great, huge birds with ferocious beaks that looked like they could easily lobotomize the hardest head. I did not touch the birds because I need all the fingers I was given, but one of the workers reached into a cage and began stroking a pure white bird as if it were a cat. The bird so obviously loved this attention that, losing my fear, I reached in and began petting it. I learned that I don't care for the feel of bony parrot head, but the bird seemed happy enough to take what it could get.

I don't think much of the idea of caged parrots, by the way. Or caged animals, for that matter. A giant enclosed but expansive birdhouse is bad enough, but a cage is inexcusable. I don't particularly like zoos or circuses, either. It isn't that the animals are so badly treated—though they certainly may be—but that they are forced to live in tiny spaces that are completely alien to them. Often they must perform silly human things that also are alien to them. I suppose if they are reared in captivity this is only a minor indignity, but this is assuming that they have lost all sense of the wild and know only the caged life. If captured in the wild, it is a gross indignity. This is a personal view, of course. Still, I would not put a parrot in a cage if I had the choice . . . and I do.

After walking through the sales area several times, I began to lose focus on what exactly it was that I had come for. This happens often with me. It was not until I saw a bag of the exact potting soil I was looking for that everything came back. They had the soil, I reasoned, therefore it was possible to buy something else if I really, really needed it.

I began studying the pots in earnest.

I returned to a shelf that had a round, crudely made, matte black pot about fourteen inches in diameter with no drainage hole. I have been on the lookout for potential water-holding vessels, and this was certainly one. In the spirit of water gardening, a cachepot of water with even a single sweetflag (*Acorus* spp.), Japanese iris, cattail, horsetail, or any of a hundred other aquatic or semiaquatic plants makes a small, succinct focal point. I have several such pots on the balcony, and I've been wanting to hide a few in the garden. So in a moment of weakness, I bought the pot not knowing exactly where I would put it. I knew that I could find a place where it would fit but only if I had the pot in hand.

After lugging the extremely heavy pot up to the counter, I took another ramble around outside where I had been eying a wonderful pot of architectural dimensions. It was of terra-cotta, about twenty inches tall and twenty inches across, with tapering sides and a loose bow emblazoned around the rim. Most such large pots are formal in appearance, but this one was completely informal with a degree of country charm. Knowing my general affinity for garden decoration outside my price range, I didn't even bother to check the price tag. I simply admired it and walked by. Several times. Then, out of curiosity, I looked. My teeth almost fell out (it's a good thing I keep them safely in my back pocket when not in use). The price was unbelievably affordable. In fact, the thought flashed across my mind that I could afford a pair at that price.

Then I began to equivocate. What would I do with one, let alone two, giant pots—the sort that one might find in an Italian villa? Well, I really didn't know. But what was the point? I was going to buy one anyway; wouldn't two be more symmetrical? They only had two, and they would not be getting any more in. Never. Ever. One must consider the options.

Well, to get to the point, I bought only one on the assumption that if its proportions fit within the garden acceptably well, then I could always buy the second tomorrow. It was a good thing I bought only one. · I could handle a single pot in my asymmetrical garden, but two big pots, even informal ones, would have been too formal.

And what did I do with my new pots? Well, the black one has found a perfect home, sitting on a flat, slightly elevated rock that I placed next to the path that leads to the back lawn. Right now it is surrounded by velvet red-leaved coleus and dark purple-leaved *Perilla nankinensis* with white alyssum at its base. Next year I plan to fill it with aquatic variegated sweetflag.

The other pot will take more time to place. I don't plan to fill it with soil and plant it because then I would never be able to move it—I can scarcely move it when it is empty. I am not entirely certain it is winterproof in this area. It would be perfect to hold the fancy-leaved banana that I bought earlier this year. I might put it in the pot on an upended flowerpot. Then fill around it with mulch. After oversummering in the garden, I could bring the banana inside to overwinter. Generally, empty terra-cotta pots left outdoors for the winter do not crack as do full ones. There is no earth in them to expand.

Then again I might not. It's entirely possible that I'll fill it with pansies. They were, after all, what made me buy the pot in the first place.

Week Four

Another time for travel, this an excursion of only two days to an entomological meeting in Richmond, Virginia, then a quick visit with Dee, and a return to . . . dare I dream it? Rain! Glorious rain. Never have I been so happy to see two and a half inches of the wet stuff, enough to truly soak the ground for the first time in months. The last inch of rain was August ninth and before that July seventh. Even with today's rain we are about ten inches below average for this time of year. But who's complaining? Certainly not me. At least about the rain.

Right now it is too wet to work in the garden, and it will probably remain that way for a few days. But that will not stop me from discoursing upon a subject that is rather indelicate, especially for a person in my position—an entomologist who strongly supports biological control and abhors the use of all those -*cides*. As in insecticides, fungicides, miticides, herbicides, rodenticides, and so forth. The delicacy of my position is that while I support biocontrol wholeheartedly, I believe gardeners are being taken for a bucolic ride through a maelstrom of idyllic advertising. In other words, there are some current practices that ought to be labeled "wishful thinking" and "let the buyer beware." This notion was brought to the fore several weeks ago when a letter appeared in the columns of a well-known garden magazine and then was reinforced by my colleague, Dr. Mike Raupp, of the University of Maryland, who presented a paper on the subject of biological control for home gardeners at the recent entomology meeting.

The letter's author waxed ecstatic about the use of a parasitic wasp called *Trichogramma pretiosum*. The gentleman used these wasps to effect some sort of control of an unknown insect pest on Shasta daisies and an unknown "horrid grey-green film of insects" on distorted globe thistles. In the first instance, the parasites were put out as a preemptive strike as the daisies' flowering stalks emerged from the ground (before a pest was even seen), and in the second they achieved noteworthy results in only a week's time.

To discuss this sort of anecdotal testimonial, which took only minutes to create in the first place, requires hours of the kind of documented scientific explanations that even I dislike reading, so I will cut straight to the point and say, trust me, I almost know what I'm talking about. In this instance the buyer of the control agents convinced himself of a scientific cure when, in fact, what he witnessed was more like a miracle of self-deception. Believe me, I take no pride in saying that. The fellow did what he thought was correct, aided in part by overzealous advocates of biocontrol (of which I am one) and uneducated sellers of biocontrol products (in whose producers I own no stock, so I am unbiased on the point).

As with most endeavors, it helps to begin with some facts. In the case of *Trichogramma* (sometimes also called "tricho-wasps" in the trade because there is no common name for them except trichogrammatid wasps), the known species are parasites of the eggs of other insects. Only the eggs. I repeat, *only the eggs*, and then only the eggs of certain kinds of insects. Each species of trichogrammatid wasp attacks only a limited number of similar hosts, and each is generally considered to be relatively host-specific. (While this is not entirely true, it is relatively true, and to explain the exceptions would take a book in itself. One of the basic tenets of biology is that exceptions can be found for almost any statement purporting to summarize our knowledge of a single species.) The first lesson to be learned, then, is that if you release these wasps, they will attack only the eggs of a particular host and essentially only those of that host or of a few species related to it. *Trichogramma pretiosum* attacks only the eggs of moths. Therefore, to release it to control any other insect is pointless.

It is likely that aphids formed the gray-green film of insects that distorted the leaves of the globe thistles. This is only a guess, but based upon the leaf distortion and so-called film it is reasonable. (The term *film* fairly well describes the living coating that aphids create.) Moth larvae would eat holes or possibly tie the leaves but not distort them. Trichogrammatids would not control aphids because they do not parasitize aphids. Never have, never will. Any control the gentleman observed was purely coincidental.

And even if the pesky green film had been an acceptable moth host, trichogrammatids could not have controlled it within a week's time because they attack the egg stage, not the stage doing the damage. Egg parasites reduce the next generation not the generation that is feeding. There is always a lag time between when the wasps are placed in the field and when control is achieved, if ever. In this case, a majority of eggs would have to have been at a suitable developmental stage for parasitism, then they would have to have been parasitized, and the adult pests would have to have stopped laying eggs and have died to achieve success in such a rapid time. Biological control agents are not insecticides; they are nature's balancers, and they need time to bring systems back into balance.

The case of the Shasta daisies is not as easy to assess again because we do not know what the pest was. In fact, the wasps were used only as a prophylactic measure because "nibbled petals" had been observed in the past on fully formed flowers. The wasps were put out as this year's stalks were emerging from the basal vegetation, and there is no evidence that there even was a pest to control, much less that a cure was witnessed. This is not the stuff upon which claims should be made.

The first question that should have been asked before any control was attempted was: What is attacking the daisies and globe thistles? Without knowing this there is no point of reference from which to begin a strategy of attack. You *must* know what the pest is before you can determine the correct biocontrol agent to control that organism. A parasite of the cabbage butterfly, for example, will not control aphids or root fly. In fact, a parasite of cabbage butterfly eggs will not control an existing population of cabbage butterfly larvae. A different organism, one that attacks larvae, is needed for that job. Similarly, if one uses chemicals for control, one must first identify the problem. Insecticides do not control plant pathogens, for example, any better than slug poisons can kill mites. (In fact, some insecticides have little or no effect upon mites because mites are technically not insects—they are more closely related to spiders.) Certainly there are broad spectrum chemicals, but even these must be used with a basic knowledge of a pest and its life stage. Application at the wrong time can be just as ineffective as the use of the wrong chemical. Examples of a pest and its damage should be taken to a trusted local nursery for help in identifying it and for suggestions concerning its control. Often county extension agents provide such information based upon years of experience and research.

The fellow presenting the testimonial was certainly convinced that what he did was right. In this he was no more credulous than the average gardener trying to right a biological imbalance. Biological systems are complicated, and we humans constantly upset the balance of nature because we don't realize how intricate it can be. We do so without the least intention of harm or sometimes without even the knowledge that things are going awry. But we do so nonetheless. Can we expect, then, to restore balance with even less thought and two dollars' worth of wasps? I think not.

Other insects are sold commercially for the home use of gardeners, and I am somewhat embarrassed to say that they work just about as well as if you were to bang a drum, hop up and down, and chant those mystic rites from the tax preparation instructions. Praying mantids, for example, are general predators. They eat honeybees, wasps, flies, ladybugs, spiders, lacewings, swallowtails—whatever they can catch. I love praying mantids and would have a garden full of them, but I would not introduce them to the garden to control pests because these insects are not educated. They do not know what a pest is. To them everything that moves is food, and they would as soon eat your children as a squash borer. (I've always thought it was unfortunate that praying mantids didn't grow bigger.)

Ladybug beetles are often sold for control of aphids, but again, this is a misleading practice based more upon what insects do in nature than what they actually do when you release them into your garden and expect militarily precise results. The beetles usually sold are field-collected hibernating populations that have only one goal in mind when you release them. To fly! This is not the response you want to pay good money for. Research shows that cold-adapted (hibernating) ladybugs must fly to burn off stored fat deposits in their bodies before they can feed. Indeed, experiments conducted by Dr. Raupp and reported at the entomology meeting show that ladybugs have a flight response independent of their physiological condition. Thus, if you release ladybugs to control your aphids, they will most likely fly to your next-door neighbor's aphids. It would be wiser and cheaper to convince your neighbor to buy the beetles to put on his aphids!

Much useful information is available to us gardeners in a recently published book called *Common-Sense Pest Control* by W. Olkowski, Sheila Daar, and H. Olkowski (Newtown, Connecticut: Taunton Press, 1991. Coincidentally, Taunton Press publishes *Fine Gardening* magazine). This is the best-documented research summary that I have seen to date. The 715-page book is a bible for those of us who want to do the right thing yet also get results. The authors take a very broad look at the problem of pest control and have founded a private institute, the Bio-Integral Resource Center (BIRC, P.O. Box 7414, Berkeley, CA 94707), to research solutions for better ways to integrate ourselves back into the environment. BIRC works with municipal, county, state, and federal agencies to achieve its goals of a less toxic world, and it does so with a maximum of biological and integrated approaches. The new book is an attempt to reach the homeowner, and I believe it succeeds well.

In summarizing the problem of home-applied biological control, the authors encourage gardeners to grow a wide variety of plants, both native and garden types, that encourage native predators and parasites to take up residence. By increasing plant variety in a garden, as well as in agricultural systems, we increase the possibilities for beneficial organisms to find places to survive. The idea is to keep a continuous but low population of predators and parasites in the garden at all times. These can then react to a growing pest population as it builds, which is far better than trying to control one that is already at epidemic proportions by throwing bugs or chemicals at it.

Biological control is a lot more complicated than whipping bugs out of a box and expecting immediate results. It is a method of establishing, or more often reestablishing, some sort of natural balance that has been disturbed by the way humankind screwed things up in the first place (to put it truthfully). With living organisms you can rarely correct in a day or a week what we've bollixed up in a year or a lifetime. Many noxious insect and weed pests have been controlled entirely by correctly used biological control methods. Sometimes the results are amazingly quick as in the case of citrus black-fly in Florida. Epidemic populations erupted one year (after apparently smoldering for many years), were discovered, and were effectively controlled in one to two years. Sometimes results are agonizingly slow, as in the control of various thistle species in Virginia that has taken six to twelve years.

We should approach biological controls with honesty and the ability to think for ourselves. Biocontrol works and works well in many instances, but it can only work within the realm of reality. There is no science fiction here, no magic bullet. When the results come, they bring the gardener a restorative, balanced sense of accomplishment. Rarely are there amazing, immediate results that take our breath away—except permanently, in the case of insecticides.

12

OCTOBER

Motivated largely by frustration, today I ripped apart a four-foot-diameter maple trunk section with my bare hands. In the past it had been so hard I couldn't split it with wedges and a sledge hammer, and it was so big and heavy that I couldn't even roll it to the recycling area. But temper (and four years of rot) does wonders for a trunk.

The temper was engendered by purely domestic problems: I was forced to stay home and placate the washing machine. It is the second day of annual leave I've wasted on this relatively new appliance. The part that took two weeks to arrive was defective, so the repairperson will have to come back yet a third time (if I'm lucky, that is), and I will have to take yet another day off. It seems pitiful to me that the largest store in the known universe stocks only one spare part at a time for its current machines. It does not seem to bother these so-called repair services that the inconvenience they cause is inhumane and that we have to pay for it besides. I should deduct my hourly wage from their bill if they can't test their parts before inserting them in my machine.

The only positive point in all this is that it has been a beautiful day to stay home and garden. Such is not always the case, so I suppose sometimes one must be thankful for random coincidences.

My first gardening act of the day was the removal of three more clumps of *Miscanthus sinensis* 'Variegatus'. Well, actually, I intended to take out just one clump and then determine the need to take out more, but sometimes when I start a chore I become lost in the doing and forget about the purpose. The soil was still moist from last week's big rain, and even at a foot deep was amazingly easy to dig. How obviously worthwhile two and a half inches of rain is. Much better than a month's worth of quarter inches. My guess is that in spite of watering, the soil hasn't been wet more than a half inch deep for the past three or four months. A good, long, soaking rain is better than anything else that could have happened in the garden. Lost in my reverie of rain, however, I managed to remove the two additional clumps of grass before I realized what I'd done, and I would have dug out an innocent evergreen as well if I hadn't grown suddenly hot and a bit tired.

The temperature was nearing 80 degrees and my fuel gauge was nearing empty, so I ate a bite of lunch, took a break, and then charged off to the next chore—planting out some of the twenty dozen transplants I'd propagated during the past month or so. I wonder whatever possessed me to start so many seeds? Hope, I suppose. Hope that I can still do something this year to salvage next. Knowledge, perhaps. Knowledge that biennials need planting this year for rewards next. Lack of faith, maybe. When a seed packet claims to hold 400 seeds do I believe it? Well, I do now.

I planted out all the sweet williams and wallflowers, but the area where I wanted to plant the Canterbury bells was taken over earlier this year by a crop of free-seeding anise hyssop (*Agastache foeniculum*). It also was the site of the aforementioned trunk. I pulled up as much of the hyssop as seemed appropriate, knowing full well that next spring it will be replaced by several million new plants from this year's already fallen seed.

Then the repairperson cameth, transforming an otherwise likable day into a trunk-ripping sort of day. After years of waiting, I decided to move the final hunk of tree trunk even if it killed me. The trunk was sitting on the ground, not buried in it, and I was amazed to find that it had rotted apart of its own will. It broke into small sections that I then crushed to dust in my super viselike grip. (Hey, don't sneer, a little fantasy never fails to make the job easier.) The stumpdust was removed to the compost pile where next year it will be but a memory. I returned to planting out the Canterbury bells where the soil is now nicely enriched with the frass (the technical term for insect manure) of termites, carpenter ants, and wood-boring beetles. There is no telling what those Canterbury bells might do next year.

Time once again to mention some colorful flower combinations here in the first week of October. Not surprisingly, most are asters associated with some complementary foil.

The first is the neon pink of *Aster novae-angliae* 'Harrington's Pink' cooled down with the pale lavender-blue of *Campanula pyramidalis.* Both plants are tall, reaching four to five feet, and both are floppy in my ever more shaded front garden. My neighbor's trees increase in height and spread a bit more each year, and I have little choice but to endure as best I can. The campanula grows up through the aster, which has fallen on top of it, so the effect is not picture perfect, but it could be with some staking (maybe next year). Unfortunately, this campanula is a biennial, so it will not exactly repeat the show next year because I didn't plant any this year. 'Harrington's Pink', on the other hand, gets broader and better every year. It even seeds itself about sparingly and comes true from seed. My friend Dug has planted some divisions of my plant in his garden where it receives full sun. Under such conditions it grows straight and true with no staking.

A more vibrant combination is the deep rose-pink *Aster novae-angliae* 'Alma Pötschke' with the deep blue *Salvia azurea* ssp. *pitcheri.* Again, both of these are four feet and floppy. A third flower, the pale pinkish white *Chrysanthemum zawadskii,* underlies the other two, supplying some basal color to the otherwise somewhat elevated show. All are perennials, but the salvia is unreliably hardy here.

More subdued is the rich pink *Penstemon* 'Evelyn' with deep purpled *Aster novae-angliae* 'Purple Dome'. In this case, the aster is scarcely ten inches tall with a background of two-foot-tall 'Evelyn'. I have not had much luck with penstemons: they rarely fill out and bloom for me, but 'Evelyn' is generous in this respect. She's dependable and has bloomed since August. In fact, she made up a nice combination in that month and early September with the deep blue flowers of *Caryopteris* 'Blue Mist' (at two feet) and the pale pink of *Boltonia* 'Pink Beauty' (at three feet).

A final combination, at six feet tall, is the pure yellow *Helianthus maximilianii* and the purple *Aster tartaricus* given to me by my neighbor Margaret who has had the plant in her garden for years. Both *Helianthus* and the aster are robust, somewhat aggressive plants, but not so much that they strike fear in the heart of the timid gardener. I've planted them in a hostile part of my rank garden and they have remained humble for two years. I have seen no indication of wanton spreading, but the soil is hard and little-watered. In a finely prepared bed the two of them might slug it out and produce quite a beautiful show.

These minor victories of workable plant combinations in an otherwise undistinguished year are what make gardening worth the effort. Without these few rays of hope, these rewards now and again, we gardeners might take a few more vacations next year and the garden might just find itself weed-choked and abandoned as the gardener finds greener pastures and lower fences over which to leap.

A houseguest, shortened evenings, and socially dictated necessities precluded much physical activity in the garden at least part of the week, and I must admit that I resent these minor intrusions into my normal routine. Fortunately, there is an invisible connection between mind and body so that my mind is free to wander at will. Though my body may be present, it is no guarantee that my mind is anywhere near the obligation under which I have been placed.

It is somewhat embarrassing, for example, when, in the course of polite conversation, my hostess or some other equally inconsiderate person poses a direct question while I am off somewhere in the ether, pondering more important matters. Did I plant the wallflowers too close together? Would it be OK to move the hydrangeas at this time of year or should I wait until spring? Can I move a four-foot cypress without killing it? Even if I can, should I? Is it too late to plant seeds of *Verbascum* for next year? (What, am I crazy? Who needs more seedlings?) Would it be better to let the tropical water lily die a natural death or prolong its agony trying to overwinter it? What would be a good way to prolong its agony should I decide to do so? Should I respade the front garden or just sod the whole thing over?

The proposition of social interactions between gardeners and non-gardeners is a dicey one. Let's be honest and say that observing social amenities is often difficult enough for us gardeners among ourselves, so nongardeners should not expect too much from us. Most gardeners will freely admit that we would rather be playing in the dirt than sitting at a formal dinner party trying to appear intelligent. Or that we would much rather be pulling weeds than conversing with houseguests.

I find personal interactions with numbers of people, or even single people, becoming less and less necessary. It isn't just that I don't like the company of other people—generally I don't—it is that I can mostly get along fine without it. My friends know this, and they almost never bother me except when they need some sort of help in the garden. Strangers, near strangers, and colleagues often find this indifference slightly insulting. I don't know why, exactly, but many people have a very high opinion of their rank as humans, when in fact they are much less useful than a good potato or a sheaf of wheat. I ask you, given the choice, would you rather eat a new potato with sour cream or a bank teller? A piece of bread with jam or a policeman? I think the choice is obvious, but many people don't. They insist that they are important, but in this world, nothing is more important than plants.

Why, only recently, in an informal nationwide poll of gardeners, on a scale of one to ten (ten being highest), most gardeners rated beets and rutabagas a solid three, which was just slightly above the rating they gave to nongardeners (a weak 1.8). They ranked other gardeners from a low five (when they are not around) to nearly nine (when something nice in the garden needs a compliment). Roses, I might add, were placed at one, while the gardeners' own gardens nearly always ranked ten. (I need not point out the often grotesque relationship between nongardeners and roses. I note in passing only that the rose was recently picked as the national flower. Need I say more?)

As gardeners, we draw our strength from plants and often do not depend upon others of our own species to entertain us or make our lives better. If we sometimes seem standoffish to nongardeners, it is because we dedicate ourselves to the care and betterment of plants. If the garden teaches us anything, it is that enslavement is a small price to pay for freedom.

I was somewhat relieved, earlier this week, to read that *The Nymph's* buttocks had been repaired. These minor, and sometimes finer, points of life are important to know, and I make it a habit to scan the papers for them. It is not everyday that a nymph has her fanny dimpled by helicopters and lives to tell about it. Then again, I suppose she was lucky—it's not everyday you can get your fanny repaired after something as stressful as helicopter dimpling. The repairs were performed at an undisclosed cost to the taxpayers, and we may all rest better for the taxing experience.

Perhaps I should go back a few months, when, you may recall, I commiserated with the ivy-covered dinosaur during the great war celebration-hysteria that broke out on the nation's mall. A number of sculptures at the outdoor Hirshhorn Sculpture Garden were damaged by helicopters as they landed nearby. Whirlwinds of gravel produced a sandblasting effect, pitting some of the metal sculptures. But hey, festivities are festivities, and victories must be celebrated. Who cares, anyway? It was just a bloated nymph, after all, and a few other nondescript pieces of tin.

I happen to like the sculpture garden myself. It is a bit of formal, refined, multilevel gardening with an emphasis on straight lines, evergreens, large shrubs, hedges, ponds, water, and, not least, sculptures. I do not spend a great amount of time there, but I always enjoy visiting the place and having a look at some of the modern sculpture that clutters up the fully functional garden.

As to *The Nymph*, I am happy to state that a little auto body filler (or perhaps some more professional and suitable butt-patching compound), and she's as good as new. It would take an expert eye and a long time to find any sign of damage. In fact, I walked up to the sculpture, took a good, long look at her behind, and didn't see a single extraneous dimple. Well, I don't think there was an extraneous dimple. I mean, with all those bulges it's sort of hard to tell what's extraneous in the first place. It's possible that someone maybe missed a spot or two, but I'd be the last person to know. It would require a lot more study and I don't have that kind of time right now. Maybe later in winter, when I've run out of garden chores, I'll study the problem a little further.

I suggest that the next time you're in Washington, D.C., you take a look at *The Nymph* and let me know what you think. It could be that my sense of aesthetics is not all that it should be.

Week Two

It occurs to me that you might be wondering about my qualifications to write about gardening. I must be honest and admit—not to put too fine a point on it—that I have no qualifications whatsoever. I garden and I write. Very simple. This makes me scarcely less mentally fit than any other journalist or biographer you've ever read, and I don't think it will hurt to be honest at this point. You will have nearly finished the book by now, and it's too late to return it anyway.

I have been called an "expert" in my field, but people occasionally have said nice things about me as well. I have written nearly sixty scientific papers of a highly suspicious nature, and they are painfully dull to read. (Science editors require papers to be dull.) I decided some years back that science was fine as far as it went, but if one were going to write, one might as well write something that someone else might possibly want to read. It is not pleasant to think that one's combined contributions to science have been read in their entirety by fewer people than might be found in an institution for the criminally insane.

It was this cold, harsh thought taken in conjunction with some cold, miserable winters that led me to take up the semiavocation of garden writing in spite of the fact that I am no expert when it comes to gardening. For that reason—and you might have noticed this yourself—I rarely treat the more technical aspects of gardening or the how-to or even the precise. Instead I focus on the more imponderable or improbable aspects and even the uneventful. I merely treat the garden as seen as a haven for a fellow who is mostly shot to hell at the end of a day spent being an expert in his own field.

Now that I've begun my little exposé on the subject of experts, I would like to tell you a gardening story that is true. I ought to know because it happened to me. It is a story that points out the oddly dual nature of what the public thinks about people who write and how they make of us something we are not. How they assume that writing means you are an expert or are at least smart or that you even know something about what you are writing. Nothing could be further from the truth!

The story takes place during my first trip to England in 1982. I happened, by design, to be traveling near a small English village that boasted three Garden-Open-Today signs. It could have been any English village, but let's call it Up-On-The-Down just to make the story sound authentic. Three open gardens in Up-On-The-Down sounded too good to miss, so I pulled off the main road and rolled down a narrow lane into an even narrower village. It was the sort of village that became so narrow one had to abandon one's car near the edge and walk up a considerably narrowed path to get to the even narrower houses. It was obviously built before the time of cars.

When I reached the first house on the tour, a small hand-lettered sign proclaimed that for forty pence, payable in advance, I could visit all three gardens. I have never been known to pass up a bargain, so I gladly put the sum in the box that sat near the gate and proceeded on the tour.

The first two gardens were of only marginal interest, which points up a fundamental truth: not all English gardens (even those with admission fees) are examples of the gardener's art as we Americans are always led to believe. Of course, the sky was decidedly leaden and the day overwhelmingly gloomy, and this might have discolored my opinion a bit. But not much.

The third garden was some distance away from the village (equivalent to the suburbs, I suppose) and set among rolling hills. I drove up to a private drive, parked in the lane, and from this vantage point could see an imposing house, barn, and semiformal garden astride the hill. I walked up the graveled drive and was turning toward the garden when I spotted a figure sitting in the doorway reading a newspaper. Simultaneously, she spotted me, arose, and walked toward me.

"That will be forty pence," she said in what seemed a more formal tone than was necessary.

Instinctively I said, "I've just paid down at the village," feeling immediately like a miser who'd taken a child's lollipop. The woman seemed resigned to my statement, somewhat as if hers was always the last garden on the forty-pence circuit, as if she knew her fingers would never caress the rim of a fifty-pence coin, would never know the ecstasy of returning two shillings in change. It seemed painfully sad, this apparently rich woman sitting out the entire day, reading her newspaper—rain imminent—awaiting her first forty pence of the day. And probably her last, too, judging from the inactivity of this sodden Sunday afternoon.

As if to somehow make up for the lack of cold currency, I did something I rarely ever do with strangers—I spoke. "I've been looking at gardens," I said, which must have been nearly the second most stupid thing I've ever said. In a hurried attempt to cover up the vacantness of my remark, I blurted out an additional, "I'm looking at gardens and writing about them." (This was only broadly true. Part of my purpose in going to England was to visit one special garden and to write about it— as recorded in *Thyme on My Hands*.)

At this point the woman's interest perked up a bit and she said, "Oh, you're a writer, then?"

Immediately I knew I was heading for deep waters because at the time I did not consider myself a writer. I had not published anything; therefore, I was not a writer. In my most authoritative voice I replied, "No . . . ," searching for the exact combination of words that would explain just what I actually considered myself.

As I muddled about for some sort of coherent answer, the woman's eyes began to dim with confusion, and I felt an immediate need to rescue her before she sank away completely in my quagmire of explanation. So I blurted out, ". . . but I'm writing a book on gardening."

At this the woman showed some renewed interest, and I could

predict that I'd made yet another tactical error. With a modicum of understanding (or so she imagined), she addressed me with the questioning statement: "Oh, you're a garden expert, then?"

In for a pence, I thought, in for a pound, and said aloud quite honestly, "No, I am not an expert on gardening."

"Not an expert?" she asked with as exasperated an expression as I ever want to see, "and writing a book?" She shook her head at the notion and walked off leaving me holding the conversation.

As she walked back to her chair, I called out somewhat as an afterthought and entirely in self-defense, ". . . but . . . but I am an expert in my own field." What she thought about this final, irrelevant confession was probably best left unsaid anyway.

I spent the remainder of my time in the garden hiding behind the taller perennials and shrubs and, on those occasions when I might be seen from the official watcher's chair, attempting to appear as "expert" as I possibly could. Under the circumstances, I did not remain long. The garden wasn't all that interesting, anyway. Really.

At one time, I presume, being an expert must have meant something. I don't think it does anymore. It is one of those overused, underdefined words of our time. According to my dictionary, an expert is a "thoroughly skilled person." Recently, however, I think the term has become equated with people who have only one particular skill—the ability to communicate with other people. That is, if you are a good talker, say on the television talk-show circuit, or a good writer, then it follows that you must know what you are talking or writing about. I am not convinced that this association is any indication of knowledge about much of anything.

The entire concept of expertism is slightly appalling to me because of its dual-edged nature. Generally, the experts who do the work are the very ones who can least popularize or explain it. Individuals who *can* popularize subjects often become the experts in absentia. These people are talented, to be certain. They are synthesizers, abstracters, recorders, reporters, simplifiers, communicators. But not, I think, experts.

Some years back I was visiting a local but widely known and respected azalea nursery in the Washington, D.C., area. Its owner-propagator-hybridizer-potterupper-caretaker-sales clerk was valiantly trying to take care of several customers at once as ever more were taxiing up the driveway. The fellow was answering questions at an expert's pace and collecting very little reward for doing so. As I edged closer to ask my own question, a potential customer apparently known to the owner posed the commanding question, "You know so much about azaleas, why don't you write a book about them?"

That seemed reasonable to me, too.

The owner's reply was direct and straight at my heart: "Those of us who work in the garden," he stated matter-of-factly, "don't have time to write books. It's the ones who don't work who do all the writing."

Ouch!

He was right, I suppose, at least on one point. He has a very specialized knowledge—an expert's knowledge—and damn little time to write about it. Experts become experts by doing. Alternatively, I have a very generalized knowledge . . . and not much of that. But then I'm really not trying to tell anyone anything useful about gardening, and I make no pretense about it. I just garden when I can and write when I can't—garden that is.

So let me say again, I am an amateur at this gardening stuff. I don't want to be called an expert because I am not. I have written two books, but books do not a gardener make. I garden because I enjoy it; it takes my mind off being an expert in my own field.

There is a tremendous amount of knowledge in the world and an even greater amount awaits discovery. In these days of the information revolution, there is entirely too much information and not enough revolution to suit my taste. We take what is told to us, presumably by experts, we repeat it, we might even think difficult thoughts based upon it, but we seldom question whether the facts were correct in the first place. How can we? There is too much to know about everything and little enough time to become expert in our own fields, never mind anyone else's.

Week Three

The temperature is starting to drop dramatically now, with nights in the thirties, forties, or fifties and daytimes in the sixties or seventies. The garden and the gardener are breaking from the late summer lull. The routine of summer's garden, such as it was this year, is no longer routine, and the questions arise of what ought to be done, what needs to be done, and who wants to work when the air is a frigid, barely tolerable 60 degrees? I would just as soon sit and pout as work. But I, a simple gardener, have no say in the matter. The garden has taken on its own frenzied feel this week. Frost has collected in spots, though not yet here, and where frost settles can winter be far behind? Low temperatures prompt one to get a move on before it's too late. Now is the call to planting, transplanting, moving, and cleaning up before the weather gets really bad.

Bulbs arrive, are sorted and prioritized. Lilies and tulips can wait a few days (yes, I bought another batch of tulips . . . these will be absolutely, positively the last unless they do very well, indeed). *Eremurus* must go right in. Nursery plants that should have been put out months ago finally receive their proper treatment, and months-old rooted cuttings are discovered hiding behind them; all have suffered enough root binding already. Cuttings must be taken of artemisias and rues—forgotten in the earlier haste to take overwintering cuttings. Several areas in otherwise good bloom are groomed to take advantage of what little grace and style (if any) remains in the garden. A planting of gorgeous huge-flowered deep pink and rose cosmos with white chrysanthemums and big clumps of woolly-white-foliaged senecios is made to look respectable by cleaning up the tawdry neighborhood that surrounds it. Three dozen seedlings of *Patrinia* are transplanted from their self-sown, scattered indiscretions to a well-defined patch where next year their yellow flowers will glow like a lighthouse in the garden. Fifty pounds of *Ophiopogon japonicus*, extracted from my friend Ron's garden, have been picked up and await a decision on where to put them (not to mention a work commitment). And now is the time to correct the mistakes of this year and of many past years. The time has come to pay my dues for years of indecision and procrastination. The mistakes must be faced head on.

There is nothing quite as pathetic as a plant in the wrong place. Whether it's a big one in a too-tight space or a little one floundering about in a vacuum, a moisture-lover in a dust-dry desert, or a cactus in a swampy swale, the result is the same—stress. The plant is stressed, the garden is stressed, and the gardener is stressed. There are only two solutions to this problem: move the plant or restructure the garden around it. (Well, three solutions, if you count moving the gardener, but we'll forego that option as being impractical.)

Whichever method is chosen, it means work for the gardener. Several of the largest mistakes should have been the smallest: dwarf conifers that were, according to the laws of nature—and the proprietors of nurseries—supposed to stay dwarf. Dwarf, in my dictionary, is defined as "much smaller than the usual one of its species." Well, OK, I guess so, but with plants the concept of "much smaller" is entirely relative . . . often to the space allotted to it in the garden. A big plant in a small space is relatively much bigger than a big plant in a big space. Mathematically, that is.

Which brings us to the case of the biggest small mistake I corrected this week: the too-big bun. This involves *Chamaecyparis pisifera* 'Compacta', a dwarf form of the sawara cypress. This cultivar is described in the literature as "a charming little rich green bun of a plant" ideal for the rock garden. I am quite fond of bun-type plants, so when the opportunity arose, I purchased this plant at a local nursery. It was a fine bun, too, I might add, already years along judging by its good size. Since in twenty years it was purported to reach eight inches high by twelve inches wide, my plant was surely ten years old, if not more, and a fantastic bargain at only nine dollars and ninety-five cents. Could life be any better? Well, yes, it could, as I found out.

About four years ago I placed the little bun in a choice spot next to the large pond. It would be grand, I thought, to look out over this miniature tree and see the water, to walk around the pond and see its reflection in rippling black angles. Alas, this fantasy was short-lived. The tree grew and grew to about three feet tall and equally as wide and nearly blotted out the view of the pond altogether. Evidently, the plant was grossly genetically aberrant or, more probably, simply mislabeled. My guess is the latter. Whatever the cause, it required some delicate surgery to remove it. Much more delicate than I first imagined.

The plan was to save the plant, to extract it with a large root ball. With evergreens this is not normally difficult. In this case, however, the difficulty arose because the tree was wedged tightly between the gravel pathway and the edge of the pond, which was made with one of those PVC pond liners. To create a large hole next to the pond was to risk puncturing the liner or, even worse, having the side of the pond collapse into the excavation. Neither sounded particularly desirable.

It was with gingerly strokes that I began the excavation, on one hand trying not to disrupt the pathway too much and on the other trying not to slip the shovel through the side of the pond. After only a short while I ran into what all diggers fear the most—rock. At least I thought it was a rock. It sounded like one anyway. A big, bouncy one. I kept hitting it no matter where I put the shovel. After several attempts to force the shovel in, over, and around the rock, I decided to take a trowel and explore the situation more closely. A good thing, too, as I soon discovered that I had been trying to slice through the underground plastic piping system I'd built to move water to the distant taps in my garden. The main supply pipe now ran through the root ball of the oversized cypress, and it was becoming more and more apparent that it was not likely to survive this surgery.

If I didn't flood the place by breaking the pipe, I would most likely flood it by collapsing the pond wall. I don't know what your approach to difficult decisions is, but when I'm faced with them, I usually bail out. And this was no exception. Who needed another tree? Trees are expendable, I've learned. Best just to admit defeat. So, with a few well-placed cuts, this tree was off to the brush pile. Another garden investment reduced to kindling.

I ran into a similar predicament with two other dwarf conifers near the pond. One is a dwarf white pine, *Pinus strobus* 'Nana', supposedly a slow grower at about two inches per year. My twelve-inch-tall plant grew nearly three feet in five years, about two and a half times the normal growth rate. I wanted to move it, but it was likely I'd have to kill the tree to do so. This time it was wedged between the pond, the path, and the flagstone terrace. After a little exploratory root surgery, I decided that it should remain in place. Because the tree takes well to pruning, I would turn it into a pseudobonsai. As slow as I might be, I can still prune faster than it can grow.

The other pondside conifer that needed attention was *Picea abies* 'Repens', the creeping spruce. This species is supposed to grow only one inch per year with a five-foot spread in twenty-five or thirty years. My plant grew about six to ten inches a year and outgrew its place in fewer seasons than can be counted on the toes of a three-toed sloth. This was unfortunate because it stretched across the narrowest part of the pond and soon obliterated it. I began to worry about this plant in earnest, though, when I saw one at Longwood Gardens that measured about twenty feet across. My plant could cover the whole pond, and quickly, I estimated. After a few years of delicate, half-hearted cutting-back, I whaled away on the plant this year. We shall see the results next spring, as it normally puts out a beautiful flush of soft, weeping new foliage. I may have cut too much . . . one never really knows until the following year, and by then it is too late. If so, then out will come the remains, and it will be a brutal affair because it is wedged between two great (and immovable) rocks at pond's edge. I await spring with some trepidation.

Another "dwarf" mistake appears to have only one resolution—annual pruning. It is the weeping hemlock, *Tsuga canadensis* 'Pendula'. The eastern hemlock is a beautiful tree and comes in many forms from treelike to prostrate. I have eight forms in my garden. The weeping form was one of the very first plants I bought when I moved to the garden. It is a tree without peer. Large plants (three or four feet tall) are expensive, so I purchased several one-foot-tall plants when I first moved here and put them aside until I could find prize places for them as the garden developed. The growth rate is supposedly slow vertically, but I did not reckon on the sideways growth, which is not so slow!

When I built the pond, it was preordained that one weeping plant would be associated with it. This is axiomatic: one weeping plant per pond, minimum. They seem to reinforce each other. Naturally, the plant that first came to mind was a weeping hemlock. I planted it far back from the pond as a backdrop and gave it six feet to spread out. Now, twelve years later, it has taken its six feet. So much for planning.

I am even more troubled after having seen a fantastically beautiful plant at Longwood Gardens. I was not prepared for the experience. The tree, at over seventy-five years of age, must be twenty feet across and ten feet tall. That's a fifth the width of my back garden, and I have one specimen on either side. At least they grow relatively slowly, so it will be many years before the two trees meet, and I shall be long gone. Although I prune my plant by the pond, I don't like to do so. Nature's pattern seems better than anything I might come up with.

The final nondwarf was a plant of *Chamaecyparis pisifera* 'Golden Mops', which had a prominent position in the rock garden. This is not supposed to grow much at all, yet my three-year-old plant is now almost four feet tall. Too tall for my small rockery. The plant has beautiful pendulous yellow foliage and looks entirely at home in its setting, but at its current growth rate, I would need to spend considerable time and patience each year trying to keep it in bounds. Therefore, reluctantly, one fine day this week, I moved it to the area from which I removed the large clumps of grass two weeks ago. Here the tree looks right at home and has considerable room in which to grow, if it survives the transplanting, that is. It is sited across the grass pathway from *Chamaecyparis pisifera* 'Boulevard', which, although the same species, looks nothing at all like it. 'Boulevard' is blue-green to gray, upright, and rather billowy. You would not think the plants were in the same genus, much less of the same species, but that's the way variation and selection (even manmade) work.

If 'Golden Mops' had been a little more slow-growing, I would have left it in the rockery, but then its roots might have created too much competition for the small plants in its vicinity. In any case, I already have too many trees to trim because they are in the wrong place. It is not so easy to trim these weepers artistically, nor should it be necessary if they were planted in the correct place to begin with.

I would like to point out, in defense of the gardener, that not all garden mistakes are the gardener's fault. Some are. Many aren't. In the case of mistakes I corrected this year, several of the varieties I planted were sold to me under incorrect names. If I purchase a plant called 'Golden Mops', then I have a right to expect the plant to do what 'Golden Mops' is supposed to do—stay moplike. I should not have to grow a plant for two or three or five years only to find out that it was mislabeled. Not only does the overall garden design suffer, but I must labor to extricate the plant from its surroundings or live with it. Either way, the gardener suffers, not the nursery that sells the plant. After a few years it seems too late to receive recompense from the nursery, even if I could remember which one I bought the plant from (and if I still had the receipt). It makes one wary of nurseries. Yesterday I went to a reliable nursery and purchased a new specimen of 'Golden Mops'. Now the question is, "Was this a mistake?" I shall have to wait several years to find out. By that time I will undoubtedly have a few more mistakes to add to my lifetime record.

Week Four

A week that begins in the dentist's office with four hands in one's mouth is not the envy of most rational human beings. There are better ways to greet eight o'clock on a Monday morning than by being bludgeoned in the name of yet another crown. Unfortunately, Monday turned out to be the high point of a week that ended with a funeral and included a week-long visit with a hyperactive houseguest. You might imagine my near mental collapse by week's end.

On crowning day I decided to stay home after the event and work in the garden—the only course of action, you might agree, that would be a suitable anodyne for such a beating. The last week or so the temperature has warmed toward midday, and I was not too unhappy spending a working day at home. I had plenty to do, of course, as all gardeners do almost all the time, so it was simply a matter of deciding what to do first.

The obvious choice was a relatively simple one involving the recent gift of fifty pounds of leftover dwarf *Ophiopogon japonicus* that awaited transplanting into the garden. These lily turfs (or mondo grasses, as they are also called) were the excesses of my gardening friend Ron Hodges, of whom it might be said candidly that he has given up gardening almost entirely and now merely grows thousands of plants all over his suburban lot. Whereas I am still putting more plants into the garden than I'm taking out, Ron has arrived at the point in his gardening life where he spends all his time taking plants out.

Ron is one of those gardeners that you have to respect for the amount of labor he put in simply to prepare the ground before any garden could be contemplated. He spent untold years with a pickaxe grubbing over every cubic inch of his well-hilled, solid clay property to a depth of forty-six feet (conservatively speaking), taking out every stone, every bit of tree root, every bit of endless lawn, and three layers of paleolithic Indian civilizations. Then he carted all the nonground material away and put back cubic miles of humus, built graveled pathways to the end of the earth, and incorporated tons of miniature green life forms, or plants, as he calls them, destined to live forever (or until the next spring, whichever came first).

In spite of the herculean work (or toil, if you like) of preparation, Ron is a minimalist at heart, reveling in the tiniest, most insignificant plants ever not seen by humankind. It is a testimonial to site preparation that his garden has, over the years, turned into a lush, exuberant mound of greenery designed to surprise and delight at each turn. Such a testimonial, in fact, that removing fifty pounds of lily turf created not the slightest ripple in his otherwise luxuriant patch of the stuff.

Only last week I had been eying my small planting of *Ophiopogon japonicus* with the intention of splitting it up (into a whopping three or four plants!) but then decided against it as serving no purpose. Certainly I could not replant the extensive patches I had in mind. So it was a great windfall when Ron asked me (maybe begged would be more accurate) to take the plants off his hands.

With the first one hundred plants and three hours of labor I was able to line two small walkways that needed something to break up the monotony of the bricks. With the second fifty plants and two hours of labor I was able to create several curving patches along an otherwise undistinguished woodland pathway. At this point the bag of lily turf was bigger than when I started, and I was beginning to think it was growing faster than I could plant it. A different approach surely was needed. Instead of pulling off individual plants from the mass of underground runners, I simply took the remaining five clumps (approximately 1276 plants) and in fifteen minutes created two great patches of green where before there had been only the brown stain of mulch.

After I dispatched with the lily turf, I turned to a project requiring the removal of two small Japanese maples that I had root-pruned and severely top-pruned last fall with the idea of potting them up as bonsai (or at least pseudobonsai). These trees were, coincidentally, also given to me by Ron, who was thinning out his forest many years ago. I, myself, moved them once, having first planted them in a situation that, all things considered, was about as stupid a place as I could have thought up. After the two moves and a severe pruning, these six- or seven-year-old trees now stand two and a half to three feet tall with three-quarter-inch trunks. I plan to pot them up as a double-trunked tree—if they do not die, that is. The point of the story, however, does not really concern the trees so much as the hole I created taking them out. Since I was close to the organic recycling stockpile (i.e., compost heap), I decided to grab a few bucketfuls to replenish the hole I'd created, and therein hangs the tale, as they say.

It was while gathering up compost that I found the widget. Quite by accident, of course, because I didn't even know I'd lost it. After three years one tends to forget that such devices exist at all. But to find it right where I presumably had left it—two feet deep in the compost pile— why, that is quite remarkable by any standards. Usually I never find anything where I leave it.

A widget, for those who don't own one, is a double-ended, semispoonlike dull knife that is used for . . . for . . . well, for widgeting, I suppose. It is a sort of gardening thingy, one of those tools that seems invaluable when purchased but is promptly forgotten when misplaced. I used it for prying out weeds from narrow crevices between rocks and flagstones or between rocks and other rocks. Since its disappearance some years ago, I've been using another weeding device with nearly disastrous results and had, quite frankly, forgotten all about the wonderful widget.

The replacement for the widget was a weeding tool sold in one catalog by the highly descriptive name of "weeding tool." Odd how that works. I have seen them more romantically referred to as "fishtail weeders" or "asparagus knives." The tool is a long, sharp-bladed, unwieldy sort of object with no known function except, perhaps, to aid in the spread of tetanus. The functioning end of the knife, a notched, beveled edge, is small and so far removed at the end of the shank as to require great eye-hand coordination. Unfortunately, my eye always coordinated the weeder into the back of my opposite hand. After the last and most severe wound, I thankfully managed to lose the device. But like the widget, it will most likely turn up when least expected.

After losing the second tool, I started using a short screwdriver for weeding. It worked fine and was fairly safe if I held one hand behind my back. Ordinarily, a serious judgment problem might have been created by the finding of the widget—namely, whether to use it *or* the screwdriver—but the foundling caused no such dilemma this time. That's because some time back I threw the screwdriver at a pair of rabbits who were munching merrily away in my primrose patch, and the screwdriver is now lost and likely to stay that way until I find it three years from now in the compost pile.

I don't know about you, but I think things disappearing is just about the most common problem one finds in the garden (if you discount all the others, that is). There is darn little you can do about it, too. Labels, for instance, disappear as if some garden sprite had better use for them than you do. During the course of weeks or months, freshly lettered labels leak out of the ground like water from an old tap. Eventually, by way of gravity, I suppose, all the metal and plastic labels collect at the nearest low point in the garden where they may be gathered for some purpose unknown to me. Generally, the plants to which they belonged have also long since disappeared. If not, then the writing has disappeared. (Wooden labels disappear entirely, providing an increment of humus and no worry whatsoever about where to replace them. Wooden labels, then, are much preferred to plastic ones.)

Watering devices are frequently lost—the more detachable the more likely so. I am particularly fond of a fan-type sprinkler that puts out a fine mist of spray over a pie-shaped area. The head sits high up on a spike that is pushed into the ground. Each spring I poke in one sprinkler at each tap to insure the nearby convenience of such a device. Simple mathematics would indicate that after ten years each tap ought to have somewhere between six and fifty-seven sprinklers by now, but I am doing well to find a single one on any given attempt. Whenever I travel to the West Coast, I bring two or three of these sprinklers back with me. (For some strange and un-American reason they may be purchased only out that way.) I haul these back discreetly in my suitcase (they do look like a set of stilettos, after all) by wrapping them in some offensive item, such as a Christmas tie or last week's underwear, to prevent too much finger-prodding by airport officials. I do not know where they disappear to in the garden, but I know they are out there, somewhere, lurking behind some shrub or other, awaiting the time I might kneel on the ground or fall over. I've started wearing armor, just in case.

Hoses are much harder to lose than sprinklers, and they're a lot easier to find, too. No matter where I put them or how neatly arranged they might be, I always manage to trip over an unseen coil or two. I'm told by eminent herpetologists that this is their way. They lie in wait for prey to come along, fling a hidden coil at the feet of the intruder, and hope that he or she falls into a trap made of sprinkler spikes. Vicious. Simply vicious. And even if you should see the viper in the grass, there's not one chance in two that you will find the end that does the spitting until you turn the tap on. By then, of course, it is too late. Your shoe will be quite full, or a long, wildly gesticulating section will have spat water in your face or, even worse, smacked you in the spectacles. The garden is a jungle in case you didn't know.

There are a good many temporary losses that may be aggravating but are not necessarily as life-threatening as the hose. Occasionally, to cite an example from my own record book, I put the hand pruners (aptly named, those) on a stone while weeding and then promptly forget which stone. When I put the trowel down to use the pruners, they are ten feet away and require an endless search to find. In the meantime, I have lost the trowel.

In fact, the largest tool I've ever lost in the garden—that I've found, anyway—is the hand trowel. Normally when I'm interrupted, I push the trowel headfirst into the soil. One time it apparently fell over before I returned. There it remained among the weeds in the side yard until I found it quite by accident when I was weeding the area for what must have been the second time in as many years. I learned a valuable lesson from this: do not put a tool down until you've finished the job. Make that two lessons: if you're interrupted, take it with you.

The most valuable tool I've lost in the garden was a power tool of sorts—a gin and tonic! This is the power unit for all my other tools. I sat it down and somehow (don't ask me how!) forgot it. It wasn't until the next afternoon that I found it quite by accident while mowing the lawn. It is a startling proposition, really, to hear grass shatter when you cut it . . . startling indeed. It's unnecessary, I suppose, to say that glass does not readily lend itself to mowing. I mean, you don't end up with juice glasses, for instance, if you start with the iced tea variety. You end up, if you are very lucky, with minutely slivered glass ground into the lawn; if not, with deadly gashing objects flying all about the landscape.

Losing things in the garden is generally no great shakes as life goes. Most of us do it on a regular basis. Whether this is due to indifference or inattention I know not. I would guess that losing the tools one needs the most is a type of psychological self-denial. That is, it denies the self an opportunity to work. Not a bad sort of illness if you can develop it, and much preferred to afflictions such as anglophobia (fear of tea cozies), claustrophobia (fear of dependent clauses), or widgetophobia (fear of widgets).

I once tried to solve the problem of losing things in the garden by tying each piece of equipment to a long cord and then tying all the cords to my belt. When I needed a tool, I just hauled in the line. This worked fine until I lost my pants.

But that is another story entirely.

Week Five _____

Although the growing season might appear to have come to an end, there is still evidence that some plants wish to continue their idyllic quest for self-replication. A number of handsome patches of *Cyclamen hederifolium* are blooming with apparent delight and bright white-marbled foliage. They appear to have no intention of letting a little frost stop them, here at the end of October. I noticed last week, while putting out the mondo grass, that some seedling cyclamens were sprouting in the pathway. This is a sure indication that my seed-grown cyclamens, now about three years old, have accepted their situation in life and have decided to stay awhile. I have three dozen corms now, some of which are three inches in diameter. It took four tries to get a colony firmly established. Before that I'd managed to keep only one or two corms from among a dozen or so nursery-bought stock. This is a good lesson to the gardener: never give up on the first attempt. Or even the second or third.

Many years back I planted *Cyclamen coum* in the garden and never saw it come up, so I naturally presumed it had died. I was startled one year to see a few small pink flowers waving about near the ground in the woodland garden. *Cyclamen coum* was alive and well. "A miracle," I thought. "It must have seeded in from Turkey." Then I remembered that I had planted the corm several years earlier. It has come up for the past five years but has never seeded itself. I would guess it is only marginally happy where it is, but I know better than to transplant it. I once convinced myself to transplant an old corm of *Cyclamen hederifolium* during dormancy. I knew exactly where it was—or so I thought—only to discover that I was off by about six inches. The corm was sliced in half and never recovered. I've made it a rule not to move cyclamens. If I need one somewhere else, I grow it from seed and plant it there.

Cyclamens are not the only plants happily blooming away this week. Two species of *Erodium* seem to be quite beside themselves in this cool October weather. *Erodium reichardii* ssp. *flore-plenum* with its prostrate creeping habit and double pink flowers is doing better even than in the spring when I first put it out, and *E. chrysanthum*, flowering at some six inches in height, is a delight with its dissected leaves and pale yellow flowers. The former is not hardy, but it spreads so easily that I just pot up a few pieces and overwinter them in the greenhouse. By spring I will have more than I'll know what to do with, so back it goes into the garden.

An uncommon plant with flowers partly white and partly the same yellow as *Erodium chrysanthum* is *Asarina procumbens*. This is sometimes called *Antirrhinum asarina*. Whatever its name, its flowers are exactly like snapdragons, but the plant is quite different, having trailing stems with softly hairy, gray-green foliage. Everything on the plant is sticky, including its seeds, and for this reason it gets itself into the most obscure places. Sasha, the fellow rock gardener who gave me my first plants, has the things sprout and live in the masonry between bricks in a vertical wall. The roots do not have the tenacity to match the seed's audacity, however, and it is easily uprooted. My plants have been blooming all summer in the rock garden, and in spite of heat and drought and now cold, they continue to bloom contentedly as they tumble all about the rocky outcrops. They have never stopped looking exceptionally proud of themselves all this year.

Several varieties of *Cimicifuga racemosa* are in their best bloom now with pure white bottlebrush flowers. At three feet in height they stand out as beacons in the darker regions of the garden. Insects flock to them as if it were midsummer when the air warms up enough for them to overcome their normal stupor at this time of year. Another plant of the purest white is *Nicotiana* 'Domino Hybrids'. These annuals grew from last year's self-sown seed when I had quite a few plants in the garden. Sometimes if plants want to come back for a repeat performance, I leave them alone to see how well they can behave. In this case the progeny were just as good as their parents—better even—because I did not have to do a thing except have enough sense not to weed them out when they came up.

Another self-sown plant, the perennial *Calamintha nepeta*, was left to grow in a gravel pathway, and there are now four healthy specimens blooming their collective stems off. It seems quite late for such a show, especially as I equate these with the height of summer, but who am I to argue with success? Next spring I will move one or two of the plants to make a little room to walk on the path—or perhaps next fall would be more realistic.

As wonderful as it is to have these flowers in full bloom, I know that the gardening year is drawing to a close. I have been preparing as best I can this week—and it is not the least bit welcome preparation. I've taken down the terra-cotta wall fountain so it will not freeze and break. For the same reason I have moved the pots of *Canna* and *Acorus* indoors, as well as the new black pot that decorates the path to the back lawn. It now rests upstairs holding the umbrella palm (*Cyperus alterni-folius*) that I removed from the main pond. Both the pot and the plant, united for the first time, would freeze if left out. This way I can enjoy both all winter long. I've moved several terra-cotta pots of sempervivums into the greenhouse, not because the plants will freeze—they won't—but because the pots will crack if left out all winter. It's one of the best reasons not to live in an area where it freezes too much.

In some cases I bring the plants in not because the pots will freeze and crack but because the plants in them will freeze and die. I have a concrete pot planted with a wonderful perennial marigold called *Tagetes lemonii*—the pot will withstand freezing, but the plant won't. It is just now coming into bloom, but even if it never bloomed, I would still keep it standing by the greenhouse door. I have to brush past it to enter the greenhouse, and its exotic fragrance of crushed spices is one of the few winter pleasures I can count on from day to day. In warmer climes I've seen this marigold grow to four feet tall with large clusters of golden yellow flowers. I would like to grow it outdoors in the ground because in a pot the foliage and flowers do not get as massive as they would if left to their own habits. This is not too practical, however, because the plant does not bloom until very late in the fall, and it would invari-ably be killed by frost before it could come into bloom. Then, too, if I tried to move it inside late in the year, the root mass would be too big for a pot.

Some plants need to be moved not inside but out, and these I've put off for too long. The eight dozen pansy seedlings I started months ago have become root bound awaiting their turn in the sun (or more likely snow). They seem to prefer this cold weather, and they can have it. I have planted three great patches of them, two in blue and one in rose red. One patch is planted between the daylilies and lilylilies. These pan-sies will cover most of the bed, flowering in very early spring before the herbaceous and bulbous plants break ground. Then, as they start to cook in the heat of late spring and early summer, the daylilies and lilylilies will come up and push them aside. This is the theory at least, and we will see soon enough what the reality might be. Gardening represents a very fine line between the fantasy of theory and the fact of reality.

The first hard frost is predicted for tomorrow, somewhere in the midtwenties. Snow is predicted by week's end. One week it is pansy-planting time and then it is the great black death of frost—it seems a befitting end to the gardening season. This week brings to full circle a quest begun last November in a moment of delirium. The quest to capture a year in time. Why, it scarcely seems as if a day had passed since I sat on that November-warmed bench dreaming about what future direction the garden might take. It is such thoughts of warmth, of past pleasures, and of interesting times to come that keep me gardening. I know that the winter may discourage but not conquer. Not this year at least.

In reviewing the many weeks that have passed since last November's benchmark, I am amazed at how much was accomplished when I thought I was doing nothing. This is the value of plodding. Both nature and I are plodders. A little work every day and mountains are built, trees grow, and the gardener's empty palette fills up. Plodding is not such a bad habit, really. If you can convince yourself that the future is only minutes away instead of years, then you have won the battle over haste. You know that whatever you do will eventually come to fruition and that it's not so important whether it's done today or tomorrow or next week. Just so long as a little something is done today and a little something else tomorrow, then before you know it, paradise will be yours. Today's acorn is tomorrow's shade garden. When looked at in this light, plodding has much to recommend it.

Those who believe that gardens are built in a day are sadly mistaken. And they are missing the point of gardening entirely. As are those who believe a garden is ever finished. (A finished garden is one made of plastic, and even that will fade in time.) Landscape designers, earth-moving equipment, full-sized specimen plants, gaggles of workmen, acres of perennials and annuals in bloom—none of these creates a garden. Time does that. Time decides what will live and what will die, what will flourish and what will sulk, what will grow twice as big as is genetically possible and what will remain dwarf, what will flower and what will not. We gardeners are only the catalyst that brings plant and earth together. After that, time is the master, and we have practically no influence except to trim a little here and there, to dislodge a few plants that come up in the wrong place, and to try our best at orchestration.

Oh, we may plan, of course, and design and do a damn fine job of it. We may start out with great detailed maps, plotted down to the last square inch. And we may expect to spend focused hours at hard labor executing these ideas, but once the preliminaries are over and the grunt work started, we are simply the housekeepers—the tidiers. Perhaps the enforcers and bouncers on occasion. Our minds are free to wander at leisure, to find some little-trod path in the mindscape and to take this path through zigzag, fuzzy memories or unclouded future splendors, through present problems or around them, through reality's certain hold to a dreamer's unsullied cosmos. Gardening is a tear in the day's pocket that lets us fall to earth where we belong. Time is the gardener. If we can realize these truths then we are free *to* garden, but more importantly, we are free *of* the garden. Few of us reach this Nirvana of the gardener's life, yet we all strive.

And now, sadly, we are running out of time, you and I. The weeks of October come rushing toward their fiery climax. The garden is crashing down all about us as tons of leaves fall—weary of their well-fought battle with this year's drought yet defiant in their last breath. Spots of color to rival any in the flowering world come drifting down in reds, oranges, yellows, greens of every description, even varying shades of brown. Winds blow and leaves fall. Rain falls. Still there will be a few good days left in this year before winter takes center stage. Indian summer days. Few, but all the sweeter for it.

This week my two Japanese maples exploded into flame, their twisted trunks like so much stacked kindling. The blaze was ignited by a nearby burning bush (*Euonymus alatus* 'Compactus') that smoldered for a week before igniting. The combination was glorious but alas short-lived. A night's winds knocked the embers to the ground where, fanned by a gentle breeze, they sheeted everything in the red warmth of a dying fire. Today's capricious gale extinguishes the glow. A few ashes linger on, caught between ivy fingers. Soon they, too, will disappear, but only for a time. Next year they will arise, as does the phoenix from its ashes.

Next year may seem to be a far distant time, but it is only tomorrow in the garden's province.

Plant Index

19

21

24

28

29

27

30

31

32

33

34

37

35

5

36

Chetco Community Public Library
405 Alder Street
Brookings, OR 97415